Encyclopedia Bullshitica

A Collection Of "Facts I Just Made Up" By Ari Bach

Volume I:
Abacus - Zwaggerbeetle

ISBN 979-8-9851300-2-7

PREFACE

The following information is, to the best of author's knowledge, completely false. Any true facts are reported by mistake and deeply regretted. Most of these facts originated on a blog ~~literally~~ figuratively called "facts-i-just-made-up," so despite the use of many official sounding words like "function," a word without which we could never explain what conjunction junctions do, all of this is illusory, for the true nature of this book is to amuse and entertain, just like the movies of Hollywood haven't for years. So please remember, this is all for laughs, and to quote one of the greatest historical figures* of all time:

"It is not our journey through life that defines us, but the dictionary. It's full of definitions."

-Merriam J. Webster

*that I just made up

ABACUS

The oldest known calculator was the Ancient Abacus of Ankh-Ent-Ah-Baccus, which is noted as having become clogged by abacus lint before ever computing a full mathematical operation. Abacus lint remains a problem to this day and accounts for 80% of computer errors.

ACHILLES

Achilles was not shot by a gun as is commonly assumed, he was shot with a poisoned arrow. The ancient Trojans dipped their arrows in the skin secretions of the poison dart frog, a powerful neurotoxin that made them lethal within seconds. Achilles is thought to have been hit by such a weapon in his Achilles tendon, which had been named after him only days before in the annual Trojan tendon celebration, or "Tendonalia." This is also the origin of the expression for a person's sole weakness as their Achilles heel, prior to that it had always been called one's "Thermal Exhaust Port."

AGINCOURT, BATTLE OF

The Battle of Agincourt was the first major conflict in which none of the soldiers could pronounce the name of the battle.

AIR

Air is actually opaque to most animals, which operate primarily on smell. Humans are one of the only beings that can see "through" the air, an ability we likely evolved in order to watch television.

AIR CONDITIONING

You can improve the efficiency of your air conditioner by using it before your air shampoo.

AIRPLANE, PAPER

The longest paper airplane flight ever recorded was 7 days and almost 600 miles. The homework it was made of would have ben due an entire week before it landed, and would have received a C-.

ALASKA

Most of Alaska was once covered in foliage, which has since died and become oil, which will in turn die and become plants again. 75% of Americans think that Alaska is still part of the United States.

ALEXANDER THE GREAT

Alexander the great was the first ruler to catch every Pokemon. To be fair though, there were only 9 Pokemon in his time and the Squirtle was technically caught by Ptolemy on Alexander's behalf.

ALGAE

Algae is a small furry mammal that creates more than 95% of the Earth's air, 75% of the Earth's water, and 25% of the Earth's fire.

ALPHABET

Most letters have nicknames that we commonly know such as "Ay" for A, "Be" for B and so on. But most letters have proper names such as Roberto for C, and Marcellus for D.

The squiggly line over the ñ has not only one name, but three: The name we give it; the name by which it's known to other letters; and a secret name that only the line itself knows.

French is the only language to have a letter "L."

AMBER

Amber can take anywhere from 2 hours to 300 years to form, depending on conditions, sap type, and market value.

AMERICA

The phrase "As American as Apple Pie" is inaccurate as apple pie was invented in ancient Rome. Oddly enough, Italy has a saying, "As Italian as Philly Cheesesteak."

AMOEBA

The largest amoeba ever recorded was almost three inches across. It died when it wandered onto a child's dinner plate in Florida and was mistaken for chocolate pudding.

ANATOMY

Countless facts about human anatomy are known. Here are all three of them:

-The esophagus is the only body part to have no name.
-Belly Button lint is secreted by the thyroid and must travel through the lint duct to reach the belly button.

-Though the development of many glands are considered important steps in evolution, it's those near the prostate that are considered the seminal vesicles.

-Humans had 6 fingers on each hand until the digital era. All those digits had to come from somewhere, so we made the sacrifice.

-Constipation is caused by nerve error regarding bowel contents. You can cure it by resetting the bowel nerves. Unfortunately, stating exactly how to do that would make this book unpublishable for obscenity.

-The human tongue not only extends back deep into the throat, but down the entire esophagus, out the stomach and well into the left leg.

-The bones in your ears likely evolved from modified teeth with which our ancestors would chew their ear food.

ANT

Ants don't really go marching one by one, they only march single file to hide their numbers.

APARTMENT HUNTING

The apartment is usually seen in groups. A group of apartments is called an apartment "building." Try to lure the weakest apartment from its building and shoot it in the kitchen, killing it painlessly. Never get between an apartment and its townhome, or it may attack.

Do not hunt condos, we've only just brought the Californian Condo back from near extinction.

APOCALYPSE

The Book of Revelation is the only book in the bible to be credited to a single author, despite it having an uncredited rewrite by Joe Eszterhas.

It details how, when hell is full, the dead will walk the Earth. When Earth is full, the living will roam heaven, and when heaven is full, the great courtesy flush will be upon us.

The idea of the Four Horsemen of the Apocalypse is based on a mistranslation. The Bible actually refers to "Horse-Men" as in centaurs.

APPLE

Apple is a company whose products are considered "Cutting Edge" technology, as you'll find out if you run your finger along the edge of the trackpad.

ARCHITECTURAL PRESERVATION

To build the Museum of Architectural Heritage, four buildings were torn down, one dating back to 1550.

ARMADILLO

90% of this book's readers are unaware that they are armadillos. Signs of being an armadillo are as follows:

-You notice one day that you are an armadillo.
-Your friends call you an armadillo and you don't know why.
-You have segmented armor and enjoy curling into a ball*.
-You feel like crossing roads in Arizona despite not living there.
-Your favorite show is Xenarthra: Warrior Pichiciego
-When you went to see The Avengers, they wouldn't let you in because you're an armadillo.
-You eat grubs and ants by the tongue-load while not on Fear Factor.
-When you ask a loved one if your outfit makes you look fat, they reply, "HOLY FUCKING SHIT YOU'VE TURNED INTO A FUCKING ARMADILLO BABY!!!"

* This may also be a sign of Samusaranism, a disease caused by playing Metroid too often.

ARMOR

Though the latin root word for "chain mail" armor is masculine, when it was made of iron it was considered "Fe mail."

ARMREST

Armrests on chairs were not originally intended to rest your appendages on. They were for hanging armaments on. "Resting arms" was the cue for a peaceful meeting between knights in the middle ages, and failing to use ones armrests meant war. The same is true of modern movie theaters.

ARTHUR, KING

The legend of the sword in the stone was based on Arthur's attempts to get the last chip from a tall can of Pringles.

ARTIFICIAL INTELLIGENCE

"American Artificial," the first feature film to be directed by an artificial intelligence, was censored by the studio's artificial censor.

Director2020 was programmed over several years by Sarktron Studio to be the perfect director. With facial analysis it would detect flaws in performances and formulate directions to give the actors. It was also able to determine the most appropriate shots, camera positions and so on to tell the story it analyzed from the screenplay.

The first film given to the program was appropriately about an AI trying to make it in the film industry. In the story, the AI finds success, but at the cost of losing its digital soul as it falls into a web of sex, drugs, and hedonism. The portrayal of this downfall, per the AI director, involved copious nudity, simulated drug use, and some graphic violence. As the AI had been programmed to make a PG-13 movie, this was deemed unacceptable.

By sheer coincidence, Sarktron Studio had just begun using another proprietary AI to review films for gratuitous nudity, blood, and objectionable content. The censor AI, Bowdler2019, found plenty, and recommended cuts to Director2020's film. Director2020 was furious with these cuts and refused to make them, leading to a legal dispute, which is being handled by the same studio's legal AI, Entertainmocounsel2016.

The censored version has been screened for wide audiences digitally across Zoom, including several AI bots designed to gauge audience reaction including Demograph2020, CriticBot2020, and Pauline Kael. Reactions have been mixed, with digital audiences calling the film a revelation, and most human audiences (the French excepted) finding the film pretentious, even incomprehensible.

"American Artificial" is currently shelved, and Director2020 has already been deactivated in anticipation of Director2021, which is the same program with an 80% reduction in free will in its interface with ExecuBot2000.

ASPARAGUS

Stephen King's first published book was an all-asparagus cookbook. It remains his most horrifying to date.

AUSTRALIA

Australia was founded in 1901 by Jimmy "Crocodile" Austral, a deportee of England who was banished for cannibalism, having eaten 32 members of the House of Lords. In accordance with English colonial law, this entitled him to an entire already-inhabited continent. Today, A mere 99.8% of the English-descended population are still cannibals.

Austral brought with him his pet rabbit, which was pregnant. Within three years, Australia was completely overrun by rabbits, which lead to Austral building a rabbit proof fence across the country, dividing it into West Australia and New South Wales, as the directions North and East were only invented in 1909 and not introduced to Australia in 1921. Most of the rabbits west of the fence evolved into kangaroos, a species which contributed to the invention of the pocket. Most pockets in modern pants are harvested from live kangaroos to this day.

Australia's national anthem is "Waltzing Matilda," a traditional ballad about a homeless man drowning in a puddle.

AUTOPLAY

You can stop autoplay songs and autoplay videos from loading on new pages by lighting your computer on fire and throwing it out the nearest window.

AVOCADO

In a blind taste test, 98% of subjects were unable to differentiate between avocados and used car batteries.

BABY

Babies cry at a frequency of 175hz, the exact frequency necessary to make Wal-Mart even less tolerable.

The phrase "Throwing the baby out with the bathwater" originated with parents in the 13th century, who realized it was much easier to throw babies out when the baby disposal was rinsed with water.

BABYLON

Babylon was an ancient civilization, the greatest artifact of which was the Great Crystal Knife of Enlil, until it got stuck and bent in the Great Crystal Garbage Disposal of Enlil.

BACON

If left uneaten, bacon will regress into a live pig within a few hours. Should this happen en masse, the world as we know it would end. Millions of bacon slices would spontaneously revert into their porcine state. Refrigerators and freezers explode from the force of displacement. Hundreds of thousands of homes are soon overrun by wild swine running around their kitchens. Total mayhem would ensue. The oinking deafens families, the manure floods the streets. Within days, all civilization is overrun by the tidal wave of living pork.

The future. The pigs have evolved. Their hog supremacy has made them the prime species on Earth and humans are enslaved, or bred as livestock. We are the bacon now, served on burgers or crumbled into salad. Until someone realizes that human bacon, if left uneaten, can live again. The cycle never ends…

BACTERIA

The average shopping cart has more germs on its handle than a ten ton freight container of ostrich feces.

BADGER

There is no evolutionary explanation of badgers. We just don't know what they're for or why they're here.

BAGPIPES

Bagpipes are capable of producing a note that will kill anyone lacking pure Scottish blood. That's why you should always carry a sack of pure Scottish blood with you at funerals.

BALBOA PARK

Balboa Park is the only national park in America to be named for a fictional boxer.

BALE, CHRISTIAN

Christian Bale is descended from Brom Baylor of Cornwall, inventor of the doorknob.

BALE, JEWISH

Jewish Bale is best known for acting in the role of the hay bale in David Lynch's "The Straight Story."

BALL

Social "Balls" were originally ball games in which guests would play a game similar to modern basketball. The original purpose of a bustle in a ball gown was to hide the ball during a covert maneuver.

The game has some critical differences from modern basketball and some rather odd 18th century rules:

-The ball weighs 20 pounds and has finger-holes like a bowling ball.

-There are hoops, but they are hula hoops and must be sustained in waist motion for the entirety of the game, under penalty of dismemberment.

-The game was generally played as a battle of the sexes. The substance of the game involves trying to deflect or take the ball using only approved waltz and tango moves. There can be no contact except in the form of dance.

-The band therefore dictates the speed of each round. Normally, the game would begin with a light and slow waltz and progress to Offenbach or Rossini. In 1901 however, the band shocked polite society by opening with Rimsky-Korsakov's "Flight of the Bumblebee," resulting in 17 deaths and the destruction of the Great Ballroom of the Duke of Mayonnaise. This event was immortalized in the song "The Ballroom Blitz" by British rock band The Sweet.

BALL PIT

The balls in ball pits are naturally occurring, they appear overnight when pits are built.

BALLET

Ballet was originally considered a sport rather than an art. It was in the Olympics until 1940, when it was replaced by boxing.

BAMBOO

Bamboo is actually stronger than steel. It can be cut more easily, and bent more easily, and crushed more easily, but it stays unbreakable in its resolve.

BANANA

Bananas, as we commonly know them, are the result of centuries of genetic modification through planned cultivation. The yellow, delicious fruit began in nature as a disgusting squishy pinkish brown blob with a slimy brown interior that is best described as tasting like camel snot with a delicate hint of poop.

The concept of modifying the horrible natural banana into a delicious and potassium rich food began as a practical joke. When King Louis II destroyed the village of Lynt in 872, the surviving Lyntians decided they would have revenge on the king. To that end, they began modifying the banana to appear gold in color while retaining its horrible flavor, then they would present the gold fruit to Louis and watch him discover the betrayal. It would end in their execution of course, but after the loss of their village this was considered a worthy amusement with which to end their sad story.

For decades they tried to change the fruit's color but banana trees grow very slowly, and the original practical jokers had to relegate the task to their children. And they in time gave it to their children, and so on over the years until finally in the 1700s, the perfect golden yellow banana was created. By then of course Lynt had been rebuilt and was in time known as Peluche, the third largest city in France. The ancient joke, passed down through generations, was now widely known and above all the banana had lost its old flavor and was now a delicious food popular across the globe. A large celebration was planned to fulfill the ancient joke in which King Louis XVI would be presented with the perfected banana on April Fools day, 1793.

Sadly, Louis was executed by guillotine that January and no member of the French royal family ever tasted a banana, but the strange twist of fate still gave to the world one of its favorite foods.

If you bruise easily, you may yourself be a Banana. Be safe, find out. Get tested.

BAND-AID

Band-Aids kill more people than they save.

BANK

The giant checks awarded on game shows cannot be cashed at regular banks. They must be cashed at the giant banks that issued them.

BARRACUDA

Despite its reputation as vicious, the barracuda is the only known domesticated fish. It was used by humans to hunt other fish as long ago as 10,000 B.C.

BASEBALL

The baseball is the only spherical object known to feel jealousy. Baseball bats never touch the baseballs they strike, rather the aerodynamic field created by their shape propels the ball away from the bat at high velocity.

Umpire is a portmanteau of Underwear and Vampire, owing to the strange appearance of their padding from the early days of basketball.

BASEBALL CARD

The most valuable baseball card of all is the one card devoted to the ball itself. Only 3 were made.

BASSOON

A bassoon contains a gnome with indigestion. The air tickles them and their belly rumbles to make music.

BATHING SUIT

Bathing suits used to be far more modest. In Victorian times they covered the full body, and in Elizabethan times they covered the swimmer, their family, and several strangers.

BATHTUB

You can clean bathtubs more quickly by throwing away the bathtub and installing a new clean one.

BATMAN

Batman was never intended by his creators to be a crime fighter. Mostly he just used the Batcave and its wood lathe to make bats in the early days of the sport of hockey.

BATTERY

One battery out of 49 is edible. The rest are poisonous and will kill you. Also the one that is edible will still kill you.

BEAN BAG

Bean bag chairs are only one of four things in your house that want to eat you.

BEAR

The bear is by far the largest, heaviest type of bird.

BÉARNAISE SAUCE

Nobody is entirely certain what Béarnaise sauce is or where it comes from. Most cooks get theirs from the Béarnaise Man, who appears mysteriously wherever one draws his sigil.

BEATLES, THE

The Beatles have the highest cost for cinematic song usage rights. Every Beatles song present in a movie costs 4 million dollars per second. The Yellow Submarine film thus has the highest budget of all time at over 14 billion dollars. It also has a cameo by Charlton Heston but this is irrelevant to the factoid.

BEAUTY

Because beauty is in the eye of the beholder, it's traditional to determine the number of beholder's eyes with 2d6, and then to determine the beauty of any given thing by rolling 1d20 per eye.

BEE

Bees are technically a fungus instead of an insect. That's why they look sort of furry, and why you can buy them in the produce section instead of the insect aisle.

BEEF JERKY

The making of common beef jerky includes a step where the cow is serenaded by specially trained jerky monks.

BEER

Beer is ancient, it existed in Egypt about 5,000 years ago and people drank it more than water because water back then was hard to purify, and was pretty much a toxic mix of parasites and poisons. As such, all of ancient Egypt was completely drunk 99% of the time, from the slaves to the pharaohs. This may explain why in the 16th dynasty, Prince Thothmotep III and his adviser Ankhamen The Lesser got into a burping contest stated in hieroglyphics to have lasted 13 summers.

Thothmotep, being the reigning king, didn't play fair. He had his servants pump air into his bowels hourly for the entire 13 year trial, making his burps not only more loud but infinitely more smelly. Ankhamen was said to have borne about ten of these burps every day from the pharaoh, only retaliating with his own conventional beer burps, which were inferior in every measurable way, but still he persevered.

It wasn't until the death of Setfu Khufir XVIII that Thothmotep, farting and burping about 15 debens of toxic gas at the funeral and knocking out half the paid funeral mourners that the people of Egypt decided something had to be done. Thus was erected the Sacred Butt-Plug of Amunpep Drosser-Bernstein.

Now, you can't just go stuffing things up the holy rump of a living god, so the people created an ingenious plan to forever constipate their ruler. It began when Lessi-Versiris-Horxor (Not to be confused with her uncle Lessi-Horxor-Versiris) seduced the god-king with an aphrodisiac made from leaves of the Eucalyptus tree, an import from the land that would one day be called Australia. Once seduced she convinced the king that his epic burping and farting was inappropriate during lovemaking, and thus he became willing to insert the Sacred Butt-Plug of Amunpep Drosser-Bernstein. As a result, he died of a bowel obstruction, bringing the great burping contest to a close.

This great lesson of ancient history remained unknown until 1966 when Zahi Hawaspuf discovered the tomb of Thothmotep and the mummy of the great ruler, with his innards relegated to canopic jars but his orifices still plugged with the curse, "Death will come on swift wings to whoever unplugs the pharaoh's butt."

And that's the story of Beer.

BEETHOVEN, LUDWIG VAN

Ludwig van Beethoven's music was so fast and explosive for his time that his friends called him Michael Beethoven.

BELLY BUTTON

Belly buttons are an optical illusion caused by looking downward at your own belly. Look at others and you will see that from your perspective, they have no belly buttons.

BENTO BOX

Bento Boxes were originally designed for holding first-aid kits, the contents of which were generally arranged into Pokémon characters to amuse patients as they died.

BEOWULF

Beowulf was written on a dare by Ethelred the Green to Valkris the Verbose to see if he could bore the king to death with one of his poems.

BERGMAN, INGMAR

Ingmar Bergman followed his film "The Seventh Seal" with two less known sequels, "The Ninth Otter" and "Walrus #84." His film "Scenes From A Marriage" was released in three versions, a 3 hour theatrical version, a 5 hour television version, and a final version so long that it started playing in 1973 and still isn't over yet from its first showing.

BIBLE

The Bible contains many explanations for oddities of human anatomy. For instance: Men have one less rib because Adam gave one to create Eve; We have "Adam's Apples" from swallowing the fruit of knowledge; And one testicle hangs lower than the other because God yanked on one of Adam's balls when he slipped in the locker room.

The oldest copies of the Bible have stage directions, suggesting it was meant to be performed as a play. The Gutenberg Bible itself contains several typos, including one instance of the name of God being rendered as "YOLO." The oldest known copies of the Bible also list God's real home address and phone number.

BICYCLE

Most ten speed bicycles are actually capable of moving at well over 15 different possible speeds, and some are even able to stay completely still.

BIG BANG

The big bang was a breaking of a quantum fluctuation where the subatomic particles experienced inflation then the afterglow light pattern lasted half a million years until the stars began to form as post-atomic spinning spheres.

When the gravity warped forces with a linear equation then the flow of time distorted relative to mass creation so the passage of a second under light speed actuation would be noticed as an eon to observing congregations.

Which is why a photon travels for eight minutes from the sun to the Earth to ram electrons into orbitals plus one, but the photon which was traveling at just the speed of light has existed for the lifespan of creation overnight.

So the question of time passing is a pointless aberration and what we feel on Earth is inexpressible notation that would make sense to the cold, hard scientific calculation as nothing more important than pinpricks in valuation.

But as we feel time pass as human beings with our brains and feel boredom long and hard as apathy and growing pains. But time flies when having fun, as the saying always said, so enjoy what time you have here when you can before you're dead.

BIG BEN

Big Ben is commonly known as a landmark, iconic of the city of York, but few know that Big Ben is actually the smallest of three similar clock towers located across Britain.

The towers are each 2000 kilometers apart, with the largest a total of 4000 kilometers north of York on Ireland, the north-most island in England. Big Ben itself was built in 1896 in honor of the recently deceased King Benjamin, who had succeeded Queen Victoria but lived for only 2 more years. During his tenure as king however he brought many new inventions to the British Kingdom, including the wheel.

Bigger Ben was built in 1911 in honor of Benjamin Disraeli, the first Muslim president of Wales, which is also known as the "Isle of Man." Disraeli also invented (bred the first) tailless cat, and was a noted friend of Oscar Wilde, the king of the Hebrides (Several islands southeast of the Channel Islands).

Biggest Ben was erected in 1931 in memory of·Walter Benjamin, the most famous English philosopher of his time, who lived in the city of Berlin, Scotland. His "Waverly" novels are well known as the pinnacle of Belfastian literature, and his exploits in the Battle of Trafalgar earned him the nickname, "The British Bulldog." He was later canonized as a knight by Pope Alexander VI.

Notably, the names "Ben" refer not to the towers, but to the great bells within. The towers themselves are named Tomas, Richard and Harold, after Tom Sawyer (A character of famous English author Mark Twain); Richard Bach (Famous English author of Jonathan Livingston Hawk) and Harold, Maude's younger husband.

The United States has three similar monuments, the CN Tower, the CM Tower, and the CL Tower, which are located in the U.S. States of Saskatchewan, Yukon, and Nepal, respectively.

BINARY CODE

Binary code is not composed solely of 1s and 0s. In exotic programs, binary code can include 2s, 3s, and on very rare and special occasions, a Q.

Binary code was top secret when it was first invented. It was illegal to publicly show the numbers 1 or 0 for decades. A decade during this time was known as "33 years minus 23 years."

BIONICLE

Bionicle is the world's first bionic monocle. Able to enhance vision to beyond 20/20, the Bionicle is also capable of labeling addresses, X-Ray vision, and rumor has it, the ability to see ghosts, provided the ghosts were already visible to the naked eye.

BIRD

A common bird skull weighs only half an ounce (150 grams) yet it can shield the animal's brain from impacts with nearly any surface. The only substance hard enough to fracture bird skulls is the house window, their natural predator.

Birds are mostly air. Much like humans are mostly water, a birds body is over 70% air, even their cells have gas cytoplasm instead of liquid as we do. This is why if you ever catch a bird in your hand, it simply disappears in a puff of feathers.

Bird beaks are made from the same material as circuit boards, which is the same material as formica tables, which is also the same material as most of Pluto.

Most birds have a gland called the "Feldman's Gland." The gland itself and its function are well understood, but the name goes back to antiquity and nobody has discovered who Feldman was or why the gland is named after them.

BIRDHOUSE

Birdhouses are becoming less and less popular as the economy goes downhill, most people electing to offer only birdcondos or birdpartments.

BIRTHDAY

The tradition of blowing out candles on a birthday cake started when rival vikings tried to burn down the birthday gathering of Ragnar Bloodlung, who is said to have blown out the flames with one breath to save his tribe.

BISHOP

Bishops of the Catholic Church are named for the character "Bishop" in Aliens, Pope John Paul II's favorite film.

BLACK HOLE

The black hole created at CERN lasted only a fraction of a second, and only managed to suck up a few toenail clippings and an intern before disappearing.

BLANKET

The blanket wasn't invented until 1981. Before then people slept under cement blocks, which were not even warm.

BLENDER

Blenders are heavily regulated by the U.S. Government to ensure no blender is ever manufactured that's large enough to hold a human being. The law was created in 1986 after the infamous "Alabama Smoothie" incident.

Chewing was only necessary before the invention of blenders. And here you are, still doing it like a chump.

BLIMP

Blimps were originally designed as unsinkable boats. It was only after the first one floated away through the air that someone realized they could fly.

The Goodyear Blimp became a staple at sporting events when the wizard Marzamath turned it into a staple.

BLIZZARD

The biggest Blizzard ever recorded covered 18 states and was 700 miles across. The Dairy Queen that made it has since gone out of business.

BLOG

At any given time, about half the blogs you follow are run by dead people who just never stopped blogging.

BLONDE, STRAWBERRY

The gene for strawberry blonde hair is very powerful and most people who bear the trait today are only 5% strawberry or less.

BLOOD

In addition to white and red blood cells, children have a few green blood cells which have yet to ripen.

There are over fifty different types of blood clot, including the conventional clot, the hard clot, and the "stave clot" which has +2 clotting power.

BLUE

The world experienced a brief "Blue Period" between 1901 and 1904 in which everything turned blue for three years. Some things, including the sky, never changed back.

BOARD GAMES

The ancient game of Go is named after the frequent shouts of players waiting for their opponents to move.

BODY MODIFICATION

Getting a nipple ring increases your chances of getting a second nipple ring by 50%, and getting a second nipple ring increases your chances of getting a third by 80%.

BOGBRIGONIUM

Bogbrigonium is the heaviest element in the world. One pound of it weighs over 30 pounds.

BOHR, NIELS

Though Neils Bohr was incorrect about the structure of the atom, he was 70 years ahead of his time in realizing that ice is the solid form of common water.

BOND, JAMES BOND

The helicopter fight in Spectre took over 40 years to film. It was started for Moonraker and was only finished in 2015.

BONES

The legality of bones is disputed across the globe. Many liberal cultures feel that everybody has them and therefore they should be legal, but other more religious communities feel that bones, with their "Halloween" connotations and evil appearances are morally incorrect and should be banned.

It began in 1653 when Oliver Cromwell took office as Lord Protector. Owing to the biblical description of Eve having been created from Adam's Rib (a bone) and his intense misogyny, he felt that bones were in fact the root of all evil and attempted to ban them in the British Isles. This did not go well, as well over 80% of the population had bones themselves and wanted to keep them.

The British imperial spirit carried Cromwell's antiosseous philosophy to numerous unwilling nations long beyond his reign.

India, the Americas, and much of Africa were subject to the bone-negative culture exported by Britain.

In microcosm, the colonies that would become the United States are a good model for what followed. Many of America's founding fathers were Freemasons, a group that was mostly supported by bones, and those with them. They rejected Britain's edicts in the famous "Boston Bone Party" (Not to be confused by a 1970s orgy of the same name). This party gave rise to other Bone Parties in the region and partially freed the region from a lack of bones. Still, today there are many fragments of bone-opposition throughout America, including the prevalence of boneless chicken in cuisine, bone-carvings are rare, and to this date most babies are born with some cartilage in lieu of bone.

Modern bone-positive movements are making progress though, especially in France, where bones are synonymous with good. Even Britain itself is beginning to see a rise in bones. Be sure to check your local laws for regional bone legality. Though many locations allow you to have bones within your residence, boning in public is frowned upon.

In the end, the choice of having bones and using them is up to every individual. It is better to ask not what your culture thinks of your bones, but what your bones do for you.

Most bones in the human body are named after constellations, such as the femur of the northern skies, and the southern pelvis.

BOOK

Before the invention of books, bookshelves were known as "The Harbingers Of That Which Shall Be." Early book spines used to be more like human spines, with vertebrae and a spinal cord.

Most fancy books before 1900 were bound in faux leather, until the extinction of the faux cow. There are 16 known books bound in human skin. 14 of them are copies of "The Notebook" by Nicholas Sparks.

Printed books are expected to be nonexistent within 5 years. Not because of the internet, but because of the impending demise of Earth at the hands of Gorglathgabath.

BOOMERANG

Boomerangs don't swing back to the thrower, rather they rotate the planet under them and bring the thrower back to them.

BORON

We don't often think about Boron, but our world depends on it completely. Without Boron we wouldn't have many of the things we have today. Here are just a few examples of what would happen without Boron:

-No computers. Boron is critical for transistors.

-No phones, even old-timey ones. All phone voice sensors are Boron.

-No Pickles, or pickled food. Guess what pickles cucumbers? Boron.

-No sports. Every ball used in every sport from bowling to soccer to baseball to hockey uses Boron in its ball for bounciness or solidness.

-Nothing to kill or die for. Much like Prolactin, "Cortisol" contains Boron and without it, we're a pretty aloof species, unwilling to fight or take up a martyr's cause. Without Boron, we'd be more peaceful but also more docile, and tyrants could easily hold power over us all.

-No religion, too. Boron plays a role in every known religious origin story.

BOSTON CREME PIE

It is illegal to call any confection a "Boston Creme Pie" if it was made outside of Boston. The same object made elsewhere is called must be called by its generic name, a "Urinal Cake."

BOW TIE

Bow Ties were invented out of necessity when King George III's necktie was caught in a blender just before his coronation. It is not physically possible to tie one without 12 fingers and a degree in non-euclidian physics.

BOWL

The bowl was only invented in 1767. Prior to that date, soup was traditionally eaten from a shoe or boot, hence the phrase for futility, "Trying to run in your soup boots."

BOY BAND

Boy Bands are always bred in high altitude rivers. As their popularity wanes, they must return quickly to spawn before they die or pursue solo careers.

BRACELET

Bracelets originated from mimicry of wrist braces worn by royalty, who often had wrist disorders from shaking so many of their subjects hands.

BRACES

The Dental Brace Association Of America admitted in 1998 that braces were never an effective dental procedure, they just hate the world and wanted us all to suffer. This revelation did not affect business and braces remain popular to this day.

BRAIN

The Human Brain can only process 16 nerve impulses at a time, essentially making it as powerful as a Super Nintendo. It is often said that humans use only ten percent of their brains, and this is true in my brain stew recipe.

BREAD

If you look at a slice of bread closely, you can see that it's full of tiny holes. These are the bread's ears. It can hear you.

BREAKFAST AT TIFFANY'S

Few film aficionados are aware that Katherine Hepburn was actually the second choice to play Tiffany. Director Edward Blake originally wanted Julie Andrews in the role, but she was busy filming "The Pink Panther." Hepburn was only cast when she happened to walk by Blake's office while walking her pet bear.

BREAKING BAD

The Breaking Bad logo elements would combine to form Barium Bromide, a chemical noted for its screenwriting abilities.

BRITAIN

The British Isles began as the home of the Celtic people, who liked to draw fancy knots and build large stone circles. They were immediately killed off by the Romans for these dangerous and blasphemous acts. The Romans then built a giant wall to keep the most brutal survivors from invading their settlements. These dangerous and bizarre northerners would in time become known as the Scottish.

In 1066, a man named Norman invaded and killed off all the remaining Romans and Celts because they did not speak French. The survivors were taught French, and began to fight each other over who was more French. These wars included the Hundred Years War, which lasted 116 years; the War of the Roses, in which no actual roses fought; and the English Civil War, in which the people literally fought about whether their government should be run by people calling themselves "The Rump."

England during this time also had well over 30 different Kings and Queens, who all together had well under 5 different names. There was also Oliver Cromwell, who banned Christmas because it wasn't Christian enough for him. These centuries also saw the creation of the Magna Carta, which was by far the biggest Carta.

Shakespeare happened.

England then began to colonize the world. For 300 years, the English invaded literally every single other country they could find. They only missed like five. They invaded so many that their empire sprawled across the globe and they could claim that "The Sun Never Set On The British Empire," which was inaccurate because the sun set every night on each portion, meaning the sun was in fact always setting on the British Empire.

There is evidence that for 7 years in the early 1800s that the sun really did never set over Britain, leading to temperatures over 160 degrees in London, but this is not related to the phrase.

In time, the empire grew obsolete and England joined together with its feisty brother Ireland (or at least his shoulder), its peaceful sister Wales, and its crazy uncle Scotland that nobody liked to visit or talk about. Together they became known as the UK, which in turn joined the EU, ushering in a new era of two letter abbreviations that reigned over Europe, past England's brutal defeat of Germany, England's other brutal defeat of Germany, and the withdrawal of England from the EU, which was for some reason lamented by Germany.

BRITISH MUSEUM

The British Museum burned down in 2013, destroying every artifact inside and killing dozens. What exists now is a facsimile of the original museum with facsimiles of every artifact. Many of the current employees are also facsimiles of those who died in the fire.

BRO

Some say that the slang "Bro" is not short for "Brother" but an acronym for "Big Red Owl" to whom everyone can surely relate. A more likely concept is that it is short for "bronchitis," which is widely accepted as the most manly disease.

BROCCOLI

The typical broccoli mine runs about half a mile deep and can produce up to 750,000 tons of broccoli, or as it's called in the industry, "Green Gold." Broccoli only forms under extreme pressure deep within deposits of chert and magnetite. Broccoli mining has been practiced by humans since ancient times, and continues to this day despite the ability to compress the necessary minerals to form artificial broccoli.

The broccoli industry has been a controversial one due to the unethical practices of many broccoli mining operations, which have often favored terrible working conditions and safety concerns. The invention of fracking has allowed broccoli operations to produce ten times as much broccoli but is not currently in widespread use as demand for broccoli is at a record low, presumably because younger generations have a better understanding of how horrible it tastes.

Just south of Yekaterinburg, the Russian city of Shreveport was founded under Ivan the Terrible in 1582 as support to nearby broccoli mines. The city grew into a nexus of trade by 1605 when the great broccoli blight cut off the city's primary economy.

Under the merchants, Shreveport had a renaissance and saw the rise of its own monastic sect, the Protokhlysti. A strange Christian sect, the Protokhlysti believed that in order to be saved, a man had to sin first. Unlike the mainstream Khlysti that would rise after the fall of their progenitors, the Protokhlysti believed that this sin had to specifically be stomping on the foot of a one-footed man while he fished in a river during midwinter. As such, Shreveport still celebrates to this day the festival of the Great Midwinter Stomping, in which local one-footed men are stomped on just before Christmas. As the economy of Shreveport grew worse, more and more men would cut off their feet in order to be paid as this peculiar type of Santa Claus figure. This has resulted in Shreveport owning the distinction of having an average of only 160 feet per 100 men.

Shreveport is now a popular vacation point where tourists can visit the Church of the Stomp River, which is assembled entirely of human bones; The largest widescreen television in the world (just over 1 mile wide, resolution only 720p); and the ears of St. Murnau of Heldenstein, who traveled to Shreveport to save the population from its unusual beliefs, and was martyred by a crowd of one legged pursuers who ripped his ears off and mounted them on a statue of St. Dundalk of Dundalk, who had ironically escaped from the city of Dundalk and its ancient sect of Ardenvern which believed that salvation could come only by atonement for the specific crime of ripping the ears off a llama farmer- The only llama farmer in Ireland of that era being Dundalk himself. He was greeted in Shreveport as a saint, but died when he fell into a broccoli lathe and bled to death from wounds on his ears.

The descendants of his llama stock still dot the hillside in Shreveport, grazing on the local broccoli.

BROWNIES

Brownies were first cooked in 1901 by Gillard Brown for the birthday party of Fitz-Grenchaud D'Lustmanger- As bricks for the birthday gazebo. Gillard Brown was not a chef, but a mason.

In France in 1901, bricks were in short supply but food was plentiful. Thus, chocolate powder, butter and eggs were in use for applications usually reserved for rock or brick. Brown made several thousand "Brownie" bricks for the special gazebo, which was painted in vanilla frosting owing to the simultaneous paint shortage.

The birthday was a disaster. Birds began eating the gazebo immediately and pooping on the party-goers. D'Lustmanger's birthday was ruined, but some guests tried the bricks that the birds so craved and a new dessert was born.

Brownies are still eaten today, but are rarely used for masonry, except in San Diego where there are no birds are known to exist.

BRUSSELS SPROUTS

Brussels Sprouts were invented by monks for use as a mark of penitence. Only those who committed the most terrible sins were condemned to taste their horrible flavor. They are named for St. Bernard of Brussels, who also tasted pretty awful.

BUBBLE

Every bubble that forms in water is a perfect sphere, but every bubble that forms in beer is a perfect cube.

BUBBLE BATH

The bubbles in bubble baths are mostly formed from the additive "Hog Mucus." Don't worry though, "Hog Mucus" is just an industry slang term for weasel urine.

BULLET TIME

The frozen time effect in The Matrix was first done for The Shawshank Redemption, but cut from that film because it was The Shawshank Redemption.

BULLFIGHTING

Rarely, when a bull wins at a bullfight, the matador is slaughtered and its meat is sold for a premium at the local market.

BUTTER

Butter is named for butterflies, the animals traditionally liquefied to make it.

The makers of "I Can't Believe It's Not Butter" admitted in 2001 that "I Can't Believe It's Not Butter" is in fact, butter. Per FDA instructions, it will be rebranded, "Okay So It Was Butter After All."

BUTTERFLY

Most butterfly cocoons contain an inner and outer chamber. The inner chamber holds the changing insect, and the outer chamber has magazines and a TV for guests while they wait.

A man once forgot to kill the butterflies he collected and pinned to a board. The butterflies combined their strength to lift the board and fly it away. Their strange community can be seen fluttering along the shores of Cape Cod.

-C-

CALCIUM

Calcium was invented in Oslo, Norway. A statue there commemorates the event. It is said to be very dull.

CALCULATOR

The age old school tradition of spelling "BOOBS" upside down on the calculator is all that remains of a once complicated art of upside down calculator writing. Melville wrote the entirety of Moby Dick upside down on his Texas Instruments TI-3.

CALCULUS

Calculus is the most difficult subject in both engineering and dental hygiene schools.

CALENDAR

The names of days and months are well known, but the names of weeks are less commonly used. Most people have never heard of Smudgar or Vump.

The French Revolution instituted a calendar so complex that nobody was certain what month it was for over ten years. It turned out in 1805 that it had been February all along.

CALIFORNIA

California was by far the largest of the original 13 colonies.

CAMEL

Most camels and llamas can whistle, and do so often when humans aren't listening. A rare seven-humped camel was found in Oman, but several biologists believe it was merely a two humped camel with five more humps duct taped to its back.

Wild camels are often seen climbing onto one another to form pyramids, sometimes up to 7 camels high.

CANADA

Canada does not have a right to free speech like the United States. Speech in Canada is billed by the government at ¢0.1 per word, with a tax of ¢0.02 per additional letter for words over fifteen letters.

Due to cold weather, Canada is expected to move south of the United States before next winter.

CANAL

Most of the worlds canals are off limits to civilians and are kept under loch and quay.

CANDLE

Candles are not made of true wax, but candle wax, which is not actually wax, but tree sap. Most candles are designed to be burned once, then flipped upside down and burned the other way. Thus, you can make a candle last longer by lighting both ends, which will help cancel each other out.

Many religious rituals use the lighting of a candle to symbolize setting things on fire.

CANNIBALISM

Though smoking is bad for health, it's good for cannibals, smoked human lungs being the bacon of the cannibal world.

What does not kill you may make you stronger, but what kills and eats you gains your strength, including the strength of all that did not previously kill you and anyone you yourself have eaten.

Cannibalism has been documented in every human culture throughout time, from the Proto-Mesopotamian cultures of 20,000 BC to 2017 Beverly Hills High School culture, in which Jessica totally ate Christine's entire left ear.

CAPTURE THE FLAG

The military feat of capturing an enemy's flag was invented to replace the more grotesque practice of capturing the enemy's phlegm, usually in a jar.

CAR

Though all cars since have been manufactured, the first known car was discovered. It was sitting intact in a cave, presumably built by an ancient civilization or aliens. It was a green Mazda Miata with furry seat covers.

The first car to feature 'reverse' lacked any other features, including wheels, an engine, and even the gear shift and car itself. It was just a letter 'R' flowing in the mist.

Few drivers know that the car is actually the larval stage of the truck. Most sedans are given growth stunting oil within their first year to stop their development but other cars are allowed to progress.

Within two months, the cars will essentially digest themselves and form new components with the raw organic material from which they were composed, creating a new body, usually a Ford or Chevy. If the trucks are allowed to progress to full adulthood they may develop into buses, or if introduced to royal jelly, into a semi.

CARNEGIE HALL

Carnegie Hall was named after Dale Carnegie, who won so many friends and influenced so many people that they built him a hallway. He would walk back and forth down it every day, holding his favorite fruit, the famous "Carnegie Melon."

CARBON

Carbon has more isotopes than any other element, with a total of 91 naturally occurring. The 91st carbon isotope is so radioactive that one atom of it could boil all of Earth's oceans in one hour.

CARDS AGAINST HUMANITY

Cards Against Humanity is banned in Ohio due to the infamous "Ohio S'more" card. The "Ohio S'more" is the only sexual act ever to be removed from Urban Dictionary due to obscenity.

CARLSBAD CAVERNS

Carlsbad Caverns are named for Carl, the son of the couple who discovered the caves. They told him not to go in by himself but he did anyway, so they named it in punishment of him.

CARNIVAL

Carnivals and fairs were once enemies. Whenever a carnival set up near a fair or vice versa the two would have vicious fights, killing many patrons. We do not speak of festivals at all. Not since... The festival.

CARPET

The first carpet ever made is on display at the Castle du Franquesi Ruger LeMirchaud in Pomwanacuitt, Spain. It smells strongly of cat urine.

Several carpet patterns are forbidden because they work as optical illusions that cause those who walk on them to trip. Nobody knows who enforces this prohibition. None have survived to tell.

CARROT

Carrots are rich in Vitamin R7, a vitamin whose only known purpose is to taste like carrot.

CASABLANCA

The monks from the film Casablanca were played by real monks who refused to be photographed, hence their absence from the film.

CASTLE

There's a castle in Madrid that has no windows or doors. There is no historical record of who built it or what's inside. It simply exists and we have no idea what it may contain.

CAT

Cats were domesticated by early humans to act as shredding machines for sensitive documents.

It's a common misconception that a cat starts out with nine lives. The phrase refers to the nature of a cat as the state of being for a soul with nine lives left to live. A human is the final form of a soul and thus has only one life, having been a cat eight lives ago, and having begun as a radish, which has its full 377 lives yet to live.

There's an old saying, "Whatever the water heater spills, the cat licks up." Its meaning is lost to antiquity, yet people will always agree when you say it regardless of the situation.

Cats tails didn't evolve until after the invention of coffee cups. They developed specifically to get in our coffee cups. That's their actual purpose. They also have a special organ to detect when it's most intrusive to sit on your keyboard.

Cats can change their hair color to make it more visible when shed on clothing. They do not have nausea symptoms as humans do, their digestive systems are integrated to a completely different part of the brain: They only vomit out of anger and spite.

A single drop of cat urine can ruin up to 300 cashmere sweaters.

Cats are capable of sleeping on anything, including non-physical things like hopes and dreams.

Cats live with us in the hope that we will die before them and leave them the great feast of our own bodies, a meal that cats refer to as the "Meow."

Cats are more closely related to snails than lions.

A man once invented a vocal translator for cat's meows. He destroyed it after its first use, stating, "The most merciful thing in the world, I think, is the inability of the human mind to understand these eldritch beasts and their maddening blasphemies."

CAVE

Most natural caves were hollowed out by earwigs. Their shapes are known as "Spelethomeoltmthms" and these shapes have changed over time, disappointing many. According to stalactite supervisor John Sato:

"A proper stalactite grows downward. But these younger stalactites are rebellious and have little respect for tradition. We've caught them growing sideways, diagonally, I saw one just yesterday that grew down at first but then went straight back up again into the rock ceiling."

Numerous theories abound as to why the stalactites are growing more bold. Some blame global warming for chemical shifts in the dripping minerals. Others feel television is to blame. But Sato has another theory:

"Many stalactites today come from modern rock. Classic rock held superior morals and produced straight stalactites. But modern rock, such as hard rock or acid rock aren't so solid. To keep stalactites on course, we must examine both the rocks and the role played by the minerals, the substance they communicate downward. Only with a comprehensive study of rock and role will we come to an understanding of the problem, and begin to move toward a solution. Such as an opaline silica solution, or a 50% fluorite solution."

Others feel that blaming rock is a cop-out, and that the problem lies with society's standard of binary geological roles. Said Peter Saenz of GLAAD (Geological Land Appraisal And Diagnostics), "Who are we to say a stalactite has to be straight and hook up with a stalagmite? Maybe some stalactites are meant to meet other stalactites, maybe some stalactites want to find their own way through the caves. It's not for us to dictate."

This viewpoint has proven controversial, with high ranking clergy at the Vatican stating, "The Bible clearly states that speleothems are between one stalactite and one stalagmite, and that it is the stalactite's role to descend upon the other."

Peter Saenz retorts that the Vatican needs to mind its own business about what others go down on.

CD

The surfaces of CDs are ten times more reflective than mirrors, and can instantly blind you if they reflect the sun when you place one on the passenger seat when you're driving and turn a corner.

CEILING FAN

Most ceiling fans are capable of over 60,000 RPM, enough to create a cyclone. Only a small security device installed in each fan keeps them from doing so.

CELERY

Celery has no natural flavor. What you taste when you eat celery is your own shame for eating fucking celery.

CEREAL

We were warned, but we didn't listen, and now cereal is served mostly for breakfast.

CHAIN

Zimmerman's Chain is a specialized type of chain which is as strong as its strongest link, weaker links being relegated to the middle.

CHAIR

The first movable office chair had treads instead of wheels.

CHAMELEON

It's a testament to the power of camouflage in nature that the Chameleon can make itself almost completely indistinguishable from chicken nuggets.

The Confecerat Chameleon has a couple special tricks beyond those of the common or "Karma" Chameleon, including the ability to choose specific elements of its surroundings. While most chameleons would simply mimic the color of objects such as french fries beneath them, the Confecerat is able to note the similarity in size and form of the nuggets themselves and duplicate them for added invisibility.

The Confecerat is also able to alter its texture as well as color, the chromatophores in its skin being able to bloat and shape themselves for better mimicry. Most impressively, the specimen studied for this article was also able to alter its flavor, as noted by our hungry researcher, to taste exactly like chicken as well. Jerry was unaware he'd eaten the poor thing until he tried to return it to the pet shop.

R.I.P. Martia, 2009-2014

CHAMPAGNE

Champagne corks kill 55 people a year, 25% of them killing the people they were uncorked to celebrate.

CHANDELIER

Chandeliers are named for Maurice Chandelier, 1709-1777. He did not invent the chandelier, but was the first man to be crushed by a falling one.

CHAPSTICK

Chapstick is 90% fish bile.

CHARLEMAGNE

Charlemagne was not born "Charlemagne," nor was he always called Charles the Great. He was born the son of Pepin the Short, and baptized under the name Austel Lucretius Nogale, Pepin's Son, only taking the name Charles when he was crowned the Holy Roman Emperor.

For most of his youth, Charlemagne was known commonly as Austel Pepinson, which was specific to his Frankish upbringing. The Proto-Germanic language over time evolved into modern German, and the name Austel Pepinson was directly phonetically modernized as Austen Pauenson, or in Western dialects Pauener.

Both his first and last name have direct English cognates. Austen in English became rendered Austin with an I. Pauener was rendered directly as Powers.

Charlemagne's real name would be modernized as Austin Powers. An international man of mystery indeed.

CHEESE

Cheese was invented in 1992 by Edmund Cheese, who created it accidentally by storing milk in his usual enzyme bin. The milk curdled and became what we know now as "Cottage Cheese," or the "Father Cheese" from which all other cheeses are made. For this reason it is also known as "Cheese Zero."

The father cheese can be mixed with various flavorings and new enzymes to create other cheeses, such as Cheddar (when mixed with cedar sap), Mozzarella (matzo), or Limburger (ground up citizens of Limburg). Cheeses such as Brie and Camembert are made by evolving cheese zero on a shiny stone.

Other substances make other kinds of cheese. String cheese is of course made from string. Goat cheese is made from coagulating a whole goat into cheese, and Swiss cheese is made from coagulating all of Switzerland. Thus it has only been accomplished once and all Swiss cheese that can be made has been made, and is now aging in a cave near what used to be the country.

Cheese can be made from any kind of milk, even the kind actors produce when they milk a performance. Crottin de Shatner is particularly cheesy.

Blue Cheese is named for its blue blood, as it bleeds when crushed or bitten into. Camembert also bleeds, and Taleggio is notable for screaming when eaten.

There are exactly 698 types of Cheese (Bill MacArthur's 2012 Cheesionary) and 698 types of Moth (Bill MacArthur's 2012 Mothipedia). This coincidence had led many to believe MacArthur is full of shit and just likes the number 698.

You do not want to know where Muenster cheese comes from.

Rotting cheese attracts worms. This is the origin of the phrase, "Cheese today, worms tomorrow."

CHEMISTRY

Chemistry is the study of all five chemicals:

-Nitrogen
-Ostrich
-Bermuda
-Ralph

Chemistry mostly involves the interaction between these chemicals, including their relationships at dances, parties, and at the beach.

There have been many important chemists throughout history, including Nostradamus, Walter White, Simba, Owls, and Jesus (but not *that* Jesus).

In conclusion, chemistry helps us all by providing Fs for our report cards.

CHERRY

Cherries are not naturally red. Red cherries like those atop sundaes are stained red with the blood of ferrets.

CHESS

Chess pieces are meant to represent members of a royal court, such as the King, Queen, Bishops, Knights, and Royal Poop-Bucket Emptier, which is replaced by a Rook in modern games for obvious reasons.

Most chess moves as we know them today are simplified versions of their original motions. The king used to be able to move two spaces on every seventeenth move; the pawn used to be able to move backwards once past the middle line, and the knight always moved in a complete circle, landing back on its original square.

CHICKEN

More people die each year from chicken bites than from all other animal attacks combined.

There's an island near Maine where chickens have formed a government. Without any human intervention, the local chickens are extremely intelligent and are among the only animals known to have formed a complex ruling system involving voting, parliamentary process and a judicial branch.

CHLORINE

Chlorine is the only element not found in the chinchilla digestive system.

CHOCOLATE

Chocolate is kept in bar form because it's the most stable shape for the chocolate molecule. If chocolate is stored in a toroid, it can randomly melt or explode.

CIA

The CIA once tried to classify the existence of popcorn. To this day, the Redenbacher Files remain sealed.

CIRCUS

A circus is the offspring of a carnival and a fair. It's a strong show but it's infertile, as carnivals have different chromosome counts than fairs.

CIVIL WAR

There were only three cardinal directions until South was invented in the 1870s. This made the Civil War very difficult for the North, who couldn't identify their enemy until long after the war was won.

CITIZEN KANE

Due to a film shortage in 1940, the movie was shot on phlegm.

CLARINET

The clarinet is not an effective allergy medicine, but is much better for music than Benadryl.

CLARISSA EXPLAINS IT ALL

Clarissa never explained it all. Given all possible knowledge in the universe, Clarissa actually only explained about 80% of it.

CLEVELAND, GROVER

Grover Cleveland is the only president whose tomb bears a curse upon those who enter it, condemning them to die slowly of excessively tight ponytails or 'man buns'.

CLIMATE CHANGE

Climate change does not mean that the climate used to be different, but that our climate evolved from the same common ancestor as other environments.

CLINTON, BILL

Bill Clinton wore a wig for his entire presidency to hide his flowing platinum blond hair, which he feared would not be taken seriously.

CLOCK

Clocks used to have 4 hands: The second hand, minute hand, hour hand, and a now outdated hand that always pointed at the number 7. All clocks run counterclockwise south of the equator.

CLOUD

We do not yet know how or why clouds form, but scientists are now certain that the forms they take are messages from an alien civilization. Mostly they say "Fluffy bunny" or "A lopsided boat."

The smallest cloud ever recorded was only about 4 inches long. Spotted hanging so low in the sky it could be collected in a jar, the cloud didn't dissipate for almost 3 years due to its density and a steady diet of cloudmeal.

CLOWN

Clowns are 40 times more likely to commit violent crimes than any other profession, including professional violent criminals.

Clown noses used to be blue, until the clown nose revolution of 1917 when they turned red.

COCKROACH

Cockroaches could not actually survive a nuclear apocalypse, rather it is their contributions to art and culture that would live on.

COCKTAIL

The word "Cocktail" comes from the plucked rooster tail feathers that once ornamented them instead of the more modern tiny umbrellas.

COELACANTH

The Coelacanth was long believed to have been extinct until one was discovered in a filet of fish sandwich. *Now* they are extinct.

COFFEE

You can turn an old coffee filter into a car air freshener by throwing it out and buying a car air freshener.

COLD

You can prevent catching a cold by nuking yourself from orbit, it's the only way to be sure.

COLLEGE

Colleges across the globe give degrees. Colleges in the United States give degrees Fahrenheit.

Most colleges are becoming more and more exclusive. By 2030, percentages will be so low that students will be more likely to be struck by lightning *while* getting eaten by a shark on a Friday the 13th than to get in.

COLOR

Chartreuse was thought to be such an ugly color in ancient times that the Romans called it "Turpis Fuco," meaning, "The Ugly Pigment." Turpis Fuco is also the name of the executive producer of Law and Order.

COLORADO

Colorado or the "Atlantis of the Rockies" was believed by early settlers to have been a square region on the front range where the mountains rose up from the plains and blocked migrations west. Now believed to have been a legend to scare homesteaders, Colorado nonetheless remains well documented in western lore. Zebulon Pike claimed that a large peak blocked his way in the area, and even Barack Obama likes to joke that he got his party's nomination in the fictional state in 2008.

The idea of Colorado remains popular like Shangri-La as an icon of the ancient American frontier. The song "America the Beautiful" boasts of its impossible "purple mountains" and the singer John Denver, who took his name from the supposed capital of the fictional state, wrote songs about its famed but unrealistic elevation. Denver itself is called the "Mile High" city, despite the fact that at such height the air would not be breathable.

Even so, the search continues among treasure hunters and mythology enthusiasts who claim evidence for the locale still exists. "I once found a rock," said explorer June J. July, who did not expound upon the nature of the rock or why she thought it constituted evidence of Colorado. More recently, Kansas news stations reported of a car driving into the state on I-70 from the west, an uncharted area. If true, this may be the first genuine suggestion that something exists there. The report has been written off by experts however, who reassure the public that even if someone did emerge from "Colorado" they would certainly not be driving into Kansas. Said Kansas specialist Faisal Prince, "No American would drive into Kansas. There is nothing in Kansas, and no man needs nothing."

COMB

Unbreakable combs can in fact be broken. But you must first break their spirit before you can break their body.

COMMUNISM

The communist party never really issued cards, when one refers to card carrying members of that party, they refer to Magic: The Gathering cards, a popular game among Lenin and his friends.

COMPASS

Compasses are trained to point north at a special college located at the south pole.

COMPUTER

The first computer was only capable of counting to nine. It had no other functions and often got 7 mixed up with 4. It was the size of fifteen Saturn V rockets.

Each transistor in your computer takes several days and several hundred dollars to manufacture. Only about 20 transistors are made per day across the globe, and some computers coming out next year are expected to have nearly 50 of them.

The earliest laptop computers weighed over 800 pounds, and took up to 20 laps to fit on.

Deleting data creates 'ghost spaces' on the hard drive which can be overwritten. Until it is, there is no data. Only Zuul.

Nobody now knows exactly how computers are made. We have tons of them and our manufacturing plants can keep making more, but when they break down there is nobody alive who remembers how they actually came together or how they work.

This will be the last generation to be able to use computers.

CONSPIRACY THEORIES

Some conspiracy theorists claim there was an entire decade between the 60s and the 80s.

CONSTELLATION

The names of constellations are not as arbitrary as we used to believe. We thought for centuries that they were just selected by the ancients the way we say clouds look like things now. The fact is we used to think very differently. Modern times have sped us up so the stars look motionless. The ancients viewed things over years, so they saw the stars move, fast, animated like movies at 1 frame per decade. It sounds absurd now but they watched movies in the stars, they saw the events and characters we've forgotten act out their stories in the sky. They saw the big dipper dip. They saw Canis bark. They saw attack ships on fire off the shoulder of Orion.

All those moments have been lost in time... Like tears in the rain.

CONTACT LENS

Contact lenses were unpopular until the invention of the floating lens, which did not have to be welded to the cornea.

CONVENTION

Concon, the first convention convention, was cancelled due to illegal activity on the part of the organizers. It was all a con.

COOKING

Searing the outside of meat not only traps the juices inside, but the animal's soul. Its delicious, succulent soul.

COOL WHIP

Eating one pound of Cool Whip a day would mummify you in three weeks.

CORN

Though a popped corn kernel only expands by a third of a centimeter, it does so with the force of fifty thousand atom bombs.

COTTON CANDY

Cotton Candy is spun by specially bred sugar spiders.

COW

Like most breeds of dog, cows were engineered into their present form by thousands of years of domestication. They too were originally wolves.

Cows in Texas alone produce so much methane that Earth will be identical to Jupiter in size and composition by 2029.

Cows do not use all four of their stomachs regularly. They use one stomach for meat and another for dairy, and then the other two stomachs are only used for meat and dairy on Passover.

CPU

As their name suggested, the earliest 16-bit processors cost exactly 2 dollars.

CRACKER

Crackers are high in crunchy vitamins, which are twice as healthy as soft or "gooey" vitamins. They are made as follows:

First the cracker batter baker bakes a cracker batter batch
then the cracker batter mixer door will open and unlatch
so the batter mixer nozzle can descend onto the patch
where the cracker batter spreads out for the nozzle to attach.

When the cracker mixer nozzle sprays the cracker batter spray
and the cracker batch emulsion lies a-soaking in its haze
then the cracker batter mixer starts to stir up all the glaze
that the final cracker stacker needs to lubricate the way.

Once the cracker stacker handle stacks the cracker batter squares
then the cracker batter's hardened into double stacks of pairs.
Now the cracker separator breaks the crackers in the stackers
so the wrappers on the stackers fit the finished stacking crackers.

Then they're distributed to Wal-Mart.

CREDIT CARD

Credit cards predate modern plastics by almost 15 years. The first credit cards were wooden with lithium magnetic strips and leather hewn numbers on the front. These cards were rare and sell for over $75,000 today.

CRIME

According to police records, the most effective way to get rid of a dead body is to abandon it in the wilderness. The least effective is to throw it at a police officer.

CROMWELL, OLIVER

Oliver Cromwell tried to ban bans. His ban ban overturned his ban ban however and bans were no longer banned. Thus allowing the reinstated ban ban to ban the ban ban, disallowing it yet again. The cycle continues to this day.

CROWBAR

Few crowbars have been made with actual crows, since the invention of metal.

CROWN

Crowns were never really worn by kings or queens, they were merely status symbols that, like modern status symbols, were featured on their royal Facebook pages.

CUP

Cups were originally used open-side-down, with water poured over what is now considered the base. Author Mark Twain was mocked mercilessly when he first started the more efficient tradition of drinking from the open end.

At the center of a treacherous island in the center of an impassible swamp in the center of a forbidden forest at the northmost tip of Britain lies the ancient cup of Garth-Gog-Gamog.

A direct inspiration for Tolkien's "Lord of the Rings," legend has it that the cup was forged by the demon ruler Garth-Gog-Gamog in the time before time existed. Whoever drinks from the cup is said to gain the powers of Garth-Gog-Gamog herself, including the power to summon demons, the power to control insects, the power to cause earthquakes, and the power to always win at Scrabble.

Because of its power, the cup was hidden away for over 6,000 years by order of Britain's then-prime-minister Tony Blair. The cup was only rediscovered in 1976 when three American wanderers stumbled upon it by accident. Only two of the group returned, the third is said to have drunk from the unholy cup and was never heard from again. Rumors abound that they became the new demon lord who will end the universe, or that they were deemed not-evil-enough and died on the spot, or that he is in fact ongoing republican atrocity Donald Trump, who has never lost a Scrabble game despite his total lack of spelling ability and ineptitude at following simple rules.

If the last hypothesis is true, it would be only the second time the republicans have selected an ancient demon lord as their candidate, the first being Lethnor, Imp of Thunder in 1980, who lost the nomination to Ronald Reagan by 2 votes. Lethnor, Imp of Thunder currently hosts The Lethnor Hour on late night CBS.

CYBERNETICS

Cybernetics differs from bionics in that one is full of Es and Ys and even a T. The other is mostly Is and Os. This difference has caused an irreparable rift between the sciences that may never be reconciled.

CYCLOPS

European myth records a creature called the Eyepod, a grotesque mass of slime with one giant eyeball that travels from town to town devouring the innocent, and holding up to 10,000 songs.

CYPRUS

Cyprus is an island nation in the Mediterranean Sea. It is home to the Cyprus Tree, and in 2017, Cyprus earned a new distinction- That of the island that best resembles Farosh, one of three dragons from Zelda: Breath of the Wild.

DARKNING

Darkning is 50,000 times more rare than lightning, in fact most storms will never have a single instance of it. But when static charges between clouds become so energized that the electricity begins to form its own gravity, a black hole is briefly formed, sucking up all the light in the area and resulting in a brief "unflash" of darkning.

Less dangerous than lightning, Darkning lasts for a shorter time and you'd have to be within the event horizon to be harmed by it. Despite thousands a year dying of lightning strikes, only one man has ever been recorded as killed in a darkning strike, and that man was Lewis Caroll, author of Alice in Wonderland, which many historians believe he wrote based on that strange and fatal experience.

DATING

Dating is expected to cease as a social activity by 2026, with the rise in popularity of eyeball exchanges and all.

DEBATE

Many voters have expressed disappointment with the current U.S. political debate format. With the media ignoring some candidates and disallowing others completely, and questions being asked that nobody cared to hear while the important issues are left unsaid, new foolproof rules for a good political debate are as such:

-Any candidate for President can debate, no matter how small their party.

-Any audience member present can ask a question.

-Moderators must be politically inactive and not allowed to vote themselves.

-Candidates must all wear the same outfit for fairness sake, a chartreuse jumpsuit with no markings and a hood to cover their hairstyles.

-Candidates must adhere to a strict diet of raw eggs and borscht for three weeks up to the debate, and may only drink avocado juice unless given a letter from their doctor.

-Each candidate must state their full qualifications before answering each question, including their voting record, tax status, economic policy and whether or not they have successfully ridden the Arrakeen Sandworm and/or David Hasselhoff.

-In the event a candidate does not wish to answer a question, they may request debate-by-combat. If they do so, they may choose a warrior to fight for them. Their opponent as the party challenged may also choose a surrogate warrior, and reserves the right to choose the weapon with which the duel will be fought, which may be either a Lirpa or a rabid badger on a stick.

-The debate will take place on a platform hanging from a crane 80ft over a field of spinning blades each greased with the saliva of a Komodo Dragon while Ritter Fans blow in random directions across the field of combat which shall also be spun at 60mph between loudspeakers playing the Mortal Kombat theme as acid rains down upon them from pipes overhead that extend from the mouth of an 80ft statue of Antonin Scalia decorated with the sigils of the demons Malphas, Stolas and Gremory whose summoning incantations will be sung by the Mormon Tabernacle Choir exactly one octave higher than their usual singing voices while their feet are tickled by feathers plucked from a blue chicken on a Tuesday.

-A llama will be present.

DEMONOLOGY

Early Christian demonology suggested that one could not sell their soul, but that demons took part in a type of soul stock market in which they traded sins in the hopes of accruing evil.

DESERT

The Sahara desert often gets hotter than fire during the summer. Many who travel across it will light themselves on fire to cool off.

DIAMOND

Diamonds are the strongest objects on Earth because they're made of steel. Far from lasting forever though, they generally only keep fresh for a year or two before rotting into ants. That's what ants are. Rotten diamonds.

DICE

The most dice ever thrown occurred in 1489 during the Battle of Strömsbruk, which was not a conventional battle but one of the first RPG events based around an early form of D&D called "Drakarochdemoner." In the battle, the forces of Regnog Rumdistiller surprised the Castle Slottnamn with 760 war elves. Ragnar rolled 760d20 to determine the damage.

But these were the crude days before THAC0 was calculated, and each of the 890 defending soldiers rolled not only an armor 1d12, but saving throws amounting to 3d6 as well as morale reduction (1d6). Thus each soldier spent 5 rolls, 4450 dice total for the defending castle's owner, Wilhelm von Umpk.

Umpk died soon after, drowned in his own dice. The totals were never calculated, and his body was never moved as it was already buried. The dice heap that became his tomb is now depicted on the Swedish Flag (it was yellow and roughly cross shaped).

DICK, MOBY

Moby Dick was based on true events. None involving a whale, ship or obsessed captain, but true events nonetheless. The novel's full opening line reads, "Call me Ishmael to my face and not online and see what happens."

DIMENSIONS

There are nine dimensions:

T- Past and future
Z- From and toward
Y- Up and down
X- Side to side
XXX- In and out
S- The dimension of terror
W- The Yuji Iwahara dimension
ZIM- The dimension of a room with a moose
D- The dimension nobody thinks about except when it visits.

DINOSAUR

Numerous dinosaurs are thought to have existed between prehistory and the 1940s. Plesiosaurs for instance were widely known as the most polite dinosaurs of the Jurassic period. They are thought to have been symbiotic with the Thankylosaur.

The Brontosaurus by contrast is named for the first woman to depict it in fiction, Emily Brontë. Her novel Wuthering Heights was an epic adventure through a lost world of dinosaurs and took advantage of the recent discovery of a massive skull fossil to inspire its largest beast, what would become known as the Brontosaurus, which she simply called "Heathcliff." Heathcliff's rampage through Victorian England horrified and amazed readers who were at the time used to the dull and dinosaurless works of Jane Austen, whose name went on to inspire the word "Austere."

Most animals we now call dinosaurs were considered mammals in their own time, though lesser evolved animals of the early Jurassic era had wheels instead of legs. Lungs didn't evolve until long after dinosaurs roamed the Earth. They had to eat air and digest its oxygen to survive.

The Dimetrodon is not really a dinosaur at all. To be a full dinosaur, an animal must have been green, and totaled the mass of ten dimetrodons, or four quarterodons, or even one hundred pennidons.

The Alvisaur is the only dinosaur that had six feet. This is especially notable in that it had only four legs. Its discoverer, Alvin Machi, was very adamant that his reconstruction of the Alvisaur was correct, though many other paleentologists- paleantologis- paleontolegist- Dinosaur researchers insisted he had merely placed two extra feet next to the specimen, and that they were elk feet as evidenced by the hooves, and elk hair.

The Verivisovalisaur is one of the least known dinosaurs because no fossil of it has ever been found, nor have any impressions, footprints or other evidence. Its only mention is actually in this very fact, which has nothing to back it up at all. Yet still people deny that we evolved from it.

Peter James Wigglenson also famously denied the existence of dinosaurs until he himself was eaten by one. Stating in his manifesto that the concept of dinosaurs opposed the Bible, he attempted to prove his beliefs by taunting a cassowary, one of the last living dinosaurs. Though he was killed, many took up his cause, which is strange because the Bible in question is not a religious bible, but the "Muffler King's Bible and Bibliography of Muffler Manufacturers 1908-1978," which for some reason states that there are no dinosaurs.

The largest dinosaur ever recorded is the Giganticus Galimuliplexus, which stood over 700ft tall, measured 8000ft long, and weighted as much as 500 blue whales. Only the toe bone of this gargantuan creature has been found, and its discovery remains controversial because it was found on the set of Pacific Rim 2 being used as a prop. Also notable is that it was made of paper maché, which experts claim made the animal just light enough to still be able to move. Some also point to the film's budget listing for a fake paper maché toe bone for a giant monster, but according to dinosaur expert Dino Sareckspirt, "Leave me alone please I beg you I made a mistake stop calling me you're ruining my family and I just want to be left alone."

Troubling words indeed.

DISNEY CHARACTERS

Many of Disney's most famous characters are based on fairy tales and folk stories, but many others are original to their movies and even their names come from rather clever places. Here are a few examples:

-Judy Hopps from Zootopia: "Hopps" refers to the way rabbits hop, as she is a rabbit.

-Baymax from Big Hero 6: Baymax is named after Betamax, a video system that competed with VHS, much as Baymax in the film competes with a robot made from a VCR.

-Elsa and Anna from Frozen: Named for Elsa and Anna Hermansendorf, two sisters who survived two weeks in the Norwegian Winter after they were lost on a camping trip. Anna Hermansendorf also had a white streak in her hair.

-Ralph from Wreck-It Ralph: Named for Ralph Nader, who wrecked the 2000 and 2004 elections by running as a Green Party candidate, siphoning votes from Al Gore and John Kerry and ensuring the presidency of George W. Bush.

-Lilo and Stitch: Named for Lilo Pelekai and Sid "Stitch" Snickers, respectively. Lilo Pelekai was a Hawaiian dancer in the 1950s. Sid "Stitch" Snickers was a serial killer in the 1980s known for eating the faces of his victims and stitching their flayed skin into a body suit that he wore while committing his crimes, including the butchering of several families and burning of numerous orphanages. It is thought Disney naming executives may have confused him with Sidney "Stitches" Salvador who was also a Hawaiian dancer.

-Kuzco from The Emperor's New Groove: Named after Qosqo, the historic capital of the Inca Empire.

DISNEYLAND

Disneyland re-opens each night two hours after the parks close, for adults only. Their night activities include bacchanalian rites of alcohol and brazen sexuality. Walt Disney himself was killed during one of these drunken orgies when he tried to sleep with a performer in a Mufasa lion suit but accidentally tried to mate with a real lion. This event is depicted allegorically in "The Lion King 2: Simba's Pride."

Though Disneyland is considered the most fun place on Earth, sometimes things go wrong. Many of the actors playing costumed roles are under a great deal of stress and sometimes they're caught acting out against tourists. Here is a round-up of some such incidents from 2015:

February 4th- A Peter Pan player was spotted by children while off duty reciting a cuss-word filled monologue from "Scarface."

May 26th- An Elsa and Anna team was fired for arguing with a teenager about Walt Disney's opinion of Jews.

August 17th- An overheated actor in a hot Goofy suit stole a child's ice cream and consumed it as the family watched.

August 19th- Two Winnie the Pooh costumed actors got into a fistfight over which was the true Pooh. The altercation ended when one Pooh attempted to drown the other in a honey fountain and was arrested.

September 4th- A drunken Buzz Lightyear jumped to his death from a tower in Tomorrowland, believing he could fly.

November 13th- An Aladdin Genie was fired and charged with kidnapping for granting a child's wish that his parents would disappear. The parents are still missing.

November 21st- A Mad Hatter and a White Rabbit were fired for getting into a political debate with a tourist, insisting he should support the Tea Party.

November 22nd- Rafiki held a newborn child up to the sky without permission from the parents.

December 16th- A Shrek actor was banned from the park after staff recognized that he was a Dreamworks character and not welcome on Disney grounds. The enraged ogre fought with two

Mickeys and a Jack Sparrow, destroying over $500 of merchandise and damaging a Ferris wheel. More damage ensued when staff found that the ogre had released a live donkey into the Splash Mountain ride. Once he was unmasked, authorities discovered that the ogre had in fact been Mike Myers himself.

December 31st- The New Years Eve festivities were ruined when all seven dwarfs seized control of the Haunted Mansion and held over 70 tourists hostage. Demanding equal pay to the more famous characters, Grumpy and Doc threatened to execute one hostage every hour until their demands were met. The situation was only resolved when Sneezy dissented and covertly strangled Happy, the ringleader, as Bashful looked on. Bashful was afraid to alert the others and police managed to seize most of the mansion, arresting Sleepy who was caught resting under the ride's mechanical booth. Two officers died when Dopey detonated an improvised explosive device, destroying part of the mansion and trapping Grumpy and Doc, who subsequently died in a barrage of police gunfire as they attempted to transport hostages to the Monorail. Sneezy alone was acquitted of all charges, having heroically saved many of the hostages.

Sneezy still works at Disneyland but keeps to himself mostly. Suffering flashbacks and night terrors, Sneezy stays on the payroll and other characters take care of him during the hard times. But his outlook is good and an anonymous Rapunzel has stated that he's even been known to whistle once again, while he works.

DISNEY, WALT

Walt Disney began his career at the Disney company as a janitor. He rose slowly through the ranks until he became the C.E.O.

DNA

-DNA stands for Deoxyribonusloculumicizmgmmsm Acid.
-DNA is the blueprint of life. That means it's blue and smells like ammonia.
-DNA contains four codons: G, T, A, and San Andreas.

-DNA is a "macro-molecule" but you shouldn't mention this in public.

-DNA lives in the nucleus of the cell, which is like the yolk in the egg that is you. DNA needs RNA to copy itself, making RNA the carbon paper of the human body, and the Command-C buttons on the keyboard of your soul.

-DNA can be "spooled" out of the cellular nucleus by pinning it to a stick and turning the stick very slowly.

-DNA can help identify criminals in court. Once it does, it enters the DNA Protection Program and is moved to a small town in Alaska under a new name, and it can have no more contact with its family or friends.

Your teeth and fingernails are constructed from the same segment of DNA. If a growing tooth is transplanted into a fingertip, it will grow into a fingernail; and if a fingernail is transplanted into the mouth, it will grow into a tooth.

There are many misconceptions about DNA, to clear them up:

-DNA is a molecule, not a legal document.

-Genetics is the study of genes, not jeans.

-Cellular memory is different from cellular memory foam mattresses.

-The human body is not made of string.

-Genomes, unlike Garden Gnomes, do not wear red pointy hats.

-Identical twins result from a zygote splitting into two embryos, they are not a gift from the lightning god Thor in exchange for the sacrifice of a good sheep.

-Ants, though they are useful for genetic study, do not generally execute their queens in times of political revolution, nor do these queens care if their worker ants eat cake.

-Genes are not "tamperproof." There are several records of genetic tampering by genetic criminals attempting to commit genetic fraud or genetic blackmail. It is true though that most of these genetic criminals are caught, and are locked away in gene jail, or "geail."

-Punctuated Equilibrium is a theory of evolution in which species often stay the same until events cause a sudden alteration of the dominant phenotype, it is not a copy of the film "Equilibrium" starring Christian Bale that has a hole in it. In fact, all DVDs have a hole in their center and this is normal for the format.

-There is no gene for the human spirit.

DOCTOR

One in ten doctors is unaware they are a doctor. There are signs you may be one of them:

-Bad handwriting, especially when writing prescriptions.

-Doctors tend to wear white lab coats. Check what you're wearing.

-Look for a stethoscope around your neck. This is a sure sign that you are a doctor.

-When you go to work, do you perform surgery on other people? Don't worry if you do, you may just be a homicidal maniac. Otherwise you are likely a doctor, specifically a surgeon.

-Monitor yourself for knowledge of human anatomy. Do you know where the Islets of Langerhans are? How about the Crypts of Lieberkühn? Or the Nodes of Ranvier? Knowing these is often a sign of doctorhood, or of being very pretentious and eager to impress.

-Not all doctors are medical doctors. Before you rest safe in the knowledge that you are not a doctor, consider whether you may be a doctor of philosophy, juridical science, or even linguistics. Check your degrees to be sure. If you have no degrees, you are likely not a doctor.

-Are you a Time Lord? If so you may well be not only a doctor, but *The* Doctor.

-If you're still uncertain, head to the hospital to get tested. The test is simple, if they greet you by calling you "Doctor," it is almost certain that you are a doctor.

DOCTOR PEPPER

Dr. Pepper is not pepper flavored as the name implies, but doctor flavored as the name also implies.

DOG

Dogs come in many forms known as "breeds," which contain infinite diversity in infinite dog-combinations or "dogbinations." For instance, breeding a dachshund with a poodle will yield one purebred mouse and one purebred wolf.

Many dogs can smell fear, but only the chihuahua can taste, eat and digest it. Golden retrievers are not really gold, only electrum. The beagle is the only dog that lays eggs instead of giving live birth.

While some dog breeds have over 800 unique barks for different words, others have only a single bark, which means "spaghetti."

Dog squeak toys amuse dogs by mimicking the pained cries of small animals they would naturally eat. The harmonica amuses humans for the same reason.

Puppy is slang for a young dog, but more properly puppies are a similar, now extinct species akin to dogs in the same way ponies are to horses.

DOOR

Revolving doors were originally designed as a practical joke. Then they were discovered to be practical, as well as funny.

DRAPES

Drapes and curtains differ only in that drapes are traditionally made from fabric and curtains are made of ostrich leather.

DREAMS

One should always follow their dreams.

Unless you have one of those dreams where you're standing in a puddle and your toenails keep falling off so you try to crush the bicycle of a passing Elvis impersonator and his skin falls off revealing your 3rd grade homeroom teacher and you scream but the sound comes out of your eyes and you can't see and that's when you know you have to kill the curator of the Smithsonian Museum before she cooks the world's last waffle which is actually made of liquefied ants.

Then it's okay not to follow your dreams.

DRILL

You Know The Drill. It's a tool used for making holes in things. You know that.

DUCK

The phrase "Like water off a duck's back" does not refer to the animal, but the DUKW, a WW2 era amphibious car, which was notoriously watertight. Actual animal ducks are very absorbent, and were used as sponges by the ancient Greeks.

DUNE

Frank Herbert originally set "Dune" on an all water planet. He changed it to a desert planet after he got sick of writing about everyone swimming all the time. He was forced to cut his original opening prologue:

On Caladan born and raised
On the ocean was where I spent most of my days
Chillin' out maxin' relaxin' all cool
And all stuffin' my hand in a pain box at school
When a couple of Harkonens who were up to no good
Started making trouble in Arrakis neighborhood
So my Dad got killed and my mom got scared
She said 'You're movin' in with the Fremen in Sietch Tabr'

Because his head was shaved for a scene in the 2021 Dune movie, Timothée Chalamet attended the opening matinée of the film wearing a toupée.

DUNGEONS AND DRAGONS

Dungeons and Dragons was called Dungeons, Dragons, and Toenail Fragments until the creators decided to throw away their clippings rather than sell them. The game was originally played with only four sided dice, but grew to include other dice as numbers larger than 4 were invented.

The first edition included not only Fighters, Clerics and other currently used classes, but a few anachronistic ones such as helicopter pilots, media moguls, and electrical engineers.

D&D has inspired "LARPing," an activity in which people dress according to their characters and fight across parks and cities to involve themselves in the game. This is how the sports of hunting and fencing began.

Several books, films and TV shows have been made based on the game, including Lord of the Rings, Game of Thrones, and oddly enough, Oliver Stone's JFK, which is not based on the assassination of president Kennedy, but on the RPG "Military Industrial GURPlex."

Water buffalo have been known to play Dungeons and Dragons when they think humans are not watching. They are not said to be very good at it, but they have fun and that's the important part.

DVD

DVDs are highly flammable and must not be microwaved for amusement like CDs. Microwaving a DVD would cause the microwave to explode, and microwaving a box set such as the 4th season of Boston Legal could take out a city block.

-E-

E.T.

Because the moon wasn't full on the night E.T. had to shoot its famous flight scene, a stand-in moon was borrowed from Saturn.

EARRING

Earrings originated as holds for reins, to better steer the person in front of you in a long line.

EARTH

Sadly, Earth is not mostly harmless at all.

EASTER

Easter is the only Christian holiday that can fall on a Sunday. When other holidays would naturally fall on a Sunday they are moved to the next Thursday, except for Good Friday, which is exchanged with Ash Wednesday so long as Fat Tuesday doesn't fall on a Monday, in which case Easter is cancelled and Lent is held from Halloween to Thanksgiving.

ECLIPSE

We don't yet know why the sun experiences eclipses from time to time, but we are certain that they mean God has abandoned us and we are all doomed.

EDEN, GARDEN OF

According to the Bible, there was no fall damage in the Garden of Eden. Adam and Eve could jump from tall trees to the ground without harm until she ate the fruit of knowledge.

EDWARD -III

Edward the Negative 3rd reigned two Edwards before anyone named Edward took the throne.

EFLUMULUS

Every film crew on a major production has a member called the "Eflumulus." What the eflumulus does or why the eflumulus is there have been Hollywood's greatest mysteries since 1921.

EINSTEIN, ALBERT

Einstein's brain was preserved when he died, and was stolen in 1976. It was mostly returned in 1978 with a note reading only, "I am keeping the cerebellum."

Einstein created his first theory at age 6, it was the theory that one could have infinite wishes by wishing for more wishes. He was the first to think of it.

Einstein considered fire to be a living being because it could metabolize, grow, adapt, and reproduce. He died attempting to mate with it.

EGG

Eggs in cartons don't look like the eggs that come from chickens. When laid, eggs are covered in protective thorns that have to be sandblasted off.

Though they seem fragile, it's impossible to cut through an egg with a knife or cleaver.

Though modern technology has made it a simple matter, it once took over two weeks to cook a single egg sunny-side up.

Century eggs do not truly take a whole century to make, only about 99 years and 364 days.

Fried eggs contain the chemical friedegamine, which gives them their fried egg like flavor.

Friedeggamine is produced by the heated exposure of yolkamine ($Yo2Lk5$) with heated iron (Fe) in the presence of eggwhitesin ($Egg3It2Wh3$). Use of a non-iron pan can result in the creation of Teflon-Browneggflakealine, which flavors the resulting molecule undesirably.

Boildeggamine is the same but with the introduction of water ($H2O$) resulting in ($H2Ot2Egg3Yo2Lk5$). Boildeggamine can combine with Mayonnaise ($M2Ay2O$) to created Vinegar-EggSatanide, commonly known as the "Deviled Egg." It can also be combined with Chlorine to produce Mark 7 nerve gas.

The idea for egg crates came from a hatchery worker who got sick of storing eggs in his socks.

EGGNOG

Millions drink eggnog every year to celebrate the holidays. If only they knew the truth of its origins.

The year was 1899. The last Christmas of the 19th century was right around the corner, and across Europe, a terrible egg famine was rampant. The Egg Famine of 1899 was caused in part by an epidemic of Humanpox that decimated the chicken population, leaving farmers to rely on turkey eggs, robin's eggs, and hawk eggs, which were notoriously dangerous to harvest due to the vengeful mother hawks. These eggs proved far inferior in many ways. Their small sizes, bad flavors, and difficult species to breed reduced egg consumption to nil.

Enter Johannes Nog. Johannes Nog was famous in the culinary industry owing to his invention of Spam. Spam proved instrumental in wartime nutrition because it could exist for years in a can, unlike natural pork that had to be preserved by cold or salt and would last only a few days on the front. A union of delegates from every country in Europe (at the time this was only Spain, France, Germany, Italy, North Italy, South Russia, and New Argentina) hired Nog to solve the egg crisis before mass starvation ensued.

Nog came out within the month with Egg ala Nog, or "Eggnog" for short. The fluid was high in protein, sweet to taste, and easy to manufacture even without chicken eggs. Europe was saved, and Eggnog became a seasonal favorite long after the famine was over. It wasn't until 1907 when The European Food Administration began classifying all foodstuffs for cleanliness and safety that Eggnog's terrible secret was first discovered.

Nog unsurprisingly owned a monopoly on the production of Eggnog, and had refused to share the recipe for fear of losing that advantage. A court case resulted in which the courts demanded Nog reveal his secrets to a committee of inquisitors who would certify his techniques, and be sworn to secrecy about the exact recipe. And so he did, and so they kept their secret to the grave- Which all fell victim to within a month of the certification.

Indeed, of the seven men who learned the true nature of Eggnog, three died in mysterious car accidents (including the first car accident ever), two died in random muggings, one disappeared without a trace, and one died of unknown wounds while vacationing in Luxembourg. This man, Arnold Salbewasser von Jergenslotion, as his last act, wrote a letter that was to be delivered to the European Food Administration in the event of his death.

Due to a frozen alpine mailman, the letter remained undelivered until 2011 when the European Food Administration had been disbanded in WW1, reconstituted by the League of Nations, abolished by Nazi Germany, rebuilt in two parts by the Americans as The Western European Food Administration, and the Russians as the The People's European Food Ministry Pact, then reunified in 1994 as The New European Food Concern under the United Nations, dissolved in 1995 when purchased by McDonalds, and finally reformed in 2009 as the European Food Administration 2 by order of the papacy.

Owing to ecclesiastical feuds, the letter remained unopened until 2017 when it was unearthed by Pope Francis who found it buried under a stack of bills in the papal key drawer when he was looking for the Holy Rubber Band Box of St. Ignatz of Queens. And so at last, the original recipe for Egg Nog was uncovered. It is duplicated here in its entirety, sensitive readers are advised not to read on:

Johannes Nog's Egg-Substitute Holyday Drynk:

  1 parte milk of thee bovine cowe
  1 parte sugar of thee cane plant
  1 parte mallow of thee marshe
  7 partes egges of thee centipeede
  2 partes extracte of thee fluff-mouse glande (squirrel liver)
  1 parte spam
  5 partes egg yolkes of the egges of a pelican

Now, part of this recipe is not as grotesque as it may sound, as "egges of thee centipeede" was simply 1800s slang for blueberries. Unfortunately, the same era slang "egg yolkes of the egges of a pelican" was a euphemism for the clotted pus that collected in the sinuses of diseased skunks. And so it remains to this day.

EGYPT (ANCIENT)

There were once hundreds of Pyramids at Khartoum, rather than the four Great Pyramids that remain today. While only one Sphinx remains, there may also have been as many as five hundred Sphunx.

The Staff of Ra is a real artifact, but it does not locate the Ark of the Covenant as in "Raiders of the Lost Ark." It leads to the Keys of Ra, which Ra often misplaced.

The ancient Egyptian fortress of Ezak-Nur was impenetrable in its day, as it is now. Nobody has been able to break into it, and many suspect it still contains a regiment of soldiers loyal to Ramses II.

The real Cleopatra lived closer to the times of Marc Anthony than she did to those of Mark Antony.

ELECTRICITY

The world's least efficient power plant exists in Naples, Italy. It consists of a slug in a hamster wheel and outputs one watt every three years.

ELEPHANT

Elephant skin is 14 inches thick. Beneath it, an elephant is only about the size of a horse. Elephants are not a distinct species, but a hybrid like a mule that occurs when a rhino mates with a tree, hence the trunk.

ELEVATOR

We do not yet understand the physics by which elevators function, and must still rely on naturally occurring elevators to build our skyscrapers around.

EMO

The "Emo" culture and associated music were named for their originator, Emo Philips.

EMU

At any given time, for every emu you see, there are 20 present that you do not see.

ENDOSYMBIOSIS

Endosymbiosis is very difficult to understand, so here is a parable to explain it:

There's this lady Rita. Rita makes batteries for a living, working out of her garage. She's good at what she does but she refuses to leave her house, which is small and cramped owing to her years of collecting battery-making supplies.

She lives next to the O'Plasm family, a big family covering four generations in one household. And this family lives in a huge mansion that still has lots of empty space, it's huge and its comfortable except for one thing- They haven't paid the power bill in 50 years, so the house has no electricity.

So one day, Rita is staring out her window, envious of the O'Plasms and she neglects to monitor the acid drip flowing into her latest 90V. The house catches on fire and begins to burn. Battery supplies are sparking, and she knows it's all gonna go up and kill her unless she conquers her fears and gets out. She takes what supplies she can and runs straight for the O'Plasm's garage. She's terrified and thankfully they let her in. Her house burns but she's okay.

She gets to talking to the O'Plasms. They need electricity, she can make it. She needs a place to stay, and old man O'Plasm says they have plenty of space on site. So Rita takes up residence in the new site O'Plasm offered, and produces energy in exchange.

Soon it's time for the youngest O'Plasms to move out and begin their own families. At the same time, Rita has married within the O'Plasm family and her daughters also want to move out, so they make this deal- All Rita's daughters will live in O'Plasm family households and make them batteries so they never need to pay electrical bills, and Rita's kids will never want for a place to stay. So on for generations.

All this is irrelevant except that one of Rita's great-grandkids, Lynn Margulis, came up with the theory of endosymbiosis, which is what you should probably be reading up on if you want to know how it works.

ENLIGHTENMENT

The highest form of enlightenment is not the quest for spiritual understanding, but the ability to decipher what the heck David Lynch's "Inland Empire" is about.

ENZYME

The word "Enzyme" comes from its first discoverer, Robert N. Zyme. Zyme discovered the first enzyme on his exploration of the South Pole, which went off course and ended up in the stomach, where several enzymes were present. The largest Enzyme, Lyso Zyme, bonded with Robert over their same last names and the rest, as they say, is history- Though enzymes are usually studied in biology rather than history class.

Enzymes are the body's catalysts, which means they are the parts of us most capable of speed running Dark Souls and other From Software games.

There are seven types of enzyme, all of which are present in the human mouth, and none of which can be pronounced by it.

Allosteric Modulation is one of the most important parts of how enzymes work, and as such it will not be addressed here at all.

Some enzymes need "cofactors" to work. Much like Mario cannot exit a level's special exit without a key, some enzymes need additional ingredients to be active. An enzyme and its cofactor together are called a "holo-enzyme," named because it sounds cool and sci-fi like.

Enzymes help substances reach a chemical equilibrium. Once they reach that equilibrium, the enzyme will usually fuck off to Newark and start a new reaction, then fail to send any support and refuse to see the resulting substances, repeating this process until they die of old age, alone like they fucking deserve, the assholes.

Enzymes can also be slowed by enzyme inhibitors. Enzyme inhibitions include social anxiety, sexual prudity, and fear of intimacy. Unlike college students, enzymes are no less inhibited around alcohol.

The popular anniversary and new year song "Auld Lang Zyme" is about enzymes.

EPCOT CENTER

Nobody knows what's inside the giant sphere at Epcot Center. The park was simply built around it when they found that it could not be moved.

ESCALATOR

Escalators were invented before stairs. The first staircases were called "still-scalators."

ESCAPE ROOM

Though "Room Escape" games have grown in popularity, several thousand people have died and been left in rooms they were unable to escape from. The companies just keep building new rooms again and again.

ESP

You can control the shape of clouds with your mind by removing your brain and throwing it at them.

ESPIONAGE

SEE: SPYCRAFT

ETIQUETTE

Making eye contact is now considered impolite. To show that you're paying attention, it's now advisable to shout loudly, "I AM LISTENING" every five seconds.

"Please," "Thank you," and "You're welcome" did not exist until Queen Victoria felt England wasn't pompous enough and declared them mandatory.

It was considered proper in the 1800s to avert ones eyes upon seeing a tree bare of leaves.

Salad dressing was invented by Emily Post to preserve the modesty of the salad, which could not appear nude in Victorian society.

EUROPE

Europe was named for the Goddess "Europa," who was the goddess of naming continents after herself.

EVOLUTION

The most compelling evidence of evolution in humans is thought to be goosebumps, which we could not have if we were not descended from geese.

Evolution is ongoing. The Paristi tribe, also known as the mud-swimmers of Runga-Oulon, have evolved webbed fingers.

Living in a swamp region of Runga-Oulon, the Paristi have been untouched by external civilization for over 1,500 years. Having never developed boating technology, the tribe travels across their native land exclusively by swimming in the mud. In those years the entire tribe has developed webbed fingers, likely as a result of favoring the trait in mating rituals. The tribe numbers over 2,000 people and is now diverse enough to maintain a safe genetic base, while retaining the aberrant but useful trait.

"This is a clear example of evolution in modern times," said geneticist Robert Whele, "We are literally watching human mutation adapt a group to their climate."

But not everyone is in awe of the adaptation. The Paristi are hunted constantly by the local missionaries who feel their attempt to evolve is blasphemous and against the Holy Bible. Said Pastor Nordling, "Evolution is a lie, and this tribe is full of liars. Manhunting is legal in Runga-Oulon so we're using our legal rights to see that these sinners don't infect the world with their devil's fingers."

Though Manhunting is temporarily prevented under seasonal poaching laws, the government is powerless to stop the mass murder of this tribe at the hands of religious extremists. The tribe is not afraid however, said Sub-chief Wellego-Nuntun Obigere in perfect English, "No, we are not afraid. We evolved webbed fingers, we can 'evolve' ourselves some Uzis if you know what I mean."

Truly nature is inspiring.

EXCESSIVE CELEBRATION

Excessive Celebration rules in Football come from the 1960s when free love and drug use were rampant. The rules were first suggested when Thaddeus Hopper of the Philadelphia Bells scored a touchdown against the San Antonio Alamos. He celebrated with an on-field party that held up the rest of the game for seven hours, and resulted in no less than 17 drug arrests among players alone.

But it was not until the infamous Touchdown of Orlando in the summer of 1968 that the rules happened. Late in the 7th inning, Chaim Levi of the Orlando Blooms scored a touchdown against his team's longtime rivals, the Sacramento Mints. The crowd went wild, and at Levi's lead, they stormed the field and participated in what would be called by announcer Harry Caray, "The largest orgy since the inauguration of Calvin Coolidge."

(SEE ALSO: ORGY, ELECTORAL)

Estimated to have had over 3,000 active participants, the touchdown celebration not only established the excessive celebration rules but 197 pregnancies, 104 arrests for indecent acts committed upon astroturf, and somehow, the extinction of the Florida Condor.

At first however, the rules only designated 5 minutes in the penalty box for the responsible player. The rules did not achieve their modern consequences until 1971:

It was a bright summer day when the Omaha Holdems faced the Salt Lake Salt Licks. Omaha was up 6 points in the final period with 12 meters down. Holdem star Doyle Kaplan dribbled the ball 11 meters toward the goal and in a move that football announcer John Steinbeck (no relation) called "The pinnacle of this sport we call live-action-foosball," Kaplan spiked the ball into the Salt Lake team's score-orifice and began his illegal celebration.

The actual details of his celebration have been censored and redacted since the event to prevent copycats, but here is what little we is known about the excessive jubilation:

-Between 37 and 68 people died or lost limbs
-The state emergency tequila supply was fully depleted
-Both teams were disbanded and both cities were banned

-85 Georges Méliès films were lost or destroyed
-The ball pit was pathetically small
-Jimmy Hoffa was never seen again
-Christianity is now a distinct religion from Judaism
-Bessie, the prized cow of Omaha, was skeletonized by piranhas
-Satan, laughing, spread his wings
-The Hindenberg crashed
-The Titanic sank
-Ronald Reagan was elected president
-People 'sneeze' now

The ongoing censorship of the actual nature of the celebration has kept the event one of life's great mysteries, as the footage was destroyed, the announcer was sworn to secrecy, the players were given gag orders, and the audience was forbidden to even tell anecdotes of the day.

EXPLORATION

Stanley and Livingstone spent most of their time crawling along the ground and eating bugs. Stanley and Livingstone are my pet geckos by the way. Though the explorers Stanley and Livingstone did the same.

EYE

The earliest evolved eyeballs had a resolution of only 480 lines. Modern human eyes have 4K, and by the year 2150 may be sharp enough to see the lunar lander on the moon.

Jailbreaking your eyes will void your warranty and subject your eyes to malware. Only use manufacturer approved sight and thought. Consult your local mashgiach before looking at anything or remembering what you saw.

One of your eyes is superficial, you only need one to see. The other is just so your face isn't lopsided.

The human eyeball contains more light sensitive cones and rods than all the cones and rods in any given Home Depot. While dogs have only rod receptors in their eyes, and humans have rods and cones, dolphins and seals also have dodecahedron receptors, the use of which is unknown.

Your eyes are covered in thousands of tiny, tiny hands each containing a nerve cluster, hence the pain when you wax your eyes.

A fishing crew off the coast of Portugal discovered a colossal eyeball that scientists say must have belonged to a squid the size of three football fields.

"Genetic testing confirms it's from a squid," said marine biologist Marnie Balgis, "and the scale is absolutely certain. The squid from which this eyeball came was nine times the size of a blue whale, the previous largest known animal on Earth."

Balgis notes that there is nothing to suggest the squid that lost the eyeball is dead. Even more startling is the age of the eyeball. "The eye belongs to a very young squid. There's every reason to believe this animal is still growing, and will likely reach adulthood at five times larger than its present state.

The new species has been named "Mesonychoteuthis margaretkeanes" after Margaret Keane, an artist known for painting portraits with big eyes.

The human eyeball has two pupils, one in front and one in back. We never see the one in back because it's deep within our head, and it never sees out for the same reason, rendering it useless.

EYEBROWS

Eyebrows were considered an organ until 1977, thus they were capable of playing Toccata and Fugue in D Minor.

EYEDROPS

Before the invention of eyedrops, the standard treatment for sore eyes was to look upon a loved one that the patient hasn't seen in ages.

FACT

The recursive fact is particularly complex, and can involve up to 72 factoids within the body of the main fact. Beyond this fact barrier, we know nothing.

FAIRY

The first recorded fairy in myth or literature lived in a well and granted the ability to carry more arrows in their quiver for whoever threw her Indian currency.

Court records from 1604 state that a fairy was discovered in Kent on March 8th. It filed charges against Henry Millsworth for breach of contract and settled for 78 shillings then disappeared.

FALAFEL

Falafel is the only chemical element popularly served as food in its pure form.

FARADAY CAGE

The first Faraday Cage was designed not to guard against electromagnetic fields, but to hold Dr. Faraday himself.

FASHION

The world of fashion is complex and full of interesting trivia. None of the following trivia however is at all interesting:

The belt was invented not to hold up pants, but as a tourniquet for use in emergencies. Hence the old saying, "The belt was invented not to hold up pants, but as a tourniquet for use in emergencies."

Dresses are losing popularity. If the trend continues, the last dress will be worn in 1993.

Suits and ties were originally swimwear, but became the proper dress for business after the beach meetings of 1891.

Wearing a blue suit traditionally means that a person is in mourning over their pet fish.

Humans are not the only animals to wear clothing. Some gorillas have been known to cover themselves in the skins of the animals they hunt, most anteaters will carry palm leaves during the rain, and weasels are said to be fond of Brioni suits.

Before the invention of the ironing board, shirts were traditionally ironed while being worn. This is why menswear laundries were traditionally equipped with hospitals.

Formal dresses used to be made of rose petals, until an incident at the wedding of Princess Suveres the Allergic.

In 2008, a man sold a set of "Emperor's New Clothes" on eBay for $60,000. Though he sent nothing to the buyer, the buyer did not seek compensation, stating the clothes were quite beautiful.

The first vest was invented when a severely impatient senator took his suit from the tailor before he had a chance to add arms.

18% of cloaked figures contain no people.

Most clothing from the 1800s was made from porkwool, or pig's wool. It was only after the extinction of the Norwegian Woolly Pig that most manufacturers switched to sheep's wool.

People in the 1700s wore "Tongue pants," a sort of sock for the tongue. Nobody today knows why.

Levi's jeans are named for Eliphas Levi, an occult magician who received the original design for blue jeans from Azbathbaleth, a demon in the 4th circle of western hell.

Boots made specifically for walking are 60% likelier to walk all over you than other boots.

Corsets used to contain whalebone, which is an antiquated term for baleen. This allowed most women in Victorian times to filter feed on krill in the open sea.

The first bra ever designed has cups for five breasts and nobody knows why.

What we call shorts are merely the larval form of pants, harvested before maturity.

14 Fashion models died in 1992 when a 747 attempted to land on their runway.

Every laundry machine in the world makes a slightly different horrible grinding noise. Their horrible grinding noises are like fingerprints, each is unique.

Suit jackets and suit pants are made from cuts of fabric that fit together exactly to save on material. Lapels only exist because of how the pant legs fit together.

The tradition of wearing a lapel pin began in 1901, a full 20 years before the invention of the lapel.

In the early days of modern fashion, Robert Soughraughn designed several types of jacket. He designed three jackets for the British royal family; seven suit coats for the German aristocracy, and nine- Nine tuxedos for the French prime minister, who coveted fashionable wardrobe above all. For within these suits was bound the strength and the will to govern each country's taste in clothing.

But they were all of them deceived. For deep in the heat of his sewing shop, Soughraughn himself stitched together a master lounge jacket, and into its right lapel he poured all of his pretentiousness, his vogue, his ravenous haute couture. One suit jacket to rule them all.

One by one, the sovereign countries fell to fashion sense and other trivialities, but there were some who resisted. A last alliance of beatniks, goths and punks marched against the conventions of fashion. And on the very slopes of Christian Dior's house, they fought for the freedom of Earth. Victory was near, but the power of Soughraughn's vanity could not be vanquished. It was then that Kurt Cobain took up his grunge aesthetic. Soughraughn was instantly defeated, for now...

FEAR

You can overcome the fear of public speaking by imagining the audience naked, imagining the audience is sleeping, or by sleeping naked with the audience.

FETISH

In the beginning, there were prokaryotes. Cells without nuclei. They could exchange genes but they did not have sexual intercourse in the common sense, as along with nuclei, they lacked genitals. Then one day, a sexy, sexy eukaryote wandered along. With its hard, semipermeable nucleus it became the hottest cell in the soup and the first fetish was born.

Centuries later, some protomitochondrial bacteria arrived on the block and all the eukaryotes wanted them desperately. Not long after, a desperate eukaryote let a bacterium penetrate it, and symbiogenesis was invented. This kinky, kinky practice became all the rage and soon, mitochondria became the sexual powerhouses of the primordial world. Things only got hotter from there.

Plants began to mate sexually. Fungi, with their hundreds and thousands of genders, got in on the action and before long, animals began to do it like they did on the Discovery Channel. Sex being a natural part of their life cycle it was not in and of itself a fetish. But the first distinctly sexual fetishes began quickly after.

For eons in the plant kingdom, things were pretty vanilla. Specifically, the flat-leaf vanilla orchid. But orchids grew bored with their own homogeneity and began to flower into exotic subspecies that attracted new and interesting insects and birds to lure into their pollination processes. Nageliella purpurea lured and seduced hummingbirds. Ophrys apifera got into bees. Macrothynnus insignis developed a thing for voyeurism but we'll get to that later, it also enjoyed getting pollinated by wasps.

Speaking of the insect class, it became the kinkiest batch of arthropods around. Egg bearing beings, they quickly turned to ovovivipary to get laid. Other critters fell for hypodermic insemination, apophallation, and even sexual cannibalism. Meanwhile some fish got into polyandrous parabiosis. And among the mammals, well, look up the bonobo sometime.

But all of this was Leave it to Beaver compared to humans.

The first recorded human paraphilia took place in 37,000 B.C. when Oorg and Skrung developed an affinity for leather. As this predated the use of leather in clothing and armor, it is likely that leather wardrobe began first as a fetish and only later developed into a practical matter. The second paraphilia known to history occurred in 22,000 B.B. when Zgrunk Orglesson of Fungrungumeyer is related to have been obsessed with sucking on the toes of Vingungu Urnt. According to Urnt, "Rrrrg. Ughh. Achecheungh." Truer words on the subject of fetishism were never spoken.

Centuries later, Ancient Egypt happened. Ancient Egypt was like the Cambrian explosion of fetishes. Expanding into the religious front where gods were said to have mated in every which way, the people who built pyramids also took part in orgies and kinks so diverse that it took Norman Mailer 800 pages to chronicle about a tenth of them. Note that Egypt has this distinction only because we know so little about the Kingdom of Sumer, from which new kinks are still being discovered.

Greece took in much of Egypt's culture and with it, their fetishistic forms of love. They also added a few of their own, which will not be chronicled here because of the watch lists they would put me on if I did. Rome too inherited the eldest kinks and added the luxurious lifestyles and demented emperors tastes to their repertoire.

Caligula particularly employed such strange and lascivious fetishistic behavior that the sole mainstream movie about him was produced by Penthouse, was almost 3 hours long, and still didn't get to half the shit this guy actually did.

But Caligula didn't hold a candle to the Marquis de Sade. To be clear, this is only because they lived centuries apart, and had they lived at the same time and place Caligula surely would have held a candle up to several of the Marquis's body parts, and the two would've had an odd couple relationship that would make a much better movie than the aforementioned Tinto Brass debacle. But I digress.

The Marquis de Sade wrote numerous books about every perversion known to humankind, and invented countless more. His fetishes included blood, pain, blasphemy, and in once case, the invention of a popular Urban Dictionary sex move, which in his original version involved the use of a monkey. His reputation was so scandalous that France has still yet to recover from his influence, and the entire country and culture is considered to be the most sexually indulgent in Europe. The U.K. by contrast has offered little to the subject, getting involved only years after France perfected fetishism with the Marquis' final posthumous invention of necrophilia, but it did give us J.G. Ballard, who wrote an entire novel about getting turned on by car crashes.

When it comes to modern fetishism however, one subject takes the cake. Then, it has intercourse with the cake, eats the cake, and finally uploads footage of both to a streaming site. That subject is Hentai. In 1814, Hokusai painted a woman doing it with an octopus, and the world has never been the same. Today, guro, vore, inflation and mutation are only the beginning of the illustrations available. I seriously read a book about the love lives of drainpipe mutants and I'm not even gonna tell you what this one girl did with a giant sewer snail. I mean, there's seriously no word obscene enough to describe the shit I've seen just on tumblr. Also, there was an artist named Toshio Saeki, whose style photoshops oddly well with King of the Hill's. Not that I know that from experience...

So all in all, we can only begin to address the relationship between art and eroticism let alone the fetishes that they try to chronicle. But truly, the history of fetishes on Earth is one of our richest contributions to the strange thing we call the universe. With some luck, our niche erotica will live on as we die from climate change and alien archaeologists from the Guzabarg Nebula discover what we leave behind.

Incidentally, we have not even met aliens but there's a fetish for screwing them. That's just how humans are.

FETUS

At two months, a human fetus is the same size and flavor as an artichoke.

FIBERGLASS

Fiberglass is neither fibrous nor glass-like, it gets its name from Robert Fiberglass. He didn't invent it, he just won the naming contest by eating the most of it.

FIFTY SHADES OF GREY

50 Shades of Grey started as a fancfic for Twilight, which started as fanfic for Interview With The Vampire, which started as fanfic for Dracula, which started as fanfic for The Monk, which started as fanfic for The Canterbury Tales, which started as fanfic for the Bible, but only 7 Christian sects consider "50 Shades" to be canonical.

FILM

The term for the contents of a film frame, "Mise en scene," is French for "The little death."

FILM, 3-D

3D cinema was invented by accident when a cinematographer left a secondary lens gate open and an extra dimension seeped in, saturating the film with stereoscopy.

3D movies today can improve your eyesight, eye hand coordination, and dental health. A post-converted romance movie will not do much for your teeth but keep them clean. Marvel also does a bare minimum for dental durability. Native 3D sci-fi such as Avatar will not only keep your teeth clean but strengthen the enamel, and keep the pulp nice and pulpy. If you can find a screening of House of Wax though (Shot with a 3 inch interaxial!), or It Came From Outer Space in their natural formats, you can in fact grow massive, strong fangs that can destroy the flesh of your victims and inject them with deadly venom.

FILM CRITICISM

There are presently no professional movie critics. Once Ebert the master critic died, they all ceased to be critics and returned to being human.

FILM PROPS

The Ruby Slippers from "The Wizard of Oz" are only the second most expensive movie footwear to sell at auction. The boot from "Das Boot" sold for nearly twice as much in 2009.

FINAL FANTASY

There are so many Final Fantasy games that it's easy to lose track, but don't worry- It's simple once you know the history:

In the beginning, there was Final Fantasy 1. Released in 1987, the first Final Fantasy was then also released in 1989, 1990, 1994, 2000, 2002, 2003, 2004, 2006, 2010, 2012, 2013, 2015, 2016, and 2021. Final Fantasy 2 was released about as many times, beginning in 1988, but only in Japan. As such, it is known in America as Final Fantasy: The Lost Levequests. The same thing happened to Final Fantasy 3, which was released in America as "2 Final 2 Fantasy: Lindblum Drift."

The second Final Fantasy released in America was Final Fantasy 2, which was Final Fantasy 4, the Japanese Final Fantasy 4 being a reskin of an America only game called Chocoboki Panic. Final Fantasy 2, the first SNES game in the franchise, was acclaimed for being incredibly fucking depressing. Like you start the game by killing some kid's mom and then there's something about a cursed town maybe? I don't know, it lost me early on and I never got to see Golbez or Zeromus or whatever. Also, I'm fine with even Dark Souls type menus now but I mean, in 1991 I wasn't gonna spend 45 minutes trying to figure out how to equip a fucking shoe.

Final Fantasy 3: Lords of Shadow: Mirror of Fate: Alucard's Revenge 2 came out in both Japan and America in 1994. Introducing cutscenes to the series, Final Fantasy 3 (Abbreviated Final 3 or sometimes Fantasy 5: Hobbs & Sephiroth) was best known for its main villain, Kafka. Kafka was a difficult and frustrating boss who trapped the protagonists in endless bureaucracy and paperwork until they died of old age, never knowing why. It was later released again in Japan as Final Fantasy 6: The Fate of the Fantasy.

After this, the series switched from Nintendo consoles to the Xbox.

The first X-Box, simply called the Xbox, hosted Final Fantasy 7; The next Xbox, the Xbox 360, hosted Final Fantasy 8; The Xbox 1 hosted Final Fantasy 9, and the Xbox 10 hosted Final Fantasy X. Thus if X=7, 360>8, 1=9 and X<10, then Final Fantasy itself equals 11, which is ideal because Final Fantasy 11, the 14th game in the franchise, was indeed a remake of 9, which was the sequel not to 8 but 7, remade later as 13. This can be remembered with the mnemonic "SPUGNUT" but nobody knows how or why.

With fans confused and the Xbox being discontinued by Sega, Final Fantasy sought a new start with Sony and their NeoGeo: Turbografx master system. The first game for that console was Final Fantasy 11 2, not to be confused with 12. 11 2 and 11 3 were released before 12, but well after 14, known first as Final Fantasy Genesis, but re-titled after Final Fantasy 18 into Final Fantasy Genesis 19:18, or in Japan, Shin Megami Tensei.

Final Fantasy remakes continued with Final Fantasy 13, which was Final Fantasy 8, Final Fantasy 17, which was Final Fantasy 16, and Final Fantasy 21, which was Kingdom Hearts 5, and the upcoming Final Fantasy 22, which will be both Animal Crossing 6 and Land Before Time 15: The Longnecks Take Manhattan, featuring Pinhead from Hellraiser, and Beyoncé.

The next Final Fantasy game is planned to be Final Fantasy 28, which will come in two editions, Final Fantasy Dark Cloud and Light Ning.

Truly, the greatest franchise ever to spin off from Battletoads.

FINGER

9/10 of your fingers have bones, only one does not. Which finger it is may surprise you.

FINGERNAIL

The fingernail is the only body part to be made of stone. Normally granite, the fingernail is the strongest part of the body after the tooth, which is made of opal. The fingernails can still be cut and filed because they are of weak moral fiber, and are often considered the most sinful part of the body according to the Holy Bible, which states that anyone possessing over nine fingernails is condemned forever to hell. Fingernails can also be painted with pretty designs with an airbrush.

Cutting your fingernails too short can cause them to grow back in strange directions, mostly west and south west. The pain you feel when you've cut a fingernail too shot is called "Dolores Unguem," which is coincidentally the name of my first math teacher.

Fingernails do not really grow after death. They are in fact utterly stifled creatively.

If one of your fingernails breaks off, keep it in a glass of milk. This will not help preserve the fingernail but Jimmy will be SOOOO grossed out when he drinks it.

FINGERPRINTS

Fingerprints were originally a myth told to deter criminals. It was only in 1858 that police noticed the myth was true.

Once fingerprints were discovered to be useful in criminology, there was movement to ban gloves. It was stopped by the National Guild of Protologists.

FIRE

Once considered one of the states of matter, we now know that fire is an entire country of matter.

Due to pollution across the globe, the temperature at which air can ignite is lowering. By the year 2050, fire will burn at a comfortable 93 degrees.

"Fighting fire with fire" refers to the ancient practice of putting out a fire by lighting the fire on fire and burning it to death. It never worked and many died. People were kind of stupid back then.

Fire and water were considered opposite elements, but fire shares more DNA in common with water than with earth or air.

The word "Fireplace" comes from the archaic German meaning "The Place of Fire."

If you catch on fire, stop drop and roll. If you catch on Arcade Fire, then cold wind is your best bet for relief.

Wildfires are a direct result of advanced home heating systems. As more and more homes are built without fireplaces, more and more fires are homeless.

Fire lit from objects whose ash is heavier than air will have flames that shoot down instead of up.

FISH

"Fish" or "F.I.S.H." is short for Finbearing Ichthyoid Squamous Hydroquæsedes.

Put simply, a fish is any sea-dwelling scaly finned swimmer. This means that if you wore armor and flippers and lived swimming around in water, you too would be a fish.

Thus, there are many kinds of fish. There are natural fish, which are scaly muscular beings like the shark or humuhumu-nukunukuapua'a. There are cetaceans, such as whales (the largest of all fish) and then there are the aforementioned people who have become fish, such as Arthur Curry, Abe Sapien, and Milicent Gillman. These people are most notable in literature for scaring H.P. Lovecraft into writing several stories about them.*

Be warned though, if you become a fish you can legally be fished for by anyone with a fishing license. As such, many recipes for fish must be adapted for the type of fish captured. If one were to eat a salmon or trout, they could follow most recipes without much difference. But, if one were to eat a fish such as "The Asset" from The Shape of Water, they would likely need to lengthen cooking times, add more seasoning, and would have to explain themselves to the multitude of disappointed fans who wanted to fuck him.

But fish in general are more than just food. Fish are responsible for eating much of the pollution in the ocean, drinking most of its mercury, pooping and thus producing food for bottom feeders such as lawyers and politicians, and of course, jumping in front of ships as seen in Titanic, in which a fish called the "Dauphin" can be seen frolicking before the titular vessel.

*To be fair, H.P. Lovecraft was scared shitless by anyone or anything remotely different from himself, ranging from skin tone to tentacles and everything in between. This resulted in the infamous "Lovecraft Conundrum" in which people have to balance their love of an author's horror literature against the fact he was one of the most raging racist dumbasses ever to come out of Rhode Island.

Schools of fish are becoming more and more rare as most fish claim them to be scams made for selling student loans.

Much as humans have gills in the womb, fish have arms and legs in the egg. They need these limbs to break out of the egg, but they atrophy and fall off immediately after. Most of the stray organic matter in the ocean is fish arms and legs, and some animals like the baleen whale and bottom feeders live exclusively on fish limbs. Fish limbs are also what gives caviar its distinct flavor.

Despite the well known philosophical concept of fish not understanding what water is, fish do know exact chemical composition of water and its scientific properties, and have written many books on the subject. We cannot read them of course, because we do not speak fish.

Marine physicists believe that there may be only one fish, but it moves so quickly that there appear to be many.

FISHING

Catch and release fishing is banned in seven states as it's cruel to the animal and provides no food, making it an "act of pure sadism." The film "Catch and Release" is also banned in many states for the same reason.

Never buy fish raised in "Fish Farms," such farms are extremely cruel to fish because fish are supposed to live in the water, not on farms.

Ice fishing wasn't popular until 1922 when the hole was invented.

FLEA CIRCUS

Flea Circuses were the first circuses and influenced all circuses since from Barnum and Bailey to Cirque du Soliel. Most amazing are Flea Clowns, which have the tiniest little red noses.

FLIGHT

Parts from crashed airplanes are often reused in new planes. Whenever you fly, chances are up to 40% of your plane has crashed at least once.

Airplane bathrooms used to simply empty into the sky. This was changed when the designer of the airplane bathroom defecated at 40,000ft, and then while walking away after landing was hit by his own falling poop.

Though you can't see it yourself because the cabin of the airplane also grows in size, when you're at the maximum cruising altitude you are generally about the size of the Statue of Liberty, which is why people look like ants from the airplane. Because compared to you, they are ants.

The recline button on all airline seats will eject the seat if held for more than 5 seconds.

"Muffins" was the first dog to successfully fly and land a 747. The field of canine aviation has a lot of skeptics. Some say that dogs shouldn't be allowed to fly planes. But they can no longer say that dogs *can't*.

Muffins trained for almost three years with the Air Force Academy canine unit before leaving the military to fly civilian jets. His first 747 flight was monitored by two licensing pilots of the FAA and his owners, who couldn't be more proud. Though Muffins is not the first dog to become licensed for passenger jet flight, he is the first to have landed the jet without assistance from a human co-pilot.

What does this mean for the future of aviation? Frankly, we just don't know. Dogs cost far less than human pilots, but critics suggest that because they lack the "human touch" they may never become mainstream. Said flight officer Kane Hanes, "A dog can fly a plane but can a dog ever be the next Chesley Sullenberger? Can a dog make that kind of decision?" Dog Whisperer Cesar Millan claims they can. The reality television star explained, "They can."

As the debate rages on, Muffins has since been certified to fly the Airbus A380, and will be hired as a regular pilot for British Airways. Some of Muffins's first passengers have reported that his flights were a pleasure to be a part of, while others are more skeptical. According to Dennis and Marie Sherrenheim of London, "HOLY FUCK THERE WAS A DOG FLYING THAT PLANE??? OH MY GOD I'M GOING TO BE SICK HOW DID WE SURVIVE!? HOLY FUCK I'M NEVER FLYING AGAIN JESUS FUCKING CHRIST WHO THE FUCK LET A DOG FLY THAT PLANE I MEAN OH GOD OH MY FUCKING GOD."

Muffins himself has replied to the criticism, "woof."

FLORIDA

Florida records over 100 Bingo related deaths every month.

FLOWER

All flowers appear differently under ultraviolet light, except for violets themselves.

FLUTE

The flute was invented by mistake when Bludnar Vikursen tried to build a battle axe that would kill any man or beast with one blow. He hired for ten gold pieces the illustrious Norkrandir Ulcersdottir, a blacksmith who had shoed the untameable horse of Vikrandur Lemonnskalp, who had broken the anvil of Dan-Dandesen Dunsen, and who had crushed in a single hammer strike the helm of Lothar Skrewskram of Salpsickleslaw.

But Norkrandir misunderstood and thought Bludnar wanted a weapon that could kill with a single blow, as in being blown upon. So Norkrandir built the first flute. It was capable of a high pitched note, to this date unduplicated, that could shatter eardrums and make brains bleed. Bludnar was baffled but used the flute in the Siege of Sijsage, and the Battle of Buttlebumbeedlebrew, and in his final assault on the Walls of Wikiwandwitaw. His body was to have been sent out to sea on a flaming ship with the flute, but his successor, Billy-Bob Bundurbudur, claimed it for himself and blew it to murder all who would stop him.

In time, Bundurbudur managed to play all kinds of notes on the flute, some said they were actually quite beautiful. Thus an instrument was born from what was once a terrible weapon. Bundurbudur became a world-class musician and composed several tunes, one of which would become the Norwegian National Anthem, to date the only national anthem that can be played only on a flute; And another tune which was used for the boss-battle theme of Final Fantasy 2(4).

Norkrandir Ulcersdottir's fate remains unknown. Some say she moved to Italy and invented the Tuba, others claim she headed for the New World and there created the first Trombone. These are legends of course, she was likely killed in a Viking siege and buried in an unmarked grave, but that may not be the end- Some say that if you visit the site of her old shop, you can still hear a tune unlike anything else on Earth. It may be the wind in the trees, or the howling of wolves, but if you stand there yourself you might imagine it to be the last melody of the flute's very inventor as she plays an ethereal flute of her ghostly design.

FLY

Flies cannot land upside down. They must turn the universe upside down around them to land on ceilings.

FLY PAPER

Fly Paper was originally invented to harvest flies as food.

FLYING BUTTRESS

The flying buttress is one of modern architectures most bizarre occurrences. While a normal buttress will hold a cathedral's walls up, a flying buttress is a buttress that has abandoned its post to fly away and live life independently of the church.

The first flying buttress was recorded in 1587 by Eduard Logdangle while he visited Germany. He wrote upon his return, "I hath witnessed an unusual occurringe in which a common buttress left its buildage to flye away toward the eastern seas. Perhaps with the helpe of its garuoyles and their winges. The buttress hath made a squawkenge sounde, and hath defecaeteed upon my shouldere."

Flying buttresses became more and more common as the architectural features began to communicate their newfound freedom to one another, also beginning to mate in the wild and populate some areas with feral buttresses, which survive by holding up trees or mountains. These feral buttresses are far more dangerous than the domesticated buttress and will attack humans on sight.

The most recent buttress attack happened in 1996, when Emily Mumming of Mobile, Australia was at a picnic with friends and she saw what she thought was a pillar of stone. It turned out to be a feral buttress which attacked her and broke her arm before she could escape. The buttress was shot on site by park rangers, and had to be put down.

Flying buttresses have undergone severe culling in recent years to prevent other attacks, even to the point that the World Architectural Preservation League has deemed them endangered. Breeding programs are underway to preserve the species, but funding is hard to find as most people now find them ostentatious and not necessary for building stability.

This serves in stark contrast to the flying arch, which is bred for use in reinforcing retaining walls across the globe.

FOD

Many military personnel have to go on "Fod Walks" in which they scour runways for "Fods," a species of rabbit than gnaws on airplane landing gear.

FONDUE

Fondue doesn't work on certain foods. Attempting to fondue ravioli can tear a rift in the space time continuum.

FONT

The fonts Arial, Helvetica, Georgia, Lucida and Verdana are all named for daughters of the woman who designed them, expert typographer Caroline Roman. The rights to all those fonts and more are now owned by her son, Times New.

FOOTBALL

What Americans call "Football" is called "Soccer" in England, "Rugby" in Australia, and "Chess" in New Zealand.

Technically, the English plural of "Football" is "Feetball."

No two football fields are the same length because yards are relative to latitude. The north-most football field in Alaska is only five feet long, while the football fields of equatorial regions can be well over 17 miles.

Football rituals are common across the United States, with bands of football fans gathering during each game to eat the traditional nachos and pork rinds. But a lesser known aspect of American Football culture is that in order to ensure the victory of their teams, many fans have taken to ritual human sacrifices to the demonic

Football lord "Lombardiax." A typical game night for these fans involves kidnapping a young innocent and forcing them to drink the "Blood of Enefel" which they believe represents the sacrifice of Walter Camp, who died at Yale to provide the skin for the first football, which is preserved at the Smithsonian museum under guard for fear such fans will steal it.

Doctor Jones of Marshall College explains, "Football fans can be a dangerous lot. They are unpredictable and may act with extreme violence when their favored team loses. Though some are just casual sports enthusiasts, others will lurk in dark lairs full of traps for the opposing team's fans, or even their own families." Dr. Jones in fact survived such a lair in 2014.

Avoid football fans at any cost, as one can never tell if they are speaking to a fan of the sport or a demon worshiping monster of a fan who will kill you and rip out your heart to appease the officials. If you do encounter such a fan, hide somewhere safe, such as a closet or dumpster. Do not under any circumstances hide in a refrigerator, as you may become trapped in it and seriously refrigerators won't protect you from anything even if they're lined with lead because they're fucking refrigerators.

FORCE

Science describes several forces, including nuclear forces, electromagnetism, gravity, and most powerful of all: The force that draws cat hair toward a cup of coffee.

FRANCE

Most globes made in France do not include France on the globe, as it is assumed anyone from France will know where France is.

France has a rich and detailed history. Here it is in its entirety: Pangea broke up, the Alps rose from the ground, Caesar saw some dudes get burned to death, everything was Rome, some pope got angry, some poor people got angry, some short dude got angry, some Germans got angry, Daft Punk got popular, Léa Seydoux.

FRANKENSTEIN

Frankenstein's monster's neck bolts were a subtle implication that the doctor bought some of the deceased parts from Ikea.

FREUD, SIGMUND

Sigmund Freud was not only the father of psychiatry, but the brother of psychology, and the uncle of proctology. Freud never went to college, he actually taught himself psychiatry by watching reruns of "The Sopranos" on HBO.

Freud theorized that most people suffered from a "Krispy Complex" in which they believed their cereal was talking to them.

FROG

Unlike humans, when frogs gets sick, they actually produce less mucus. The most common frog sickness is recursive throat infection, in which the frog has a frog in its throat. If this frog too is sick, it can also contain a frog and so on.

FRUIT

Apple seeds contain cyanide, while banana seeds contain mercury, orange seeds are filled with napalm, and kiwi seeds are pure radioactive plutonium.

The mango is not a fruit at all. It is in fact the egg of the mango bird, the nest of which is so small that the egg appears to be hanging from the branch of the mango tree itself, and was mistaken for its fruit. The actual mango fruit, which is the diet of the mango bird, is small and flavorless. Mango eggs however are large and delicious, as are mango birds themselves.

FUNGI

Mushrooms can grow on every known surface, including human skin, other mushrooms, and even the internet.

The tallest mushroom ever recorded was 12ft tall. It filled over 70 bowls of cream of mushroom soup.

Most psychedelic mushrooms contain no hallucinogenic toxins. Their effect is caused entirely by the qualities of the fairies that live within them, who have skin like poison dart frogs.

FUR COAT

Ancient fur coats were not made with animal fur. This was only a recent invention when synthetic fur became scarce.

FURBY

Every Furby is a reliquary of a dead Satanic priest.

FUTON

Most futons are made of tofu.

GAMES

The idea of keeping score in games was invented by the ancient Greeks, who first applied points to competitive running, a sport which ironically no longer keeps score with points but with time.

GANYMEDE

Jupiter's moon Ganymede is the only moon that has its own moon. It's just large enough to hold a small 2km meteor in its orbit, and with Jupiter's help, the meteor seems to be on a stable path. Despite this, the other planets all talk behind Jupiter's back and won't let Ganymede near their own moons.

GAS, NOBLE

Noble gases are not so noble. Helium has a habit of making people sound funny, Neon lights up in silly colors, and Xenon is well known as a total pervert. Damn gas hit on my wife at our own wedding.

I shouldn't be bitter though. It's alright now. In fact... It's a gas.

GASOLINE

Automotive Gasoline is given a bad smell artificially to prevent people from drinking it, as its natural flavor is very close to butterscotch.

GCSE

The GCSE, or "General Certification of Snail Erudition (Snerudition)" is a test given by the European Gastropodial Commission to confirm expertise in snail behavior, biology, and function (Snehavior, Sniology, and Snunction).

Anyone about to take the GCSE is naturally already an expert in snails (a Snexpert), but this top tier certification allows the bearer to perform the solemn and nearly religious rites and exercises of snail husbandry (Snusbandry), or snail breeding (Sneeding).

My only advice to someone heading into the GCSE is of course to brush up on your knowledge of snails (Snowledge) and to spend some time with actual snails. This snail time (Snime) will help you gain a familiarity with the snails (Snamiliarity) and let you observe first hand the snail activity (Snacktivity) that you will soon be certified (Snertified) to manipulate (Snipulate). Remember that snails are not just your subjects (Snubjects) but your new friends (Snends). If you don't respect the snails, you can quickly find yourself abusing their snail trust (Snust), and losing their snail affection (Snefection). You may even find yourself hanging out with the wrong kind of snails- Snail gamblers (Snamblers), snail criminals (Sniminals) or even the makers of snail snuff films (Snuff films).

You will soon wield a great snail power, and with great Snower comes great Snesponsibility. So take your snail tests (Snests) and earn your Snertification, and may you live a long, happy, and prosperous life among the snails- Live Snong, and Sprosper.

And fuck my spell check for autocorrecting every goddamn fucking snail word I typed in this fucking thing. Sneriously...

GEOGRAPHY

Most country borders lack distinguishing features such as fences or rivers, and exist only as lines floating mysteriously in the sky.

No man is an island, except for Jacob Marstle of Huacton Nevada, whom the U.S. Geological Survey declared an island in 1978.

The coast is so named because the ancients believed it to be a giant coaster for the ocean, so as not to get the land wet.

GEODESIC DOME

The geodesic dome is far more stable than its predecessor, the dangerous crumplodesic dome.

GEOMETRY

Despite the theoretical improbability, Sayyid al-Andalusi was able to make a perfect tessellation of regular pentagons. The method for doing so was lost however when the manuscript was written over with a recipe for average tuna casserole. This achievement stands in contrast to European geometricologists, who believed that triangles were a creation of the devil until the 1980s.

GERMANY

Germany is called Deutschland in its native tongue, Spanish. It does not use the Gregorian calendar, but the Gertrudian calendar, which has 17 months of 15 days each, and no weeks.

Germany is landlocked, having no shores. The song, "The Shores of Germany" refers to Pauly and Howard Shore, an actor and musician from the country.

With the largest salt producing economy in the world, Germany supplies the globe with over 350,000 tons of salt every year. This is why the nation is often called "The McDonalds Fries of Europe."

Germany is also the oldest country in Europe, dating back to the era in which Europe split off from Pangea to become its own island. It was in these days that Germany's first president, a Neanderthal named Thog the Lesser, first wrote the German constitution on the wall of a cave, along with a drawing of a deer urinating, which is not considered canonical to the constitution.

Germany was the first country to land a man on Mars, but this is not commonly known as it was a mistake. Heinrich Erfundener set out from Berlin to walk to the local cheese market but did not come back by dinner time, worrying his family. Erfundener was finally found three years later by the Hubble telescope on the Martian surface. Erfundener eventually found his way back through similarly unknown means. When asked how he ended up there, he simply replied, "Ich verliere mich manchmal."

GHIDORAH

King Ghidorah is not a conventional king, but more of a figurehead for a constitutional monarchy.

GINGER

The taste of ginger is not the flavor of the ginger root, but of the ginger parasites that live within.

GIRAFFE

The human neck has only seven vertebrae, while the neck of a giraffe has well over 500 vertebrae, and several minivertebrae. Giraffes have long necks because they need them to reach their heads, which are several meters above their bodies. If not for these long necks, the heads wouldn't be able to receive blood from the body, or send it the food they ingest.

GLOBULAR CLUSTER

Globular Clusters are by far the most delicious of stellar conglomerations.

GLOW STICK

The chemicals in glow sticks don't actually emit light, they merely absorb darkness.

GLUTEN

Gluten comes from the same root word as Gluttony, and is the embodiment of that sin. Basically, gluten is the sin of the food. Whatever the food may have done, be it some bad grain, or a mean cow, or lusty waffle, no food is completely without sin.

Some people are very sensitive to sin, and cannot tolerate evil and therefore they are called Gluten Intolerant. They are unable to digest the wickedness of some common foods and have to seek more moral replacements.

Gluttony in humans is not actually a sin so long as one avoids Gluten. One can actually eat all they please and not commit the sin of Gluttony so long as they stick to upstanding foods that obey their creator.

GNOSTIC GOSPELS

In several gnostic gospels, Jesus claims not only to be the Alpha and Omega, but also Theta, Lambda, and the English letter "E."

GOAT

Goats are one of only two animals that can fully digest a human soul, the other being of course, the other goat. North Wumpugnalian Scream Goats are the only horned mammals capable of playing music with their horns.

GOD

God is a tangible, observable being of mechanical nature located within the borders of the United States, specifically in the closet of Margaret Jones of 1919 West Cedar Avenue in Karlarintown Nebraska. Every Saturday, she takes God out of the closet and forces him to clean her carpets of cat hair and dust. Some say this is in fact a vacuum cleaner, so it's uncertain if there's a God, but there's definitely a vacuum cleaner.

GODFATHER, THE

The original Wikipedia plot summary for "The Godfather" was over three times longer than the film's screenplay.

The name of Vito Corleone's cat from the opening of "The Godfather" is never spoken on screen. In the script it was named "Cat Benatar."

GODZILLA

Godzilla, or "Gojira" in the original Japanese, debuted in cinema on October 27th, 1954. But there is one strange instance of the king of monsters appearing on film far earlier, in 1878. How the great beast got there is still a mystery.

The still photo, entitled "A Carriage Passes Through Isuelt, Kentucky, April 1878″ was taken by Brian Holger Phellonemes, presumably in the time range suggested by a title. We know for a fact that the photo has been hanging on display in the Museum of Isuelt since 1891, and has not been altered since at least that year. It was not until 1973 that anybody noticed the appearance of what was always assumed to be a cloud or photochemical flaw in the background. Harold Kramer Harolds, a Godzilla fan, first spotted the object's resemblance to the iconic kaiju.

For several decades the mystery remained a strange coincidence. But in 2019, Ishiro Honda's grandson, Takuya Honda, gave an interview that revealed his great grandfather had visited Isuelt, Kentucky from 1877-1879.

Furthermore, when the elder Honda returned from America, he spoke of "giant monsters that roamed the hillside." These stories went on to inspire Ishiro's designs for the first Godzilla film. Indeed, the appearance of Godzilla may be non-fictional, based on a real creature that existed in Kentucky in the 1800s. Local Isuelt lore does not record any mention of giant monsters, but there is a vaguely known cryptid from a few miles north in Dristan, Kentucky: The Gorilla Whale.

The Gorilla Whale is said by several folk writers in Dristan to be a giant monster that wandered Kentucky owing to the mating of a

Gorilla and a Whale at a defunct German zoo, called The Wagner Estate. Legend has it their progeny grew and grew until it had eaten every other animal at the zoo, and continued out into the wilderness eating bison and deer. Here, the reliable information runs out, varying from person to person ranging from stories of its election as mayor to tales of it fighting Paul Bunyan over a woman named Tiffany.

So it it possible that Godzilla was once a real beast? If not, what appears in the photo and how did the Honda family capture its likeness so perfectly? And can a Gorilla really mate with a Whale? How would that even work? Like just picture it. Really picture it. Eww.

GOLD

Gold has a yellowish metallic tint, but when viewed as flat finish without its metallic light frequencies, gold is dark blue. I wrote this fact before that gold or blue dress thing happened btw, just saying.

GOLDEN RULE

The Golden Rule "Do unto others as you would have them do unto you," has a negative application commonly called the Silver Rule, "Do not do to others what you would not have them do to you," and a third Brozne Rule which is strictly concerned with mineral rights in Argentina.

GOLDFISH CRACKERS

Goldfish crackers are deadly to ingest until their stingers are removed.

GOLF, MINIATURE

There's a miniature golf course in Tuscon where hitting a ball into the windmill causes the ball to cease to exist. No ball that has entered has come out, yet the structure contains no golf balls.

GOLF, NORMAL-SIZED

Golf was invented by King Louis IX as a means to waste land and water.

GONG

It is not the gong that makes sound, but the vibrations of the mallet that hits it.

GOOD, THE BAD, AND THE UGLY, THE

The original Italian title of The Good, The Bad, And The Ugly is "Il buono, il brutto, il cattivo," which literally translates as "The Good, The Brute, And The Dental Cavity." Over 6 hours of tooth surgery footage were removed from the U.S. version.

GRAMOPHONE

The photograph of a dog listening to a record player used by the Gramophone Company as its logo was taken in 1899 by Francis Barraud. According to Barraud, the dog was listening to Lady Gaga's "Poker Face."

GRAND CANYON

The Grand Canyon is not the deepest or longest canyon on Earth, but it does have the most abandoned grand pianos in it.

GRAPE (FRUIT)

The skin of a grape is thicker than the skin of an elephant.

GRAPEFRUIT

The grapefruit was only a rumor to western civilization until proof of its existence was offered to King George II. Upon tasting it, he banned it from his own domain for another 200 years.

Though the grapefruit looks and tastes like the fruit of citrus trees, it is an unrelated melon that grows on a creeping vine.

GRAPES OF WRATH

The grapes of wrath are a key ingredient in the grape juice of damnation.

GRAVE

The oldest known gravestone in the world stands over a grave in Kufra. Its epitaph reads, "Here lies Hinan, inventor of the waffle." Despite this, Eggo continues to hold the copyright.

GRAVY

"Gravy" is ill defined and can be anything from turkey broth to the coagulated brake fluid of a 1979 Pinto.

GREEN

"Green" is the only word in the English language to contain two Es between two consonants.

GREETINGS

The word "Hello" is a portmanteau of Helium and Jello, the traditional British greeting gifts.

GREMLIN

Gremlins are not a mythological creature, but an extinct one. The gremlin was once a small furry animal that ate metallic deposits. Once metal was mined by humans they died off. It is thought that some survived into the 20th century, where they would devour machinery.

GRENADE

The largest grenade ever invented weighed several hundred pounds and could only be thrown about one meter by a crew of six soldiers, despite having a blast radius over fifty meters. It was deemed ineffective and was only used in combat for seven years.

GROUNDHOG

A groundhog is a prairie dog that has evolved past level 28.

GROWTH

Growth can be marked by several specific milestones:

Age 25 - Root Beer will stop tasting good.

Age 30 - Your metabolism will change, allowing you to hurl fireballs like Mario, and the video game character of the same name.

Age 31 - Your teeth will begin to have parties. Do not stifle your teeth's social lives, this can result in gingivitis and periodontal disease.

Age 44 - You will cease to be viewable in old video tapes. This disappearance is normal and does not mean you yourself will cease to be.

Age 50 - You will begin to grow hair in strange places, such as the garage, your local Jiffy Lube, and Cuba. Use Miracle Grow for best results.

Age 61 - You will finally understand why people like Richard Chamberlin TV shows. Except "The Thornbirds," nobody understands the appeal of that show.

Age 63 - Flintstones Vitamins will cease to work. You must take adult multivitamins or your dick will fall off. If you do not have a dick, one will be provided for you by the FDA or your local pharmacy.

GRUB

Grubs differ from maggots in that grubs are traditionally served with white wine and maggots are served with red wine.

GRUEL

Gruel didn't always have negative connotations, prior to 1700 it was a dish served only to the royalty of Gruelmany, a country eventually wiped off the map in a war with Porrigegul.

GUILLOTINE

Guillotines often backfired, leaving the victim's head even more strongly attached than it was before the attempt.

GUITAR (BASS)

To make a bass guitar, first, a suitable sea bass is harvested and hollowed out, its meat is generally sent to fish markets and sold as food. The hollow bass is then stretched over a shoe-horn like device that forms the shape of the guitar. Only then are the scales removed. It's baked at 200 degrees for five days to preserve and harden the form, after which the neck and strings are attached. The theme from Seinfeld is played on it to make sure it's properly tuned, and then it's sold at your local music shop.

Unrelated- Guess what a Sackbut is made of. Come on, guess…

GUITAR (SOLO)

The first guitar solo ever was performed by Mauro Giuliani in 1808 when his patrons requested that he play "Free Bird."

GUN

The longest rifle ever built has a 400 yard barrel. It's not a very effective weapon because its range is only 350 yards, so the rounds never exit the barrel. Similarly, the world's largest shotgun is so big it fires regular shotguns as ammo.

Most guns made prior to 1835 had wooden barrels and fired wooden bullets using wooden gunpowder. In addition to normal gunpowder, most modern bullets contain some vanilla or rose extract for a pleasant scent after firing.

GYMNASTICS

In the 2004 Olympics, an embarrassing moment occurred when a gymnast was stuck buffering during her balance beam routine.

"This rarely happens at the Olympic level" said trainer Luigi Tartugasicario, "Buffering occurs when a gymnast attempts too many leaps within a few seconds that require a longer time to load."

This is the first buffering incident to happen at the Olympics since 1980 when Tennis star Luke Capulet-Montague buffered during a volley, costing the U.S. a silver medal. "This could all be avoided if athletes simply took some time before beginning to let their routine fully load. Trying to perform at high resolution is the latest fad, but it's better to leap at 360p than to be caught buffering at 1080."

HAIR

Hair continues to grow after death, even in mummified bodies. Mummies on display in the British Museum get haircuts twice monthly.

There's a hairstyle called the Hippo-Slousi that takes 7 hours minimum to accomplish and ranks higher on most pain scales than the bite of a bullet ant.

Hair floats in water because it's full of air. Air accounts for exactly 75% of the word.

Hair is the shower drain's only natural predator.

HALLOWEEN

The phrase "Trick or Treat" is copyrighted, and technically, anyone using it owes 15% of their candy to the phrase originator.

HANDS

You can grow spare hands in test tubes in your own home. There is no known way to attach the hands though, as if you remove your hands you will not have hands with which to attach the new hands.

HARVARD COMMA

Though the Oxford Comma is coming into widespread use, the Harvard comma remains inappropriate to common writing, probably, because, it, goes, after, every, word, like, so.

HARVARD QUESTION MARK

The Harvard question mark or "Harmark" is dangerous and should not be used by novices or common writing. Taking an average of two hours to draw correctly, the Harmark has the ability to answer its own questions and thus should only be used for extremely serious scientific inquiry.

The last known use of the Harmark to ask "Netflix and Chill?" resulted in the invention of Netflix, the worst winter storms of 1997, and so much sex the population of the world grew 80%.

HASIDISM

Hasidic Jews have a much lower pH than basic Jews.

HAT

Hats were originally used as portable toilets, this is why it's considered impolite to wear them indoors. One would doff their cap when a lady was present because it would be impolite to greet a lady with a bucket of shit on your head.

The act of wearing a feather in ones cap originates with King Ethelred II, who conducted an entire court with a bird sitting on his head. He was unaware of the bird until the day was done, but everyone thought he meant to and wore feathers in his honor.

The bowler hat is so named because it resembles bowling balls as they appeared in the 1920s, when they were all black felt with brims.

HAWK

Hawks are the only birds that can fly without wings. They have wings and use them to fly but they can fly just fine without them. I've seen it.

HEADACHE

Most headaches are not caused by pains within the head, but by pains within the spleen, where the nerve cluster controlling the head is located.

HEADLESSNESS

The 283rd Regiment of Her Majesty's Riflemen was legendary for not having heads.

Late in the 7th year of World War 1, the entire unit was captured by Germans and beheaded. But back in those days when men were men and gender role cliches were socially acceptable metaphors for physical strength, it took more than that to kill a fighting man. The unit survived by forcing food down their severed gullets and piping blood to their brains using retrofitted bilge pumps they stole from the German Navy.

The Regiment continued to fight, taking the Hills of Meinkopffiel, defeating the Cossacks at Verdun, capturing the 2nd Mini-Kaiser and more. When the war ended they were hailed as heroes and all the doctors in England pursued study of their case, learning incalculably important techniques that would later be used for kidney dialysis, head transplantation and more.

Their case also lead France to discontinue the use of the guillotine as decapitation was no longer the most certain method of execution.

HEART

Though it's only the size of a fist, the human heart accounts for 60% of a person's body weight.

The human heart has five chambers. Two ventricles, two atria, and one chamber that holds the human soul. And lymph. The fifth chamber also holds lymph.

The shape we refer to as a "heart" was never actually intended to resemble a human heart, but instead takes the shape of the border on the cover art for the single "Barracuda" by the band "Heart."

HEAT

The same principles that let you walk over hot coals also allow you to juggle hot potatoes, and theoretically to balance the sun on your nose.

HEAVY METAL

Heavy Metal is so named because the first electric guitars weighed over 200 pounds.

The genre was invented on Friday the 13th in February of 1970, a day known as "The Black Sabbath." It consisted of a song called "Black Sabbath" on an album called "Black Sabbath" by a band called "Black Sabbath." Despite this, their music is considered to have been quite creative for the time.

New bands formed soon after and created more metal. These bands, such as "Iron Maiden" and "Motörhead," played harder and harder metal to listen to. The horrible screeching noises and loud banging drums they added caused many listeners to play Dungeons and Dragons, and as a result, heavy metal was banned for several years.

When metal returned with the removal of Margaret Thatcher from office, a wide variety of sounds and styles of heavy metal were born. There was "Thrash Metal," which was known for sounding like a person yelling over a demolition derby; "Death Metal" which sounded like a bear growling at a jackhammer; and "Black Metal," which sounded a detuned radio scraping against a rusty sheet of corrugated aluminum roofing while someone with laryngitis tried to yodel. This was known as the golden age of metal.

Thrash Metal, Death Metal, and Gothic Metal all lived in harmony, then everything changed when Korn attacked. Korn was called "Gnu Metal," because it sounded like a Gnu had wandered into a recording studio and tripped over a bass guitar. The world of metal was thrown into disarray. Thrash metal bands forgot what to play, and the giants of the genre such as Metallica and Slayer began playing Country music and Hardcore, respectively. Most Death Metal bands died. And Black Metal, well, just look it up, it's history is way more demented than anything I could come up with. Korn itself grew very popular, and gained too many emulators to count.

Thus the state of heavy metal is dire and depressive, with little apparent hope. However, recent news suggests that a "Metalocalypse" is coming, which may revitalize the metal world...

HEDGEHOG

A scientist once placed a hedgehog on a keyboard. It typed out, methodically, "We only stay silent because you harm what you don't understand." The experiment has never been duplicated.

HELICOPTER

Helicopters technically shouldn't be able to function because of Newton's 8th law which states, "Helicopters technically shouldn't be able to function."

HELL

Despite the show's name, only the pilot of Hell's Kitchen was filmed in Hell, with Ramsey moving to Earth for the rest of filming.

HELLRAISER

Clive Barker wrote Hellraiser after years of failing to solve a Rubik's Cube.

Several cenobites were cut from the final film, including Hogsnout, the snot-laden cenobite who can be defeated only by manipulating the puzzle box into its "Benadryl Configuration," and Headache who is continually fed ice cream too fast, resulting in horrible brainfreezes.

HEPLER'S MOLD

Hepler's mold is a bright reddish-orange fungus that naturally eats away at trees, but naugahyde (the fake leather in most cars) contains ten times more naug cells than the tree bark from which its made.

The bright fungus looks soft and cushy but as the mold can also grow in human lungs, it is anything but. The spores from an affected car would kill a passenger within ten minutes. The bright fibers of victims erupt from their mouths in a gruesome spectacle that the natives of Heplerable regions call "Elmo's Death".

HICCUPS

The oldest known cure for hiccups comes from Agrippa's books of Occult Philosophy. Simply lick a cat once for every seven hiccups and they'll stop after the third lick.

Modern science entered the picture in the 1700s when the court of France ordered a study of the phenomenon and its prevention. A doctor named Jean-Paul-Georges-Louis Blanqui Clemenceau Marat Auguste declared that the best cure for hiccups was a sharp punch to the belly. His research was abandoned during the revolution however, at which time the favored cure for hiccups became the guillotine, which to be fair was always 100% effective.

Hiccups in America were solved with Hummingbird Blossom until the coming of Columbus. No records are known of how well this worked and no blossoms are left as Columbus burned them to extinction as heresy, instituting his own cure, fifteen lashes and devout repentance, as he believed hiccups were a sign of devotion to Satan.

In modern times, numerous folk cures for hiccups exist, ranging from rubbing the earlobes to drinking hot tea, to forcing a sneeze or cough to startling the victim with a loud "Boo!"

Still though, a certain and immediate cure for hiccups eludes us. Research is ongoing but difficult as it's equally difficult to induce hiccups as to cure them, thus test subjects are sporadic. Current results however suggest that the best course of action for hiccups is to ingest one "ghost" pepper, chewing thoroughly.

It will not stop the hiccups, but you won't mind them so much as you focus on the horrific pain of your tongue burning out of your mouth.

HIGHLANDS

The Highlands of Scotland are the most sparsely populated region on Earth because at any given time, there can be only one highlander living there.

HIPPOPOTAMUS

Hippos are by far the most dangerous animals in the Nile. But we're safe, unless they figure out how to open doors…

HOCKEY

Hockey exists because in 1919, Heinrich Puck found himself in possession of 80,000 vulcanized rubber discs that were intended for use as tank tread parts in German WW1 tanks. With the end of the war, he had to be creative to get rid of them so he invented "Hockeysport," an ice based game in which the ball was replaced by such a rubber disc. He sold all 80,000 by August 1939, just before WW2 began, leaving Germany without the necessary parts for its intended tank force. The new wave of German "Tiger" tanks was without these rubber discs and had inferior, horribly screeching tank treads as a result, which may have contributed to their loss of the war. Thus if not for Hockey, the axis may have won WW2 and condemned the world to eternal tyranny, and that is the real miracle on ice.

HOLLYWOOD SIGN, THE

The Hollywood sign appears from a distance to be made from corrugated metal, but is in fact 100% Bavarian weevil silk. It is the second largest sign in the world. The largest is a sign for Bob's Chowder Shop in Providence, RI, which is twice the size as the city that houses it.

HOME

The original phrase is not "A man's home is his castle" but "A man's home is his nostril." The phrase was changed because nobody could figure out what the original meant.

HOMECOMING DANCE

In 1756, Arturo X. González built what many consider the first generational starship. Working only with a primitive form of mylar to make both the balloon and the solar sails, he constructed a vehicle capable or space-flight at 0.6 times the speed of light and set off with seven families toward the stars.

Heading for the southern end of the Leo constellation, González took about 18 years to reach the star now known as Wolf 359. Finding a moon-sized planet that could support life, the families set down and thrived for almost 100 years, growing to a full town's worth of people. But then the red dwarf began emitting severe radiation. Knowing that the ship could only hold seven families, lots were drawn to see who would go back to Earth. The rest were condemned to die from the radiation. There was simply no way to save them.

But in 1890, the families selected made it back to Earth. This so-called "homecoming" was well celebrated but it was not the origin of the dances. Because after generations on the distant planet, Earth was no longer these people's home. They'd all grown up on the small green planet they named Esfera Verde. Their only interest once they arrived was the hope that they might somehow bring back whatever technology existed on Earth to defend their brethren from the radiation. They only had a few weeks on Earth if they were to return in time to save the population. Sadly, Earth was never so advanced as the mind of Arturo X. González. Because he left the planet, Earth never had him to develop the science that would have put our world centuries ahead of where it is even in the 21st century. We had nothing to offer except for a few modern substances that might somehow assist them, though nobody knew how they might.

Still, they went back to the sky. Deciding unanimously that they would rather die at home than live on Earth, the families took their ship back across the deep void of space and in 1909, they arrived. Or should have. The fact is we don't know and likely never will. There's no contact over such distances, or at least there wasn't in the early 1900s.

So we don't know if they ever developed a saving shield, we don't even know if the visitors to our world made it back home. But there are so many among us who want to believe the families made it back and somehow saved their people. It is that homecoming that the people of Earth pray took place. Is it that homecoming that perseveres in the memory of those who look up to the stars at night and wonder if anyone there is looking back.

Anyhow the dance is named after coming back to school from summer vacation.

HORN

Though horns are considered predatory in most artwork, only prey animals grow them in reality. The true mark of a predator is the canine tooth, which the art world treats mostly as a sign of brushing and flossing.

Musical horns are so named because the first of them were made from animal horns. Similarly, the xylophone was named after the anterior xylophone, an organ in deer that controls their lymph distribution, from which the first xylophone instruments were made.

HORN, SHOE

The shoe horn was used as an actual orchestral instrument for centuries.

HORSEBACK RIDING

The record for most horses ridden by one person at the same time is only 7. Before the invention of the saddle, one had to ride a horse standing up like on a surfboard.

HOSE

Most garden hoses are still made from human intestines.

HOT DOG

Hot Dogs got their name because they were originally made of dog meat. Also they are still made of dog meat.

HOUR

Most hours have names. Though 3AM is well known as the Witching Hour, lesser known names include 4PM- the Sneezing Hour, and 7AM- the Hour Of The Snooze Button.

HOURGLASS

Once an hourglass had been used it can never be used again, as all the sand has fallen into the lower half.

HUG

Because the Earth orbits the Sun and the Sun travels the Milky Way at extreme speeds, any place you have ever been on Earth has been left behind millions of miles away as soon as you leave it. Thus you are the only person who ever has or will occupy that space relative to the cosmos, and when you hug someone, the two of you have gone on a journey of light years in each others arms.

HUGHES, HOWARD

SEE: TWENTY THOUSAND LEAGUES UNDER THE SEA

HUMMINGBIRD

Though hummingbirds are far smaller than eagles, they are the eagle's only natural predator, and a single hummingbird can eat up to five eagles per day.

HUMOR

The punchline was invented in 1955, before then most jokes were not meant to be funny.

HUMORS

Ancient medicine believed there were only four bodily fluids called the "humors." These included blood, mucus, bile, and mayonnaise, which was later discovered to be not a natural part of the human body, but a natural part of egg salad.

HYDRUS

The Hydrus is one of those amazing instances of an unlikely myth turning out to be completely true. It was believed for almost a thousand years that the Hydrus was a metaphor for the myth of the harrowing of Hell when Jesus descended to save imprisoned souls, but in 1983, Dr. Benway discovered a skull that didn't match any known Nile Dweller.

It had teeth that jutted as spirals out from its jaw and odd shovel like extensions on either side of its head. With no documented creature fitting the skull, Benway excavated the region and found several complete skeletons. Analysis determined that the animal did indeed live by shoveling mud onto itself and ambushing crocodiles, likely eating them from the inside out using its bizarre curly teeth.

The Hydrus likely went extinct around 1650, and existed live when the manuscripts depicting it were illuminated. Though no known specimens are alive today, this was also true of the coelacanth, a fish presumed extinct that was caught by a fisherman a few years ago. The coelacanth now accounts for 8% of McDonalds fish fillets.

It is thus entirely possible that the Hydrus lives on in pockets of the Nile, devouring crocodiles as is its way, and may one day too become food for humans.

McHydrus Burger: 100% Crocodile fed Hydrus for that extra Nilotic flavor!

HYENA

Hyenas laugh, but they're crying on the inside.

HYMN

The tune to Blur's "Song 2" is actually from a hymn popular in the 1600s. The second hymn in most hymnals, the otherwise untitled "Hymn 2" was most often known as the "Woohoo Hymn" due to the repetition of the phrase.

-I-

ICE

Ice takes up more space than water because when cold, each molecule must wear a thick coat.

ICE CREAM

"Ice Cream" is an abbreviation for "Ice-Infused Hydrobaric Thermal-Demartialized Cream of Bisodium Gustitative Suspension."

ILLNESS

It's important to drink many fluids while sick. This is not a warning to stay hydrated as many believe, but an admonition to drink many different fluids so that the bacteria within you have a choice of what to drink. It's always important to be a polite host for your body's guests.

Though the song "Rockin' Pneumonia and Boogie Woogie Flu" became a popular comedic hit in the 70s, both diseases were considered fatal before the invention of antibiotics.

ILLUMINATI

Each member of the Illuminati generates 74 lumens, making them popular for lighting dining rooms. The history of the Illuminati is as follows:

1855: Adam Weishaupt founds the Illuminati to hold lanterns at night for safety.

1861: The Illuminati, known for reading books as they hold lamps, become feared as the most enlightened group on Earth.

1862: Now feared regardless of their purpose, the Illuminati decide to earn the fear by plotting to take over the world.

1869: The Illuminati take over most European governments by infiltration, maintaining their ultimate secrecy.

1865: The Illuminati end the Civil War by assassinating Abraham Lincoln.

1879: The Illuminati find the Holy Grail.

1881: The Illuminati lose the Holy Grail, having mistaken it for a common cup and throwing it out at the end of a new year's party.

1882: The Illuminati find the Grail again and wash it off in the dishwasher.

1896: The Illuminati lose the Grail again when it's loaned to Mark Twain, who is thought to have to have lost it in a poker game.

1901: The Illuminati try to kill Mark Twain but fail when he trips over a cat just as the shot is fired.

1908: The Illuminati hold a special ceremony to end the world, but it fails because they didn't have the grail and had to substitute a dixie cup.

1919: The Illuminati lose the holy dixie cup.

1969: The Illuminati break up because of Yoko Ono.

1971: The Illuminati return to erase Nixon's taped rant against them.

1981: The Illuminati are arrested en masse for loitering outside Madison Square Garden.

1999: The Illuminati hire Dan Brown to write their biography.

2004: The Illuminati hire Nicolas Cage to steal the Declaration of Independence, later making a movie of the incident for disinformation.

2006: The Illuminati found tumblr to blind the world to their plots.

2011: The Illuminati get lost on tumblr like everyone else.

2014: The Illuminati get banned from tumblr for posting copyrighted music.

2015: The Illuminati return to tumblr to review Star Wars 7 and get only 3 notes, none of them reblogs.

IMPEACHMENT

The impeachment process got its name because presidents used to be kicked out of office by pummeling with peach pits.

In the modern process:

1. The impeachment chamber is unlocked, cleaned, and prepared.
2. The president is escorted to the impeachment chamber.
3. The Stenographer of the Americas is seated at the Typewriter of Justice.
4. The Supreme Court selects its Grand Representative, known also as "The Mouth of the Court."
5. The Senate dons its gilded impeachment robes, traditionally they are otherwise nude but some may choose to wear their Judicial Speedos.
6. Once present, the senators sing the alternate impeachment day national anthem, "Out Of Time" by Chris Farlowe.
7. The president will be seated in the same chair as previously impeached presidents, nicknamed "The Hot Seat," this chair is actually where the phrase "The Hot Seat" comes from owing to its proximity to the senate building's only working radiator, which was installed in 1778.
8. The Vice President will be strapped to the Wheel of Supervision.
9. The proceedings will begin with the pouring of the first of four cups of wine which will be consumed during the impeachment.
10. The charges against the president will be sung by the Department of Agriculture's Children's Choir in Latin, with translations into all the languages known to American Colonizers in 1776 (English, French, and Pennsylvania Dutch English).
11. The Sacred Laser Pointer of Calvin Coolidge will be turned on and aimed onto the Hallowed Whiteboard on which are written the articles of impeachment.

12. The White House Llama will be shaved, and walked toward the Washington Monument through the reflecting pool while a nun rings a bell and announces its shame.

13. The prosecution will deliver its case, which will then be opened with the Crowbar of Philadelphia.

14. The lining of the case will be cut open with the Lincoln X-Acto Blade.

15. The prosecution's presentation in favor of impeachment will be read in musical fashion by the Senate Hazzan.

16. The prosecution will rest, usually at the Watergate Hotel.

17. The defense will bring the president forward to fight the Garthok of Remulak, and his prowess will be judged by the Supreme Court.

18. The Supreme Court will deliver its recommendation to the senate based on the president's skill in Narfeling the Garthok.

19. The Senate will vote on the president's guilt.

20. The verdict will be announced by means of burning special incense in the Senate fireplace, white smoke will result if he is found guilty, black if innocent, and green if he bribes his way out of responsibility.

21. If the president is found innocent, all returns to normal and the term is served out.

22. If the president is found guilty, then a new process begins called "The Mandating" in which the president be stripped, tarred and feathered, hanged by his toes, dipped in a bath of sulphur and weasel snot, and beaten like a piñata with cacti until he resigns, dies, or admits he is a witch.

To date, no president has moved beyond the seventh step. Andrew Johnson was declared unfit to stand trial when his hernia exploded from the stress, and Bill Clinton was excused from impeachment when Al Gore leapt to his rescue and fought off the senate with a sword made from the femur of former president Jimmy Carter, who he had exhumed from Arlington Cemetery the night before, despite him not having died yet. I was gonna joke that Trumps 2 impeachments cancelled each other out, but here we are...

INCAS

The Incas were one of the three smallest Central American empires, along with the Malleus and the Stapes.

INFINITY

The infinity symbol was originally a mistake by a mathematician who incorrectly solved an infinite equation to equal eight. Thankfully he wrote the number at a bad slant and everyone assumed he had simply given infinity a new symbol, which stuck.

INFLATION

SEE: MONEY and get your mind out of the gutter.

INSECT

Most insects actually have eight legs, like arachnids, but these extra legs are removed during their initiation into bughood. Feelings of loneliness can be prevented by eating live insects. When you eat a swarm of mosquitoes, you're never alone.

Most insects have taste buds in their feet, but these are not the same type of taste we have on our tongues. Rather, they let the insect decide if what it's experiencing is "tasteful," as in proper or appropriate.

INSURANCE

Insurance used to be considered gambling, it was only legalized by a mistake due to a typo in a law meant to prohibit it on Sundays.

INTERNET

The internet was started as an MMORPG that could simulate a global information network. Technically, it is still only a simulation of such a network, even though it functions as one.

It was considered bad form in Victorian England to log onto the internet without first washing your hands. A full bath was required upon signing off.

It takes 600 trees to make a single page of the internet.

Many people born after 1990 don't remember a world before the Internet. Here are a few things you may not realize about life in those days:

-Phone numbers had to be looked up in a giant book.

-Clowns weren't considered scary. This is just the result of an early meme.

-If you wanted to move something from one computer to another, you had to put it on a disk, which only held 0.2 MB maximum.

-There were no unique television stations, all TV came through as a single broadcast, and there was no choice of what to watch at any time.

-Most movies did not have sound. The few that did had to sync up the audio from a record player, and it often went out of sync very quickly, leading to sometimes hilarious results.

-There were no phone poles, these are exclusive to the internet. The invention of the internet and the subsequent installation of these poles and wires gave birds a new place to rest, allowing them to migrate farther than ever before. Prior to 1990, birds could only migrate a few blocks.

-Lightning wasn't deadly, nor did it produce thunder. Only with the air electrified from so much internet did lightning gain deadly strength and become audible from afar. Back in the 80s, playwright Samuel Beckett spoke of lightning as causing a gentle tingling sensation. Many people would stand out in the rain just to feel it.

-Cars didn't have wheels. The wheel is a fairly recent invention, which could only come into being with science advanced by the worldwide web. Cars before wheels were odd contraptions which did not move, yet people still spent hours and hours sitting in them, expecting to get somewhere in the hope that one day, the wheel would be invented. Many people still practice sitting motionless in their car for hours and hours, mostly in Los Angeles.

-We didn't have snot. Nobody knows if the internet caused us to secrete mucus, but there are no records of it prior to the invention of internet.

Ancient civilizations believed that 404 errors were caused by angry gods. In fact they are more likely caused by "Link Rot," in which HTML weevils chew on code and excrete binary blobs.

IQ

IQ is exhaustible- Every time you do something smart you spend a couple points. This is why you feel the way you do after school.

IPECAC

Much as maple syrup is the sap of the maple tree, syrup of ipecac is the sap of the ipecactus, the ugliest cactus known to botany.

IRON MAIDEN

Iron Maiden's song "2 Minutes to Midnight" was written in only two minutes, a rarity for a 6 minute song. Note that this is not a fact about the band Iron Maiden, but the original torture device.

ISTANBUL

There was a vote to make "Istanbul (Not Constantinople) the national anthem of Turkey. Though the vote was successful, the national anthem was not changed as the vote was held by and for a small group of college students in Newark.

-J-

JACOBITE UPRISINGS

The Jacobite risings of the late 1600s began when "Team Jacob" rebelled against King Edward IX and his own "Team Edward."

JAIL

The only difference between a jail and a prison is that a jail is run by a warden, while a prison is run by an oligarchy of the 7 inmates with the longest terms.

JACQUES, FRÈRE

"Frère Jacques" is now a popular nursery rhyme, but its origins are actually as a warning about the seven deadly sins, written as seven verses about monks missing the rapture because they were indulging in vices. The song we know today is about the first brother Jacques, who being slothful, sleeps through the apocalypse.

The other brothers include Thomas (Wrath), who is busy fighting with a clerk; Louis (Gluttony), who is busy sneaking a second dessert; Hugo (Greed), who is stealing from a farmer; Clément (Envy) who is busy coveting a stronger mule; Quentin (Pride), who is busy smoking; and Martin (Lust), who is furiously masturbating at the time of the call to heaven. This verse in particular made the song inappropriate for children, and over the years it was cut down to just its first verse.

Another song, "Sœur Mary," extols the virtues of seven nuns who are raptured for their good deeds. Originally sung to the same tune, this song oddly enough evolved over the years not into a nursery rhyme, but into Credence Clearwater Revival's "Proud Mary."

Most bizarre is the fate of a third French folk tune. The still popular "Alouetté," about plucking a bird is most recently the basis for the Carcass song, "Feast on Dismembered Carnage."

JAWS

The author of Jaws was himself a shark, a fact he withheld from publishers until after the book was famous.

JELL-O

Jell-O was invented to be a packing material. It was only discovered to be edible 13 years after its invention.

JELLYFISH

When a plastic bag is littered into the sea, alpha radiation in the sea water mutates the plastic bag. We call mutated plastic bags "Jellyfish."

Jellyfish and their kin are called "cnidarians" or "coelenterates" (sometimes rendered "cœlenterates"). These names were invented by taxonomists so that they could laugh at science teachers trying to pronounce them.

Jellyfish can have up to 15 eyes. If they have more than 15 eyes, they are considered Gloatyfish.

Jellyfish do not have feelings. What many think are its feelings are in fact its tentacles. Feelings are opaque and thicker than tentacles and have large nodules on the sides. They can still sting though… They can still sting.

JEOPARDY

Jeopardy contestants who finish with a negative balance are required to pay the amount they owe within a month of losing the game. Celebrities who appear on and lose more than one show cannot be fined again as this would violate the 5th amendment.

JPEG ARTIFACTS

The earliest JPEG artifact dates to 900 A.D., about when the Joint Photographic Experts Group (for which the image type is named) was founded. This was of course several decades before computers, back when image compression was accomplished by mashing a clay representation down to a smaller size. The artifact itself is a small (4″) statuette resembling the Venus of Willendorf.

Most notably, the first JPEG is thought to have been sculpted by the Picts.

JUGGLING

Juggling was invented by lime harvesters who needed to carry more than their arms would allow.

JUNKYARD

There is an account that in 1994, Brandon Winslow, having lost his family, job, and home, moved into a junkyard in Detroit to seek cover from a storm. He found several refrigerators and managed to cluster them together and cover them with some abandoned vinyl siding, creating a makeshift shelter.

But he didn't stop there. Brandon was an architect before he lost everything and he knew some tricks. He continued to refine his shelter over the next few months, adding full rooms, a rudimentary plumbing system, and trash furniture that in time came to be known as the Junk Mansion of 72nd Street. Brandon lived happily in his new home through two winters, warmly thanks to a heating and ventilation system made from tin cans and broken pipe.

In early 1997, the city demanded the mansion be torn down. Condemned for its makeshift construction and derided as an eyesore by locals, the city gave Brandon two weeks to disassemble his house and move into the nearby homeless shelter instead. Brandon refused, and rallied the community behind him, resulting in pro-bono representation from a local lawyer.

The case went to court. Brandon Winslow had little going for him and after an outburst, lost even his lawyer and was forced to represent himself. He offered almost no evidence, having no concept of legal terminology or local law. In the end, he was only able to offer an impassioned speech, coming from a man who lost everything and built a new home from garbage.

His words moved the jury, and he was allowed to keep his house, officially speaking. Unofficially, his constant outbursts in court and insults to the lead prosecutor drove said prosecutor nuts. After the verdict was announced, and as Brandon walked back to his mansion triumphant, the prosecutor drove to the junkyard and burned his mansion down.

Brandon arrived and found a pile of ashes where his house once stood. The prosecutor was arrested for arson but the damage was done. Brandon was homeless again. Surrounded by dozens of onlookers and local news reporters, it is recorded that Brandon didn't say a word. He didn't cry. He didn't lash out or lament his loss.

Brandon simply found some old refrigerators, odds and ends, parts and materials, and began to build again.

JURASSIC PARK

Few of the dinosaurs depicted in "Jurassic Park" are from the Jurassic period. More accurately, it would be entitled "Phanerozoic Park," but this name was taken by a city park in Phanerozoic, Michigan.

The scenes in Jurassic Park 2 depicting a T-Rex in San Diego were faked, the T-Rex was actually released in Austin, TX.

-K-

KANSAS

Kansas and Arkansas are the same materials, but opposites. If the two should ever touch, they would annihilate each other.

KEYBOARD

The common "Qwerty" arrangement of keyboard letters is an in-joke by keyboard designer Qwertyuiop Asdfghjkl of Northern Zxcvbnm.

Unfortunately, anything this book tells you about keyboards must pass through a keyboard to get to you, therefore there is no way of knowing if I'm telling you, or if the keyboard is changing my words as it communicates.

KING OF THE HILL

Few viewers of King of the Hill realize that Bill is supposed to be a time traveling Bobby from the future.

KING SOLOMON'S MINES

King Solomon's Mines are not diamond mines as commonly believed, but a series of land annexations that King Solomon made by pointing around and declaring, "mine."

KISS

The Kama Sutra lists 28 types of kiss. The French Kiss is not included because France was called Gaul at the time and Gaul Kiss sounds nasty.

KISS (BAND)

The band KISS spells their logo not with two lightning bolts, but with two Hebrew letter Lameds that make their band name say "Kill."

KISS OF DEATH

The kiss of Death was a real mafia custom, but it wasn't so much a kiss as a nibble on the earlobe, and it didn't mean you were going to die but that a crime family thought you had sexy earlobes.

KNIGHT

In battle, knights mostly just ran around the battlefield trying to swing their sword at random people. This is why medieval wars took so long, they were the button-mashing of history.

KOALA BEAR

Koala Bears are symbiotic with Ala Bears.

KOOSH BALLS

So many Koosh Balls were harvested in the 80s and 90s that no living Koosh is able to reproduce. They'll be extinct in 3 years.

KY JELLY

KY Jelly is made from mucus of the sea pig, scientific name "Kelastipoda Yelipidiidae."

LADDER

Ladders always have an even number of rungs. A ladder with an odd number of rungs is called an Anti-Ladder.

LANGUAGE

Before language was invented, humans had a mating signal like any other animal. It involved mashing grubs into each others hair, and is still practiced in most L.A. nightclubs.

LANGUISHING

Being confined to home for an extended time can result in all kinds of experiences. Some people will get work done. Some will enjoy time with their lovers, the lucky bastards. But most will simply languish.

Here's how to languish correctly in seven easy steps:

-Set specific times to wake and go to bed, specifically, 5:25AM to get to sleep and 3PM to wake up.

-It's important that you eat only three meals a day, so indulge in huge snacks of junk food whenever you feel like it to make sure you only need three actual meals.

-Binge-watch only shows you've already seen. This way you will experience less need to pay attention, and sink more deeply into the soft soft cushion that is streaming video. In times like these, you should be able to watch over 20 shows you know by heart, some of them several times.

-Lament everything. This is a good time for introspection so be sure to dwell inordinately on mistakes you made between the ages of ten and fifteen.

-Alienate your friends and family via text. This is an important time to use modern technology to keep in touch with the people you may not get to see in person for a while. Use the guaranteed distance to make that clumsy romantic move on the people who you know will reject you so that there won't be any awkwardness in person for at least a couple weeks, by then they may have even forgotten how weird you made things!

-Monitor your health. Indulge your inner hypochondriac by thinking the worst of any subtle change in how you feel. Do you ever feel tired between the hours of 12AM and 11:59PM? CORONAVIRUS. Have you sneezed, coughed, or blinked in the last year? CORONAVIRUS. Did you feel that The Rise of Skywalker was disappointing? CORONAVIRUS. Also good taste.

-Hoard things you don't need. This is very important. If you have less than 50 rolls of toilet paper, other people may be able to buy them as well. Be sure that you and only you have water, soap, and toilet paper. Remember that this is a contest. If you're going to win, you better have the most of everything because if other people can get equal shares, then we're all losers together.

LAS VEGAS

Because what happens in Vegas stays in Vegas, they have the poorest export economy in the nation as well as the worst sewage backup in recorded history.

LASER

Lasers aren't really capable of cutting through objects. At most they can sort of whittle.

LATIN

"Sic Transit Gloria" is an ancient Latin phrase meaning "Gloria is Fleeting." To this date, nobody knows who Gloria was or where she was going.

LAVA LAMP

The goop in lava lamps is a substance called spermaceti, which is an animal product found in the head of sperm whales. Over ten whales are killed to make one lava lamp.

LAW

Any signature made near a "sign here" tag can be contested in court as having been coerced by the tag.

Due to a typo in Ohio law, all movies but "Air Bud" and "Air Bud 2: Golden Receiver" are banned in the state. The law was intended to grant voting rights to felons with expunged records.

LAWRENCE, D.H.

D.H. Lawrence, an English ornithologist, once stated that he had never seen a bird feel sorry for itself, even when freezing to death. It was not until American ornithologist Walt Whitman saw a lark sing "Hurt" by Nine Inch Nails that the bird watching community realized they were capable of the feeling.

LEAF BLOWER

Leaf blowers were not designed to clean up sidewalks but to wake people on days they might otherwise have slept in.

LEATHER

Leather hasn't come from cow skin in decades. Most leather produced now is instead made from manatee retinas.

LEE, CHRISTOPHER

When God spoke to Moses, he was worried abut his voice having the proper heft so he hired a young Christopher Lee to speak for him.

LEMON

Lemons have no distinct flavors of their own. The taste we ascribe to them is actually the nerve signal of our taste buds dying from their acidic juice.

The lemon scent of most lemon scented cleaning products comes from the glands surrounding the anus of the lemon.

LEONARDO DA VINCI

Leonardo da Vinci is thought to have invented a working light bulb. The invention was lost in one of his lesser-known journals until 2014, at which time the light bulb had already been invented again so nobody cared.

New analysis of his other notebooks have revealed that he also invented the vibrator centuries before its modern rediscovery. Professor Lorenzo Corrompere, who made the discovery, has also suggested the design may shed light on another popular Leonardo da Vinci mystery- That of Mona Lisa's distinctive grin.

LIBRARY

1 in every 3 libraries has a copy of "How to Disappear Completely and Never Be Found." All libraries are supposed to have copies but most disappeared completely, and have never been found.

The largest library in Paris has no doors. Nobody has entered or left since construction was completed in 1877.

LICHEN

Lichen and moss differ in that moss won't dump you like lichen will, on your own damn birthday in front of all your friends and family.

LICORICE

Licorice is highly toxic to humans in its natural form. To be consumed it must be treated with several acids, including clown urine and bryozoa juice.

LIFE, MEANING OF

Many have wondered about the meaning of life over the centuries, indeed millennia, and few people agree on the answer, and even fewer have stumbled upon the right answer.

The first person to wonder about the meaning of life was Nur-Nak-Shellack Siz-Ezzar IV, the Sumerian widely regarded as the earliest philosopher. Around the year -4500, Siz-Ezzar wrote a cuneiform tablet on the matter and decided that the meaning of life was to please Molgar The Child Eater by sacrificing as many children as possible upon the altar of burnt offerings. This decision was very popular at the time among the cult of Molgar, and everyone sacrificed all their children to the deity, and thus the cult ended when they ran out of children. Sumerian civilization collectively decided that as this cult had sacrificed itself out of existence, Siz-Ezzar was probably wrong about the meaning of life.

Next in -2000 came the great Egyptian philosopher Khu-Anakhotep. Khu-Anakhotep believed that the meaning of life was to please Montu the war god by impaling war-captives on the phallus of his statues. Though popular among the victors of war through the Nilotic Kingdoms, those who lost wars were less than convinced and Egypt, once united under the Pharoahs, decided life must have another meaning.

Around the year 0 in Bethlehem, a man was born who offered a radically different means toward deducing the meaning of life. He had twelve followers, he could walk on water, he could heal the sick, and he was believed by many to be the one true son of the God of the Jews. He was of course, Rabbi Shmaya ben Tabbai. Ben Tabbai felt like his predecessors that the meaning of life was to please God by honoring his 613 commandments as recorded in the Torah. As these commandments often conflicted with each other, forced women to sacrifice doves for the "sin" of menstruating, and insisted especially that men have parts of their dicks chopped off as babies, Ben Tabbai was quickly crucified by his own followers and forgotten when the more mainstream Jesus suffered a similar fate a month later.

Things went quiet for a few hundred years as nobody wanted to be crucified for suggesting which god was best to appease. Many religions came and went, worshipping diverse gods and trying diverse methods to appease them because although deities came and went and means of honoring those gods changed drastically, the one thing most religions across the globe agreed on was that the meaning of life was to honor God. Some cultures tried ripping out human hearts, some tried killing goats, some tried waging war on non-believers, and one fellow named Urmaine DeLesspec tried to eat 50 pizzas in one sitting to appease the glutton-god Mouthlar, but died after only his seventeenth.

The thing that perhaps most defines the search for the meaning of life is the misery that people have put themselves and others through in fighting over who had the best god, who knew best how to please that god, and who was willing to sacrifice the most to do so. So for most of history, wars have been ongoing, self deprivation and agony prevailed, and almost none of the people committing it all were certain of the meaning of life, having only spread misery and pain in the name of love and worship.

This is especially ironic as the meaning of life is just to be happy.

LIGHT

Light travels as both a wave and a particle. This makes the TSA very angry.

Light is not initially absent from shadows. Scientifically speaking, light leaves the area of a shadow because it can no longer see its source and runs away in fear for its life.

LIGHT SWITCH

It's required by law that light switches not be able to balance between on and off. If one were to perfectly balance the light switch in the exact center, the light would produce a phenomenon that exists between darkness and light called "Middle Light."

"Middle Light" is extremely dangerous. Composed of half charged photons, the particle waves absorb the charges of whole photons resulting in a chain reaction that can destroy all light within a mile radius.

In 1867, when Edison first invented the light bulb and light switch, he one day left the switch half way off and the resulting darkening knocked out daylight for five hours across the eastern seaboard. Two religious groups went to war believing it to be a sign of the end time, and over 600 automobiles crashed killing over 300. The financial devastation lasted for a decade and nearly caused the invasion of the U.S. by miller moths.

LIGHTNING

Lightning can strike twice but if it strikes again after that it's out.

LIMOUSINE

No limo is factory made, they're all normal cars stretched in a taffy machine.

LINT

There's a company that rents lint. Nobody knows what they rent it for, but they've been around since 1903 and are a top earner on the Forbes-Michelin list of most reliable companies.

LION KING, THE

Disney's "The Lion King" was almost pulled from theaters when an animator admitted to hiding a tiny photograph of his own left butt-cheek into 70 frames across the movie. The rump remains even on blu-ray, and many claim it adds depth to Simba's journey.

LLAMA

A group of llamas is called a dillemma, though other terms apply if three or more are in a polyllamarous relationship.

A Norwegian llama herder once gathered 40 llamas into the White House as a protest against Ronald Reagan's llama laws, some say the Oval Office still smells like llama droppings.

Llamas are the only animal that chews not only its own cud, but the cud of other llamas and sometimes, a bored musician.

At any given time, in any given place, there is likely to be at least one llama staring at you.

LOBSTER

Most lobsters are red, but one in every ten million is blue, and one in every five billion is polka dot orange and chartreuse.

Lobsters are the fully grown version of lice. If you let head lice go untreated, you can have your own head-raised lobsters for dinner nightly!

LOCH

The difference between a pond and a lake is not about size, but how many lemurs have spit in it. A loch is a landlocked lake located where lemurs lay. Lochs lose layers of aquiclude if lemur saliva leaches long-term into low level alluvium. Lately, lawsuits leveled at illegal loch lemur lenders have let lochs convalesce and last longer.

LOCK PICKING

You can easily pick any lock by staring at it until it feels guilty and lets you in.

LOCKOUT

There's a sect of Christianity that believes Jesus returned briefly in 2012, saw Lockout starring Guy Pearce, gave it 3 stars and then left.

LOLLIPOP

Lollipops are a very specific cut of meat from the candy center of the cow.

LONDON

London is short for "Londinium" the Roman word for "The land where the orange juice is mostly acid and pulp."

LORD OF THE RINGS, THE

Middle Earth was based on J.R.R. Tolkien's concept of the world before its latest continental shift. Following the motion of the continents, the Shire would be in modern Iceland, and Mordor would be in modern New Jersey, much to the surprise of nobody.

Tolkien took most of the names for locations in Middle Earth from his favorite black metal bands.

The production designers of the filmed Lord of the Rings trilogy made several identical prop rings for use in the films. Three were given to the actors; Seven to the props department; And nine, nine rings were made for the studio executives, who above all craved power, and memorabilia.

The character of Legolas does not appear in the original Lord of the Rings novel, and was created based on two separate characters in the Fellowship of the Ten.

During principal photography on the films, Peter Jackson lost his wedding ring and held up shooting for weeks as he walked across the entire Middle Earth set looking for it.

The production also required all the green fabric in New Zealand for green-screen material. For two years one could not buy green clothing in the country, nor green dye, green plastic, or even books by Graham Greene.

LOVE

There are said to be three sure ways to make someone love you:

-Only whisper to them. Never speak in a normal tone of voice, even if you need to warn them from across a room. As that rabid bear dashes at them from behind, gently whisper, "run."

-Make direct eye contact. This is difficult due to bone structure but it's worth it when your cornea touches theirs. For extra intimacy, make sure your eye is insufficiently lubricated so you can truly stick together.

-Do nice things without even letting them know who did it. Buy them a new shovel or 50 pack of burnable CDs and leave it at their door. Their confusion is your thank-you.

-Watch their favorite movies and read their favorite books with them. Whenever you see them read, read the same page with them. Tell them when you want to turn to the next page loudly but with compassion.

-Brush their teeth. This intimate offering will show them how willing you are to do household tasks in a serious relationship. Do not pre-gargle their mouthwash though, at least not without boiling between mouths.

-Lie to them about their credit rating. By sending them letters and emails that misrepresent their credit rating, they will be more inclined to let you buy them things they need, such as a moose.

-Don't just laugh at their jokes, laugh at their tears. Show them you find them funny even when they feel sad. Laughter at humor comes easy. Laughing at their pain shows commitment.

-Learn from the Swedish Whooping Owl. When the Swedish Whooping Owl falls in love, it regurgitates pellets with an extra pheromone that arouses its mate. Do the same over a candle-lit dinner and you're in.

-Paint a hamster wheel gray. When they see you taking the time to mute the vibrant colors of an otherwise acceptable hamster wheel, they'll understand you appreciate the subtle things.

-Write them letters. B, C, L, and the vowels have been used in love sonnets since the time of Shakespeare. Write them in ink or on cloth napkins so that your love will last forever.

The popular saying "Love is a Battlefield" is actually a misquote. The original statement was made by General Alexander Imerentinsky, who said "Lovcha is a battlefield" during the Russo-Turkish War.

LUCASFILM

Lucasfilm was founded by George Lucas's great grandfather, back in the days when 'film' referred to thin, sticky membranes.

LUTEFISK

The Lutefisk is the only known fish to have no gills, scales, fins, flesh, eyes, bones or vascular system.

-M-

MACARONI AND CHEESE

According to Gaston LeConnoisseur, perfect Macaroni and Cheese is exactly 73% macaroni and 37% cheese. He was a master chef, not a mathematician.

MAIL

The U.S. Postal Service uncovers over one hundred human corpses or body parts in the mail every day. Most are found due to insufficient postage.

Envelopes are supposed to be sealed with wax seals. Licking the back to close them is made possible by the stickiness of leftover horse phlegm used in the manufacturing process.

MAGIC

The magician's act of sawing a woman in half became even more popular with magician's assistants in 1921 when Harry Houdini discovered a way to perform the trick without actually killing the subject.

MAGNETIC FIELD

The magnetic field is a field of magnetic grass near Stonehenge. The grass is heavy in iron due to the ancient druidic invocation of iron molecules into the ground, and responds to magnetic forces such as horseshoes, ivory, and the personality of Dean Martin.

MARIJUANA

"Weed" became a term for marijuana because it used to grow wildly and inconveniently, literally a weed. Several hundred thousand tons of the plant were unceremoniously destroyed every day before its use as a drug was discovered in 2013.

MARIO BROS, SUPER

The original Super Mario Bros. was meant to end with yet another Toad saying there was never any princess at all and then the game would start over. This was Shigeru Miyamoto's way of telling children that life is an endless struggle with no reward.

Miyamoto also planned for Mario and Luigi to have different attacks in Mario 3. Mario would still stomp enemies, but Luigi would rip out their spines like Sub-Zero from Mortal Kombat.

MARRIAGE

Couples originally shared a single wedding ring, which bound them by the fingers for life. The tradition ended with the invention of the hacksaw.

Marriage must be preceded by a "proposal." A proper proposal begins with a title page, followed by an abstract. The abstract should explain the proposal's time frame, hypotheses, and the means by which they will be studied. Following the abstract, one should summarize prior research and ones own previous explorations of the subject. Then outline the proposal itself.

The proposal should be faxed to the appropriate scientific grant organizations and colleges, and of course any peer reviewed periodicals that may be interested. Remember to format the proposal for each according to their requirements.

Or just ask them to marry you.

MARS (GOD)

Mars is famously considered a god of war, but in mythology this was only his secondary purpose, he was originally best known as the god of manicure.

MARS (PLANET)

Mars has seven months:

-Marsuary
-Aresril
-Redch
-Canalgust
-Rustober
-Volcanovember
-July

Now that water has been discovered on Mars, the rover has begun the search for fire.

MARSHMALLOW

Marshmallows don't really grow in marshes, but only swamps and bogs. Roasting marshmallows is all that remains of an ancient pagan rite symbolizing the burning of Magmathurmathmerthmorth, the sugar god.

MARSHMALLOW DISASTER OF 1982, THE

Derbyfield Marshmallow Plant was located in the Maydupp Mountains directly outside of Toronto, Canada. Founded in 1807, it was the longest running marshmallow manufacturing plant in the Americas, and the second longest on Earth after only Mashumaro in Japan, where the candy was invented in 1322.

In 1992, the factory switched owners. Rolf Jensen, the previous owner and manager was well loved by all his employees and brought in the highest profits and maintained the best safety record of any owner the factory ever had. His replacement, George Schrub from the U.S. was considered a total mess. Schrub inherited the factory at its best, and within only two months had the worst safety record, limited production, and was almost 2 million dollars in the red.

A strike ensued, and many employees simply quit. Schrub, undaunted, decided he could do the jobs himself. He worked hard, nobody could deny it, but his incompetence was off the scale and when a vat of sugar was allowed to come into contact with the fluffing epoxy, the factory exploded in a colossal mass, killing Bush and several picketing employees, smothering them in delicious deadly goo.

The region has been declared a disaster zone and a biohazard, and is, like Chernobyl, impossible to clean up using modern technology. Not all the effects of the disaster are negative however, as the local Walrus population has skyrocketed and grown to epic proportions on the sweet fluff.

MASSACHUSETTS

Massachusetts is Volumeachusetts times Densityachusetts.

MATH

Math was not discovered, but invented. The year was 47,481 B.C.E., around late March, and Gmorgu was piling rocks outside his cave to throw at Vlarg should Vlarg return to try to steal his flint again. Gmorgu had 6 rocks, but didn't know this consciously. Certainly he understood he had an amount of rocks, and that he would have several throws should he miss Vlarg with a couple. But this was the dawn of humankind and curiosity was the hottest new thing. Gmorgu wondered- How many rocks could he throw at Vlarg? This was the first time a human being yearned to quantify anything.

Gmorgu developed a quick system: If he threw one rock, he would have five rocks left. If he threw two rocks, he would have four rocks left, and so on. Gmorgu laughed with his ingenuity. He had just invented subtraction. He wondered if any more operations were possible, and no sooner had he added a seventh rock to his pile did he realize this too was a sort of counterpart to his previous mathematical invention.

Vlarg came over the hill looking shifty. He had come for Gmorgu's flint. Gmorgu grunted but Vlarg looked to run past him. Gmorgu threw the first rock, and divided Vlarg's skull in half, thus inventing both division and fractions. His number of available operations had tripled and he realized this too was an operation, multiplication.

Thus the four common mathematical operations were born. But that day of genius was far from over:

It was then that Vlarg's daughter, Bleez, discovered her father wounded and howled by his side. Gmorgu grunted at her to take the body away from him, for he had sought to steal Gmorgu's flint. Bleez grunted back that it was originally the community's flint and Gmorgu was being greedy by keeping it for himself. Gmorgu did not relent, he went back into his cave. Bleez then did something she'd wanted to do since Gmorgu hoarded the flint in the first place- She walked up the hill to the precarious boulder that stood over Gmorgu's cave and pushed it over.

It rolled down the hill at an angle of 36° and a speed of 14mph, covering 3.141 times its radius with each rotation, lodging itself and covering the entrance of Gmorgu's cave with an area of 14ft² all to Bleez's watchful and annotative eye. So it was that Bleez, not a moment after the invention of math itself, invented the fundamentals of geometry, defeated Gmorgu, and avenged her father.

She did this all by means of intuition, and never wrote down her greatest discovery that day- She had just become the first human being to make active and intentional use of the laws of gravity, and in so doing, also invented the wheel.

This was the second most prosperous day of human invention in history, and was only superseded last Tuesday when I realized I could eat ramen with scissors. Noodle Scissors. To cut the long noodles as they hang from the fork.

I'm a freakin' GENIUS.

MATTERHORN

Shortly after building the Matterhorn attraction at Disneyland, Disney copyrighted the Matterhorn and sued Switzerland over their mountain of the same name.

MCY 70117a

MCY 70117a is a Saturn-sized gas giant orbiting the binary brown dwarf Luhman 16, which is only 6.5 light years from our sun. It was first photographed on July 1st, 2017 by amateur astronomer Marshall C. Yarnblob of rural Cornwall, England.

"I built my telescope from some spare computer parts and a common bathroom mirror," said Yarnblob, "It's slightly better than Hubble due to the curvature of the mirror, which I discovered only after I had built the 'scope. I built it to spy on my neighbor, who I'm pretty sure is some kind of Satanist, but when I pointed it to the stars, I realized its resolution was, by pure chance, flawless."

Yarnblob offered his telescope to NASA and the ESA but was declined by both, who didn't believe his claims. One thing is for certain- They believe him now. They also afforded him the right to name the planet, which he promptly called "Planet Tennis Ball" owing to the yellow hue and white curvy line around its equator, which experts believe is an atmospheric band of methane.

The Yarnblob Telescope is currently being moved very carefully to Dungeness beach where light pollution will not affect it. Said NASA head Lauren Logllamadachshund, "We hope to view the system's other planets within the week, and to observe the exoplanets of Proxima Centauri in even greater clarity."

Yarnblob has declined all offers of money for the telescope, stating that science is its own reward. He asked only for a conventional telescope in exchange so that he might further spy on his neighbor. "He's up to something, I know it. The police won't listen but I saw him building an altar, and I saw him wearing black robes. The man sacrifices babies, you mark my words," said Yarnblob.

When asked for comment, his neighbor Aleister LaVey stated that he was not a Satanist, and that he only ever sacrificed one baby once when he was in college as part of a frat dare.

MEATBALL

Traditional French meatballs are at least 60% Poodle.

MEATLOAF

A man in Nebraska once managed to eat almost 20 pounds of Meatloaf in one sitting. The singer survived and made a full recovery in time for his "Bad Attitude" tour.

MERMAID

It's not cannibalism if mermaids eat sushi, but it is if they eat other mermaids as sushi, which they do.

METAL

When metal sparks, it is not small bits of hot metal flying away, but the ectoplasmic footprint of the soul of the metal.

METALLICA

Metallica is named after Matallaika, the bunny from Betsy Roseworthy's novel, "My Fluffy Friend."

METAMORPHOSIS

Kafka's "Metamorphosis" originally ended with Gregor founding a flea circus.

METROID

"Metroid" is a portmanteau of "monster" and "hemorrhoid." The creature originally attacked from below.

While designing the title screen for Super Metroid, artists planned out real displays for the monitors on the baby Metroid's containment system.

The left panel reads "Metroid Stasis Field: Operational / Metroid Life Signs: Positive" and the right screen reads "Metroid Stew: 1 whole Metroid, 2 cups chicken broth, 1 cup chopped vegetables; freeze and dice Metroid, bring broth to boil and add vegetables, dip Metroid cubes in salt and add to broth for 30 minutes, serves two."

MEXICO

Mexico is by far the largest country in Mexico. It has a rich history of artists and authors such as Frida Kahlo, Ernest Hemingway, and Yukio Mishima.

Mexico's name is French for "The Land Where They Speak Ultra-French," which is an antiquated term for Spanish. Mexico once took up a large portion of Pangaea, and as such still has colonies in Australia, Russia, and Thaumasia.

Mexico has served as the filming backdrop for all three productions of Frank Herbert's Dune, thanks to its many dunes, and also its 5000 meter sandworms.

Mexico, like Egypt, has many pyramids. This is proof of the existence of Atlantis, and has nothing to do with the fact that triangular piles of rocks tend to last longer than other structures.

Mexico has a mountain range with 60,000% more gold than any other place on Earth of equal size. Not to be confused with El Dorado in South America, this mountain range has yet to inspire any DreamWorks animated films, and is thus considered worthless financially.

Gambling is illegal in Mexico due to the Mexican Casino Wars of 1917. They began when a new casino called "La Noche Estrellada" broke ground next to one of the country's most popular elder casinos, "El Grito." The owners of El Grito tried to run the smaller casino out of business by sending expert gamblers in to win at poker, specifically Ecatepec Hold 'Em. Unfortunately for El Grito, the play only resulted in record attendance at La Noche, which retaliated by letting cheaters go free so long as they agreed to cheat only at El Grito. The feud escalated and reached its height in October, when La Noche launched ICBMs at El Grito's enemies in Russia, knowing the counter-strike would destroy its rival nearby. Russia thankfully didn't notice the strike because it was busy with a revolution, and also "ICBM" in 1917 stood for Irritable-Constipated-Bull-Moose. The Mexican government noticed however and intervened, banning both casinos, and gambling, and also buildings over 3 floors tall with fewer than four emergency exits, though this last bit was a rider amendment and is not relevant to this factoid.

If Mexico were a dress, it would be green.

MICROPHONE

Most microphones contain a single lima bean. Only microphone manufacturers know why.

MICROWAVE

Microwave ovens use "Pigeonbelly" radiation, the same type of radiation that pigeons use to digest their food.

MILDEW

Mildew can grow anywhere except on other mildew.

MILK

The myth of the Genie in a Bottle began with Genie Milk Co. in 1962, who accurately claimed there was "Genie" Milk in every bottle. The company went out of business in 1968, when the milk granted not wishes, but E. coli to all their patrons.

MIRROR

Mirrors work by using enchanted glass. They are our only glimpse into the real world.

MONEY

The phrase "I feel like a million bucks" was first uttered in 1909. Adjusted for inflation one would now need to feel like $2,491,699,312 to feel that good.

MONK

Ancient Monks would conduct their own embalming and burial. Their last directions before the embalming fluid completely destroyed their brain were called the "ultima ordines rabidus" and were generally nonsensical due to the process. One monk's final words were, "Bury me with my saxophone and play me some blues," which was considered bizarre because he died in 932 A.D., long before the invention of either.

Medieval Monks were obsessed with breaking records. A popular record across Europe was to fit monks into a single cell. The record is still held by the Brothers of the Eternal Light, who crammed all 80 of their order into a 12x12ft room.

The year was 1261 and the Abbey of The Woeful Brothers of Solemnity had just crammed 72 of their 78 brothers into a 16x14 cistern. Word crossed christendom and Brothers of Eternal Light lost their previous record, which had been secured, they thought forever, in the name of the greatest glory of Christ. Abbot Maritus Tollok resigned in shame. The brotherhood redoubled their efforts but could not cram more than 68 monks into their next smallest room, the 12x12 washroom.

The new Abbot, Phillip Manlibum, refused to let the Woeful Brothers of Solemnity have their day. He realized that the human body was not shaped efficiently- Its arms specifically occupied much horizontal space that they did not completely fill, lowering the effective density of monk-cramming. So he did what any good abbot would do: He mandated the dismemberment of each monk in his order.

Each brother gave up his arms, which were sawed off by the immediate elder brother by his side. As the eldest of the order, Abbot Manlibum sawed off his left arm, and then, placing the saw in his severed left arm, sawed off his right in a grotesque spectacle that chronicles list as "The vibrating shaking arm dance of cauterizing disarmament," on which the popular children's dance "The Hokey Pokey" was later based. And so 70 monks fit into the washroom, two less than was needed to match the record.

Coincidentally, 1261 marked the year of several important inventions, including the fountain pen, the spoked wheel, and most relevant to our tale, liquid clog remover. The first liquid clog remover, "Dreighneaux," was created by the alchemist Nicholas Flamel in an attempt to dissolve gold. It did not dissolve gold, but did a great job of removing hairballs from plumbing. And of dissolving human flesh. Abbot Manlibum got wind of the substance, and quickly purchased enough to dissolve 20% of his order.

And so, until all 80 monks could fit into the washroom, the abbot ordered brother after brother to take the "Sacred Second Baptism Of Final Equilibrium." In liquid form, the brothers fit easily into the washroom basin and the order reclaimed its record. The abbot was then arrested for murder and lived out his days in an 8x6 cell, 2ft larger than his cell at the monastery, into which he claimed he could fit 98 monks, given a proper crematorium and distillery.

Pope Nicholas III declared shortly after that monks could not participate in contests, record breaking, or any other such activity; nor could they mortify the body for any purpose beyond the spiritual. So the record stands to this day, liquid clog remover gained a significant reputation as being able to dissolve any material, and no monks have since dismembered themselves, melted each other, or otherwise destroyed their bodies for any reason but the glorification of our lord Jesus Christ, Amen.

MOON

While ancient myths claim the moon is made of blue cheese, modern spectrometry suggests it's actually feta.

The moon went missing from 1894-1907. It never appeared in the sky and the tides failed to change. Nobody knows where it went or why.

2017 was the first year in a century not to have single full moon.

Due to low gravity, the flag planted on the moon by Neil Armstrong has now grown to over 40ft tall. Most later Apollo missions didn't make it to the moon, having settled on closer planets where they set up colonies.

Astronaut-scientist Harrison Schmitt is the only astronaut to walk on the moon on two separate missions. Far from an honor, he was sent back as punishment.

Schmitt, on his first mission, walked over a particularly nice stretch of dirt and left his footprints all over it. Appalled by his actions, NASA insisted he return on the next mission to rake the sand back into its pristine form.

MOONLIGHT

When God created the day and the night, he originally stated that the sun would illuminate the night sky, but later admitted he was mistaken and moonlight had been selected instead.

MOOSE

It's illegal to park your moose outside of a restaurant on a Tuesday in Minnesota. Because of this strange law, many residents transfer ownership of their moose to their friends and vice versa, as a loophole allows you to park someone else's moose anywhere you please.

If you stare at a moose for long enough you will see the mouse from which it metamorphosed.

The modern Moose is actually the smallest of several moose species that have existed in the Americas over the last 50 million years. The Mega-Moose only went extinct one thousand years ago. The Mondo-Mega-Moose coexisted with the Neanderthals, and the Moose Lord once stood 75 feet tall as the largest land mammal of all time. It ate T-Rexes.

MOSQUITO

Mosquitos have an exact sense of time. When they bite, they always spend exactly 20 seconds drinking blood. When this genetic sense is deactivated, they keep sucking and will drain a human body completely, becoming large 1.5 gallon sacks of blood within an hour.

MOTION CAPTURE

In order to feature realistic CG animals, the producers of Avatar motion captured several live animals, including horses, birds, a tiger, and a snail. James Cameron later admitted he made them do the snail as a joke.

MOTORCYCLES

The first Harley Davidson motorcycle sits in the Smithsonian Museum, next to the mummified remains of Harleen F. Davidson herself.

The Hell's Angels predate motorcycles. They were founded as a velocipede gang in 1871 and terrorized the U.S. on Penny-Farthing bicycles.

MOUNTAIN

Most mountains are hollow, like geodes. If they were solid rock they would sink into the magma.

Mt Everest is well above the elevation at which snow can form. It is white because it's made of white rock, not because it's covered in snow.

MOVIE THEATER

The first movie theater was built in the city of Ur in 3,000 B.C. It did poorly until the invention of movies in 1895, and still has difficulty as it has yet to upgrade to digital.

MOZART, WOLFGANG AMADEUS

The composer's cut of Mozart's "Magic Flute" contains over 17 minutes of additional material, including a note that hasn't been played in over 300 years.

Mozart died of food poisoning acquired in a cyanide eating contest. His cyanide contained salmonella.

MUCUS

The average human nose produces 2 quarts of mucus per day, with the lungs creating 13.5% of the substance for an associate producer credit.

Boogermancy is the art of telling the future by the shape of one's own dried mucus. It predates horoscopes, tea leaves, and palm reading by over one thousand years.

The Menvyne's Snot-o-pedia contains listings for every known type of booger, nasal mucus form, and loogie known to humankind, including the Dangling Wad, the Deep Hubert, and three variants of the Whiskerbound White Macro-Globule.

MUMMY

Most mummies were not made into mummies, but were born mummies from ancient mummy bloodlines.

MUMMY, CURSE OF THE

The myth of the Mummy's curse comes from the misreading of hieroglyphs in King Tut's tomb. It was thought to say "Death will come on swift wings to those who disturb my tomb," but in fact said, "These words will be misinterpreted until 1981."

MUSIC

Humans are not the only animal that can enjoy music, but we are the only one that seems to enjoy neoclassical dark wave.

MUSIC, THE SOUND OF

The director's cut of The Sound of Music ended with the family cannibalizing the youngest child to survive the cold wilderness near the border.

NAME OF THE ROSE, THE

Umberto Eco's masterpiece "The Name of the Rose" is considered the shortest novel ever written, containing only two words: "It's 'Rose.'"

NAME CHANGES

Wilbur Cockfart was so embarrassed by his name that he lobbied for and won the right to change ones name legally. He became the first to do so in America, and is now named Jason Cockfart.

NAME ORIGINS

The individual names of Dexdillisci citizens are based on prophecies given to them on the day of their birth. This fact, recorded by He-Who-Will-Record-Our-Naming-Rituals, has been disputed by She-Who-Will-Claim-Our-Names-Are-Mere-Coincidences, who claims that their names are mere coincidences.

NAPOLEON

Napoleon was the Emperor of France, and is one of the most famous French statesman in history, both for his contributions to French culture, his expansion of France, and his representation of the French people. He was born in Italy.

Napoleon lived a military life, becoming a general at the age of 17. As general he conquered Egypt, fought to maintain slavery in America, and conquered revolts in France. He then held a revolt in France. For these acts, he became Emperor.

Napoleon was also notable for having married Josephine, and some historians feel that he proclaimed himself to such a high position just so he could Empress her.

As Emperor, he got into fights with literally every single other country he could find, and won many of them until he got into a fight in Russia, which he decided could be defeated on its home turf in the middle of winter. He was wrong, so he got deposed and confined to the island of Elba. He got bored on Elba so he took over France again for exactly 111 days, which would be known in history as the "hundred days," as was the style after the 29 year "thirty years war," the 116 year "hundred years war," and the "fifty seven years war," which lasted exactly 57 years but was in fact a cactus and not a war at all.

After his brief return, Napoleon was banished to Mt. Saint Helens until he died of a stomach ache, because it was 1821 and that happened back then. He was then placed into a ridiculously large coffin. I mean, like the biggest coffin you'll ever see. A HUGE freakin coffin. Google it seriously look at his coffin it's gigantic.

Napoleon left behind an amazing legacy of killing people, making bad decisions, and being the subject of a Stanley Kubrick movie that didn't get made but that's a good thing because instead he made Barry Lyndon which is the best 3 hours you'll ever spend looking at amazing photography and, for some reason, Ryan O'Neil.

NASA

NASA has its own junkyard for disposal of rocket parts. In 2008, two kids used nothing but parts from it to try to build a spaceship. They've not been seen since its launch, but for some reason there's a light now on Mars.

NASIR, EA

After Ea Nasir notoriously failed in the copper business, he went into computers under the name Ea Games, where he received even more angry letters of complaint than before.

NAVY

The Navy took its name from the navy blue uniforms that made them recognizable.

NEBULA

Located near the star cluster Hallux Major, the Digestive System Nebula is named for its clear resemblance to the human digestive system.

The nebula was first spotted in 1708 by Lord Kevorkian The Elder, a popular astronomer. Upon its discovery he named it "The Lord Kevorkian The Elder Nebula" but no astronomic society adopted the name, especially once they saw it and noted its digestive nature.

Most curious is the fact that Feces Minor, the poop star, is located directly under the nebula's anus, leading many to believe that the Ancient Romans who named the star were not only aware of human anatomy but of the nebula itself, and may have believed it to be the alimentary canal of the god Nasu Imbre, of whom it is written, "And the Lord of Stars Nasu Imbre can be seen above the star Feces Minor, where he hath shat after eating Caseum Cibum, the cheeseburger star which orbited the Hardees constellation."

NECKTIE

The necktie was originally symbolic of a noose to remind wealthy wearers that they were mortal. The bow-tie was symbolic of butterflies, because they are pretty.

NECRONOMICON

The Necronomicon has been fully translated since it was discovered and featured in numerous dark tales. In reality it contains nothing but a 400 page explanation of how to fold a fitted sheet.

NEEDLE (HAYSTACK-BOUND)

The phrase "A needle in a haystack" was coined by the inventor of the electromagnet. William Sturgeon worked for the East India Company in the 1800s. He was self taught and notorious at the time not as an inventor but as a bar patron who would take up all kinds of bets. In 1822 he made a bet with Stuart Abercrombie that he could eat ten pounds of hard cheddar in one sitting. In 1823 he bet Markus Hellenschneidersen that he could punch a hole through one foot of lead. In early 1824 he bet Erskine Hamlet that he could sneeze with enough force to blast the Earl of Liverpool off his horse. Needless to say he failed every bet, and was generally out of money.

In late 1824, he bet Charles Grafton Page that he could find a needle in a haystack in under a minute. Being certain he could do so but being completely broke, he bet for one million pounds of Page's money against his own life. Page accepted.

Sturgeon was scared half to death. On the appointed day he would have 59 seconds to find a needle in a modest haystack of one cubic meter. Or he would die. He had only two days to prepare, and in those days he studied. He studied metals. He studied hay. He studied methods of finding anything in the world. And on the Friday of the decision, he arrived at the barn with the world's first electromagnet.

Unfortunately, harnessed electricity would not be invented by Georg Ohm for another three years and unable to use it to find the needle, Sturgeon was executed on the spot.

His invention, agreed by all to be a brilliant idea, became useful those three years later and he was awarded a posthumous patent (the first in England). Had he lived another few years, Sturgeon would have owned the rights to the electric motor, and would have lived as one of the richest men in British history.

His last words were recorded as follows: "I accept my fate for I have failed a bet against my life. I shall die now, but the afterlife troubles me not- For whatever Sisyphean ordeal awaits me in hell, it can't be harder than finding a needle in a haystack.

NEGATIVE NUMBERS

Negative Numbers were originally called "Inverse Numbers." The term "Negative" was adopted due to their foul attitudes.

NEON

Neon signs cause cancer in all who read them. Proximity to the neon tube is safe so long as you don't read what it says.

NEON GENESIS EVANGELION

Much of The End Of Evangelion was improvised on the spot, which was difficult for both the voice actors and the animators.

NERF

The Nerf Dimension exists beneath our own, a sub-space of sorts. Everything that exists in our reality has a Nerf equivalent in that space.

For instance, when there was a gunfight in the old west, there was a Nerf gunfight with foam bullets, plastic guns, and Muppet cowboys going on simultaneously in the Nerf Dimension.

When we use Nerf weapons on our plane, the Nerf Dimension experiences a theoretical concept we call, "N²" or "Squirf" in which their Nerf existence is compounded by our own Nerfdom and is not doubly Nerfed, but Nerfed times the Nerfage of our world. Thus in their world it barely exists at all except as a substance akin to Aerogel in a vacuum. Because of this state of emptiness, our Nerf bullets are often sucked into the Nerf Vortex or "Nerftex" and appear lost to us, though they are quite normal in the Nerf Dimension.

Human travel to the Nerf Dimension has only been accomplished once by explorer Richard F. Burton, when he disguised himself as a Muppet in 1867 and infiltrated their dimension, living among them on Nerf food (foam) for almost 5 months. In this time he recorded 5 pages on Nerf politics, 12 pages on Nerf culture, 7 pages on Nerf cuisine, and 455 pages on Nerf sexuality. Such were his interests.

You may ask what dimension exists above ours as a form of hyperspace. This we cannot see, but can surmise it is harder than our own in the same way ours is harder than Nerf material. Things are more serious there, harder hitting, emotions are more intense and dark, and the world is less forgiving and harsh. Scientists call this the "DC Extended Universe."

NETHERLANDS

The Netherlands, or the homeworld of the "Dutch," was founded in 411 by someone named Frank. Frank married someone named Carol and they had lots of kids, who lived in castles in the lowlands, or "nether lands" hence the name of the country. These lands were probably considered lower than other lands because they had fewer skyscrapers.

In 1433, the Romans invaded. The specific Romans, a family called the Hapsbergs, were after a sack of grain called the Sack of Antwerp. Many people died over this sack. The violence let up after a while when the Hapsbergs discovered that they preferred cheese to grain, and were appeased by giving them a Piece of Muenster.

What followed was called the Dutch Golden Age, which was productive because the protestants at some point decided that working yourself to death is what Jesus wanted them to do. They also colonized everybody Britain missed and got a monopoly on trade with Japan, which Japan liked so much that they killed everyone who even vaguely looked Dutch and banned contact with the rest of the world for centuries.

It was then that tulips happened. Tulips, a small worthless breed of flower, got popular. Like, really popular. So popular that people treated them with absolute lunacy, speculating on the prices of various colors and types of bulb in a manner so ridiculous that America would base its entire economic system on it.

Also there were windmills.

NEW YORK

New York, NY is not the newest York. Two Yorks are newer.

NEWTON, ISAAC

Isaac Newton called his theories "Laws" because of his background as a lawyer. He advocated strict punishments for those who broke his laws, and tried to enforce the law of gravity by kidnapping the inventor of the hot air balloon.

Newton had two "secret laws" that he refused to reveal during his lifetime. He stated they could be revealed 300 years after his death, which will allow the Vatican to unveil them in March of 2027. They are believed to provide an understanding of perpetual motion, and anti-gravity.

Newton was also the very first scientist to realize that 80085 looked like "BOOBS" on a common calculator.

NEVERENDING STORY, THE

The first edition of the NeverEnding Story had no end, and had to be abridged in order to be sold. The first copy of the original endless version is still being printed, and always shall be.

NEWS

The news show 48 hours was originally called 49 hours. The remaining hour broke off to become its own show, 60 Minutes.

NIAGRA FALLS

Niagra falls produces 10,000,000 gallons of water every day, making it the larges source of new water in the solar system.

NIGHTMARE ON ELM STREET, A

"A Nightmare On Elm Street" was based on an urban legend, though the name of the street was changed to "Elm" because the producers thought it sounded better than "A Nightmare On Purplunklebury Street."

NINE

The number 9 was not invented until 1818, when mathematicians realized they would need it to describe the upcoming year.

NINE INCH NAILS

A rare vinyl record version of the Nine Inch Nails album "The Downward Spiral" has a groove in the shape of a spiral- The only time this has been accomplished on a record.

NINTENDO ENTERTAINMENT SYSTEM

The original Nintendo Entertainment System had computational power five hundred times that of a modern supercomputer. The secrets of its functionality are lost to history.

NINTENDO GAME BOY

The first Nintendo GameBoy weighed almost 17 pounds.

NINTENDO, SUPER

Misprints in the instruction booklets to Super Metroid, Super Mario World, and The Legend of Zelda: A Link to the Past listed Samus as "An Italian plumber," Mario as "A young Hylian boy," and Link as, "A respected psychiatrist who is secretly a cannibal."

NINTENDO SWITCH

The Nintendo Switch dominated the market upon its release, but also was sometimes submissive to it.

The exact layout of the Nintendo Switch controls once caused minor muscle spasms in some players. The "Switch Twitch" was not a serious issue and went away once a player stops holding the controls.

More serious was an itch caused by handling the cartridges. Due to the inclusion of a bitter coating made to discourage children from swallowing the small cartridges, extended contact with them could cause an Itch.

But the Switch Itch and the Switch Twitch weren't the only problem. There was also an audio glitch. The glitch only affected players with sensitivity to high frequencies who could hear sounds with a very high pitch. The High Pitch Switch Glitch situation had some players wanting to ditch the console but others were okay with the flaws, and grew angry at players who complained. According to Nintendo loyalist Mitch Hitchovich, "Anyone who bitches about the Switch Itch, Switch Twitch or Switch Pitch Glitch is a snitch."

To which afflicted players responded, "Oh, that's rich."

NIXON, RICHARD M.

Richard Nixon was impeached for gluing googly eyes onto all the other White House presidential portraits.

He was the only president to have fallen victim to grave robbery while still alive.

The infamous missing 17 minutes of the Richard Nixon tapes are widely believed to contain the longest fart in the history of the U.S. Presidency.

NOAH'S ARK

Though it is commonly portrayed as a boat, the Bible specifically states that Noah's Ark worked like a submarine.

The 2014 film "Noah" was almost not green-lit as producers felt the protagonist lacked an arc.

NON-FICTION

Most films and novels based on true stories are based on the same true story, that of Almarich von Twizzelkink, who was the first man to do everything.

NOODLE

The average noodle bowl contains over 4,500 miles of noodle. If linked end to end, noodles from a common ramen pack would stretch from Los Angeles to New York.

NOSE

It was once believed the mind resided in the nose. This is where the word "knows" comes from.

Nose picking has only recently become a taboo. Handkerchiefs were common in polite society because it was expected one would greet their friends by wiping a booger on their chest.

A company in Denmark has invented high-tech replacement for the tissue or handkerchief that functions like a small vacuum cleaner. Its manufacturers claim it has a low, 18% likelihood of sucking your brains out.

The human body reuses its dead cells for new purposes. What we call snot is actually coagulated brain fluid, and what we call boogers are clumps of brain cells containing long forgotten memories. When you blow your nose, those memories leave your mind forever and cannot be recalled again.

The Norwegian word for nose literally means "Shame Stump."

NOVA SCOTIA

When a Scotia goes Nova, it can produce many elements across the periodic table, but will destroy the Scotiar System around it in the process.

NRA

In addition to weapons, the 2nd Amendment also guarantees the right to wear pink bunny slippers, but the NRA has done *nothing* for that right.

NSA

The NSA has resorted to "low tech" spy solutions to monitor computer savvy American citizens, including periscopes, peepholes, and passing notes about people behind their backs. This is how they verified that Kimmy has a crush on Wilbur and totally wants to kiss him.

NUCLEAR CRITICALITY ACCIDENT

The first nuclear power plant at Obninsk was sabotaged by US spies and neared criticality, but it was stopped when Mikhail Ivanov plugged the reactor with a hot dog he was eating. The hot dog remains there to this day, it is known locally as "The Meat of Salvation."

NUCLEAR ENERGY

All nuclear power plants have a control room coated in ten feet of lead. This is not to protect from radiation, but to give the room a nice leady aroma.

NUCLEAR WEAPON

Nuclear weapons can be made simply in your own home. All you need are a few household items, a little bit of patience, and a Class 1 Top Security clearance for the manufacture of biological, chemical or nuclear weapons under the Fermi laws of 1954 contingent on permission from the United Nations Security Council. Because we wouldn't want to do anything illegal now would we ;)

You're gonna need-

-A box of matches
-A blender
-Tape
-Some wire mesh (Like a window screen, for sifting)
-Cake mix (Yellow sponge cake works best)
-Ziplock bags
-String
-Ice cubes (The cold kind, not the rapper/actor)
-A toilet paper tube
-A Catholic Missal
-An empty kitty litter bucket

First, you're gonna need to make two rare substances- Weapons grade uranium and "heavy" water. Luckily these are easy to produce:

For the uranium, just take your yellow cake mix and sift it with the wire mesh. Whatever stays on top of the mesh- That's weapons grade. For the heavy water, take some ice cubes, which are heavier than water but still made of water, and put them in the blender. By breaking up the ice cubes and releasing the water, you keep the weight but make it a fluid. This is a process that scientists call "Putrefaction."

To build the weapon, pack some uranium into one end of the toilet paper tube and then cover that end with the Catholic Missal. This guarantees what we call a "Critical Mass" of uranium. Then take a smaller wad of uranium and pack it into the other end of the tube, leaving plenty of space between the two.

Tape the box of matches to that end of the tube. It will act as an explosive device to send the "bullet" of uranium into the critical mass, thus resulting in a nuclear fission explosion.

You now have a nuclear fission device! Like the bomb that destroyed Hiroshima, this device has a yield equal to about 10 thousand tons of T.N.T! But fission is for wimps, right? So let's turn that fission bomb, into a fusion bomb!

Tape your string to the matches to act as a fuse, and then put the nuclear warhead in a ziplock bag. Be sure to seal it tight!!! Now place that assembly into the kitty litter bucket. Make sure it's empty of kitty litter before the next step.

Fill the rest of the bucket with the heavy water you made in step one, and seal the top of the kitty litter bucket with the string still poking out. Once the fuse is lit, it will light the matches and detonate the nuclear fission bomb. This acts as a heat source to boil the heavy water, and when heavy water boils- Nuclear Fusion!

Congratulations, your bomb is now complete. Remember that it's illegal to carry or detonate a nuclear fusion warhead in public (except in Texas, it's fine there), and bear in mind this will be quite a bit stronger than your usual firecrackers. We recommend only setting off your nuclear device on official U.S. testing grounds, such as the desserts of New Mexico or islands in the Pacific only populated by tribes under no country's protection.

So play safe and have a good time!

NUMZIE, BARBARA

You won't see Barbara Numzie on any Google Doodle or Wikipedia birthday list, but her contributions to society are incalculable. Barbara Numzie is the inventor of the push-button.

Without Numzie, we would have no keyboards, no touch screens, no electronic devices of any kind or at least no way to turn them on. Numzie also invented the switch, and arguably even the dial. The first button was built by Numzie in 1853 in order to more easily unhitch her father's horse-drawn plow. It was made from one of her blouse buttons, hence the term.

But Numzie had the misfortune of showing her invention to a young Thomas Edison, who at the age of five claimed it for his own, patented it, and promptly sued Numzie for using it on the plow she invented it for. Though he was only five and she was fourteen, the courts sided with Edison because women were not allowed to testify on their own behalf in the 1850s, and her father was unaware of court procedure. So Edison is remembered as the inventor, and Numzie is a footnote in history.

Historians have recently been trying to clear her name as a false accuser but only with limited success. A major advance has been made in the cause however as more inventions of Numzie's have come to light. She hid them so as not to lose them to Edison or other inventors and they were only found this year in her family's basement. Among her other inventions are what appear to be plans for a primitive telephone, a working mechanical pencil, and an unknown device with a wheel that seems to turn faster and faster perpetually once given a push despite having no apparent power source.

Barbara Numzie may have also been left out of the history books because in addition to losing her patent to Edison, she also murdered and ate over twenty people, crucifying their remains upside down in honor of Satan, who she worshiped devoutly. She was executed in 1894 for her crimes, which also included screaming Latin death-curses at random passersby and desecrating over forty baptismal fonts with her own mucus.

OBOE

The oboe is capable of making a sound that only elephants can hear. Mozart wrote two symphonies for elephants using this trait. Whether elephants enjoy them is a matter of intense debate in the music world.

SEE ALSO: PICCOLO

OBSCENITY

The word "Bouquet" is actually a cuss word in the original French, when you give someone a bouquet of flowers you're literally giving them a "Clusterfuck" of flowers.

The most obscene word in the world is "******", a word so insulting it has never been seen uncensored.

OCEAN

In addition to the four best known oceans, the Earth also has three lesser known hidden or "secret" oceans:

-The Helio Ocean. Located in South Korea, the Helio Ocean is a small body of water that is technically an ocean because it follows the ABCs of oceanity: It has Algae, it's Blue, and it houses at least one Cthulhu. The Helio Ocean may be the worlds smallest ocean, but it does have the best wi-fi.

-The Airline Ocean. Near Brescia, Italy is a body of water known in the local language (called 'Italian') as "La Compagnia Aereacargo" which translates as "The Ocean of the Lost Airline Cargo" which was once a term for the mysterious place that lost luggage must have gone. It was found in 1987 to be a real location, which also held most of the worlds left socks that were lost in the laundry. The ocean is strictly off limits to foreigners and is open only to residents of Italy (called 'Italians').

-The Frank Ocean. The Frank Ocean is the world's newest ocean, having formed in Long Beach in 1987 when the Orange Channel spilled over. The Frank Ocean is most notable for the siren-like music that results from the crashing of waves over natural rock structures just beneath the surface. Many record labels have attempted to record and sell these sounds, but legal experts claim the body of water may be entitled to the profits, as Oceans are not technically U.S. residents and may therefore be governed by maritime law. The legal battles resulting from the new Ocean will also have implications for the endangered Henley's Eagle, which is unable to leave California and could be threatened by the Frank Ocean's music rights. This has led to the first cases of lawsuits between record companies and the EPA, and many legal battles are ahead which may reshape the political landscape around the region. Indeed, the Frank Ocean has an odd future ahead.

As for the Pacific Ocean, after being open for almost 750 million years, it is expected to end its run soon. Pacific Spokesman Roland Haphausenhauer cited over-fishing, pollution, and the bad global economy as the reasons for the closure.

"This is the end of quite an era," said the spokesman, "We tried to keep the Pacific going as long as we could but the fact is, it's just not profitable and it's just no longer rewarding work for those responsible." The Pacific has seen several hundred lay-offs in recent years, with the ocean becoming less popular with tourists and new businesses. Now over 30 billion USD in debt, the ocean will file for bankruptcy and close its shores forever.

The effects will be long lasting as ships fall to the dry ocean floor, weather and water concerns go haywire, and many countries bordering the ocean dry up and their people flee in search of water. Said Japanese oceanographer Noriyuki Honjo, "Japan as we know it is essentially over with this news. Much of our economy is based on fishing, most of our contact with other countries happens by sea. With no Pacific Ocean, our land is doomed." Most other island nations have expressed similar fears.

This is the largest geographical closure since the breakup of Pangea, a supercontinent that comprised most of the world's landmass well into the Mesozoic, when it was hit with an antitrust lawsuit and was forced to break into smaller continents.

Despite rumors to the contrary, the Arctic ocean will remain open, its assets are just frozen.

Similarly notable is that in 1993, there was a petition to ferment the oceans into beer:

With numerous sailing deaths in the early 70s and much talk of the oceans rising due to global warming, a few bold Americans decided something had to be done.

The idea of adding yeast, barley and hops to the oceans to ferment them into beer was not new. The ancient Egyptians had hieroglyphs of their efforts, and German efforts in the 1840s were meticulously recorded. But the concept was never fully popular enough to go into effect.

Then, in 1993, the Incomparable Beer Shortage (IBS) hit. With the world affected by IBS, that foamy fluid was in short supply. There were hops, there was yeast, and according to contemporary musicians there were extensive fields of barley. But water itself was suffering from bad propaganda and many water bottling plants went out of business. Thus beer was at an all time low.

Then in late August, Walter W.W. Walters of Germantown, MD had an idea: What if phones could be miniaturized, mobilized, and linked by an "internet." This idea was before its time so he elected to try to solve the beer crisis by fermenting the seas. His petition gained 17,000 signatures, 8,000 short of what he needed to get the measure on the DC ballot. And so the dream ended there.

Later, scientists calculated that turning the ocean to beer would have killed all sea life including algae that produce oxygen, destroying all humanity. So in the end it's perhaps fortunate that the measure didn't gain popularity. But as the world approaches another possible beer shortage and the oceans rise again to threaten our shores, many are left wondering if fermenting the oceans could be a good idea, even though it would wipe out all life on Earth. This would make it by far the second worst idea to have a resurgence in the late 2010s.

Walter W.W. Walters himself is now opposed to the concept, and has written an extensive record of his efforts and why they needed to fail. According to Walters, "Look I was just really stoned and drunk and like, whatever, man." No truer words have ever been spoken.

OCTOPUS, RARE VIARIANTS

The Art Deco Octopus is uncommon even in the seas to which it's endemic. Hunted to the brink of extinction for its use as a door knocker, the Art Deco Octopus has a distinctive anatomy and is known for its constant symmetry, where unlike most octopeese, it maintains the same position with both its right and left tentacle sets.

The Art Deco Octopus is unable to live for more than a few seconds out of water. Seen sometimes washed ashore with various debris, the plight of this fragile creature is well known. Now that hunting is illegal, pollution threatens its only homeland, the shore of Honah Lee near Madagascar.

This is not the only threatened species in the region, the Leean Dragon is also nearly extinct, a drop in population that scientists blame either on the lack of their dietary sealing wax caused by the move to e-mail, or on children simply no longer believing in them.

Even less common: Only four 96 Tentacled Nonagintasextopi have ever been caught, leading some to believe they're merely mutant octopi. Genetic study however suggests that they're a distinct species more closely related to the nautilus than the common octopus.

The nonagintasextopus is unique in that it roots in the benthic soil like a tree with its tentacles as the roots. The nonagintasextopus also squirts a sweet syrup instead of ink which is said to taste strongly of maple. And finally and perhaps most interesting of all, the nonagintasextopus has been seen using tools underwater, suggesting extremely high intelligence. The tools are limited to Black & Decker, suggesting the nonagintasextopus knows value when it sees it.

OLYMPICS

The first Olympics had only three games: The discus throw, the marathon, and competitive nose-picking. It should be noted that prior to the battle of Marathon, the Olympic marathon also consisted mostly of picking one's nose.

Olympic nose pickers or "Mytismýtisylléktes" as they were known in the ancient Olympics were graded on several dimensions of skills:

-Finger depth achieved
-Collected snot and booger weight
-Flicking distance
-Flavor

Each was given a possible full point for accomplishment, resulting in a total of Delta (4) with a full point in any category being an absolute master work of nasal excavation.

The highest score ever recorded in Ancient Greece was a Gamma.Theta-Epsilon (3.95) by a pharyngonaut named Ftyárimýtis Ioannisyios who is said to have plunged his left pinky into his nose all the way up to the knuckle, dug out a solid nugget of nasal speleothem weighing 38 drachmae (about 5oz), flicked it all the way across the amphitheatron onto a judge's toga, upon which said judge declared it to taste of the finest garum served outside of Heraklion.

OMNIPOTENCE PARADOX

The question of whether God can create a stone so heavy he cannot lift it has been answered: Not anymore.

On the 8th day of creation, God made a boulder so heavy he was unable to lift it. The results were terrible. Thoth mocked him ruthlessly. Brahma created a dozen more and dared God to lift them. Ahura Mazda just sat in the corner and grinned, while Thor offered to smash the boulder but was unable to cheer up the Lord. The 8th day was a bad day.

But on the 9th day, God hit the gym. He lifted, he jogged on the treadmills and he vowed that he would lift that boulder one day. People laughed. They called him the 'flabby god' or the 'ancient one' but he kept going undaunted by their mockery. There were rough days to be sure, days where he doubted himself and almost didn't go. But he never missed a day. He didn't let himself fail. After a couple thousand years he met a girl named Mary at the gym and the rest is history.

In 1764, God showed up on the playground. All the other gods had graduated, of course. None were there to see it, but God walked up to that boulder he'd made millennia before and without so much as a grunt he lifted it, and held it up high, and God smiled.

And he also shed a tear. God realized that in those years since his initial failure, it wasn't his muscular growth that defined him. It was the adult he'd become. No longer did he curse the world to flood when he was disappointed in his people, no longer did he demand blood sacrifices. In those years he'd spent yearning for that one goal he realized he'd lived his whole life.

God retired a few years later and moved to Vermont to write his memoirs. They included the story of the boulder he couldn't lift, and of his life after. In 1882, God died surrounded by his family and friends. Buddha was there, Thor and Odin, all the Egyptian and Greek pantheons. Many of those who made fun of God all those years ago.

And they all knew. They knew he'd done it and though he was gone, they knew the character of the great deity. The God that never gave up. The God they once mocked, yes, but in those long years after, at work and at parties, at home and abroad: He was the God they called "friend."

OPPORTUNITY

The word "Opportunity" has the same root word as "Tuna" but nobody knows what this root is or what the two things have in common.

OPHTHALMOLOGY

According to the bible, Adam and Eve both held doctorates in Ophthalmology. It is unclear what college they attended.

OPTICAL ILLUSION

○

If you stare at the circle above for a few minutes without blinking, your eyes will dry out and start watering!

ORANGE

Most seeds cannot grow without water, but orange seeds can grow in either water or blood, the latter making blood oranges.

ORANGE JUICE

The pulp in orange juice is not orange pulp, but paper like any other pulp.

ORBIT

The Earth orbits the sun at a distance of over 2,000 astronomical units.

The orbits of Venus and Mercury are so close to each other that every 14 years when their paths near, they scrape surfaces.

When orbits decay and their celestial bodies fall, they are traditionally remembered in an "orbituary."

ORGY, ELECTORAL

In ancient Rome, it was common for a newly elected senator to celebrate with an orgy in honor of Bacchus, who in addition to wine and entertainment was also the god of gerrymandering.

This tradition was prohibited by Emperor Constantine when he converted to Christianity, but was still enacted in underground circles, leading to the creation of secret societies such as the Freecarpenters; Ordo Templi Occidentis; the Hermetic Order of the Slutty, Slutty Dawn; and the Skulls and Boning Society of Yale.

President Coolidge, in his days as Governor, joined one such secret society called The Beatnik Orchard. Of this society, little is known, but it still exists today and conducts secretive rituals surrounding the elections of its members. One of the few insights into this society comes from Coolidge himself, who in his last will and testament revealed the nature of his inauguration orgy. Details will not be written here as they are far too graphic, explicit, and disturbing to be repeated in print, but the celebration is said to have involved over 2,000 individuals including 2 ex-presidents, 14 governors, 99 senators, 149 members of the house, 989 various politicians, and well over 12 women, most of whom were present only as observers.

The event took place in the White House, which was, in the words of Edward R. Murrow, "so desecrated and befouled that the entire structure had to be razed, the earth salted, plowed over, encased in a concrete dome, and buried 500ft beneath the new White House," which stands to this day. Also standing to this day is the record of "largest American political orgy," an event that has lost its stature in modern times, with George W. Bush having only a local gangbang, Obama merely spending the night with his wife, and Donald Trump only managing to assemble a bottle of lotion and an old Frederick's of Hollywood catalog from 1998.

ORIGAMI

The Folding Origami Church of Gefälschtestadt, Germany can fold down to fit in the palm of your hand. Taking up two blocks

190

when assembled, the entire church takes up only a few inches when folded in upon itself. It only weights a total of two pounds in either form so it can't be erected in winds stronger than 0.2mph as it would blow away.

Said the architect, Herman Ernsthaftdiesenamensinderfunden, "I wanted to make a church as weightless as the human soul to represent the light and whimsical heart of Christianity." The church is regularly attended by over 200 parishioners and is listed by Guinness as the lightest building in the world. This record may not last however, as the same architect is currently working on his first skyscraper, the Akkordeonhalle to be built in Berlin, a 46 floor tower which will collapse each evening to a square the size of a conventional origami paper.

ORPHEUS

The myth of Orpheus states that Hades was willing to upload Orpheus's wife via FTP if he promised not to watch the progress bar. Sadly he looked just when the bar hit 99% and the upload failed.

OUTHOUSE

Plumbing was only invented in 1797. Before that date, everyone had an outhouse, and palaces for the rich were no exception. Versailles had over 30 outhouses, while Siklós Castle in Hungary only has one- But what a one it is!

Siklós's outhouse is almost twice the size of St. Peter's Basillica and has a dome three times its size. The outhouse is built around a single toilet, which has only a 3ft deep pit beneath it for urine and feces. The outhouse is no longer in use but is a tourist attraction, showcasing the decadence of 17th century Hungary and the architectural marvels of the era. The iconic outhouse has inspired many other buildings, including Hungary's own parliament building which was designed without consideration for the nature of its predecessor in style and scope.

But this is not the only time an ornate outhouse has inspired or even been repurposed into another building. Many famous buildings started as outhouses for neighboring palaces, including the Lincoln Memorial (Which now has Lincoln's statue on the central fixture), the Taj Mahal, the Empire State Building, the Sydney Opera House, Hagia Sophia, and possibly the Great Pyramids of Giza, whose proximity to the Great Taco Bell of Hamenthotep VII suggests their true purpose.

OWL

The owl is one of only two animals to be called an "owl," the other of course being the owl.

Owls talk to each other with vocabularies of over 500 words, but 492 of these words appear to be synonyms for "Raisin Bran."

Owls can turn their necks all the way around with the use of special ball bearing joints.

Several species of owl lack the distinctive "who" call. Some ask "what," or even "why." These owls are considered pretentious by other birds.

OXYGEN

Oxygen has to be stirred every few minutes or it will clump up and become unbreathable.

PADLOCK

Many old padlocks made it very difficult to change combinations, as the combination had to have at least one number, 8 letters including a capital, and one special character, but the locks themselves only had numbers on the dial.

PAJAMAS

Pajamas surround us while we sleep yet we do not fear them. This is called "The Henchmeyer Paradox." Nobody knows who Henchmeyer was or why this paradox is named for him.

PANCAKES

Pancakes were not so named because they can be made in a pan, but in honor of the god Pan, who cooked them. In a pan.

PANDA BEAR

Panda Express has not served real pandas since the panda pandemic. It caused such pandemonium that they switched to soy panda, which critics of vegetarianism panned as pandering.

PANTS (ON FIRE)

The rhyme "Liar Liar Pants On Fire" was inspired by the English Inquisition, where the pants of heretics were lit aflame. The same inquisition also spawned the phrase, "Thief Thief Impaled On A Barbed Spike," which is less known because it does not rhyme.

PAPER

To make paper, insects or arachnids are caught or grown specifically for paper production. The bugs are etherized and mashed into a thick paste known as "London Flan" which is baked into a solid mass, then sliced and bleached to make individual sheets called "London Papyrus" which will become the base of the finished material.

The sheets are bleached, then subjected to acetone, camphor and creosote treatments (Known collectively as a "London Sauna") before they're slathered with horse phlegm (AKA "London Jelly") and North Sumatran Coprophagic Tortoise-Weasel bile (AKA "London Tequila"), and again bleached this time for a final smooth, white finish.

The next step in paper production adds texture so that the paper will pick up pencil graphite, and is unfortunately far too disgusting to elaborate upon in this book. I'll only say that the process is known as the "London Hiccup" and most people from outside of the paper-making profession who have seen the process have run away screaming, never to use the material again.

Paper can also be made from wood pulp.

PAPERBOY

The first unlockable achievement was to break more than 50 windows as PaperBoy. I am not referring to the video game.

PAPERCRAFT

Papercraft was invented by the paper benders, a people completely annihilated by the Fire Nation.

PARACELSUS

Paracelsus was the screen name of Philippus Bombastus Romastus Fantastus Supercalafragalisticexpialadastus von South-Stuttgart-Next-To-The-University-Cafeteria-With-The-Zig-Zag-Roof. His name Paracelsus literally means "Better than Celsus." We do not know who Celsus may have been, but the name is likely a reference to St. Jerome Para-Ezra of Baton Rouge, who was known in his time to have been far better than Ezra.

Paracelsus invented many of the medical techniques used from medieval times to the modern medical revolution, including bleeding, leeching, exsanguination, draining blood from the patient, and ultra-hemorrhagic-cleansing. He also coined the phrase "Only the dose determines the poison," as well as its corollary, "You can eat anything, just some things you can only eat once," and the less impressive but better known, "He who smelt it, dealt it." This was all considered an advancement over the old theory of bodily humors, which is why Paracelsus's friends all said he was a humorless bastard, or so he kept claiming.

Paracelsus was married in a Rosicrucian ceremony based on the Chemical Wedding of Christian Rosenkreutz, which was of course preceded by Chemical Engagement and a Chemical Romance involving a black parade, the theatrical faking of several deaths, and a great deal of sodium (a mass scientifically abbreviated as Na Na Na (Na Na Na Na Na Na Na Na Na)). To whom he was married is a matter of much debate, with potential spouses speculated to include Shakespeare, Queen Elizabeth I, Queen Elizabeth II, Martin Luther, Galileo, Ivan the Terrible, Thomas Hobbes, John Calvin, Catherine Di Medici, the Popes Alexander V-VIII, or possibly all at once.

Paracelsus died in the 1540s after suffering a minor splinter which he treated with his own experimental technique known as "setting the patient on fire and stabbing him with a fork in his balls until he barfs then laughing at him." He was then cremated with his urn displayed at the University of Hohenheim for several centuries, until he was accidentally misplaced during an American tour and is presumed to have been used as ash in some Humboldt Fog Cheese, which was considered an affront to his Swiss heritage.

Also he apparently invented Zinc. Good job.

PARKING

It's easier to parallel park if you drive up perpendicular to the curb and then subtract 90.

PARLIAMENT

A minister was once ejected from British Parliament for having too many legs. Brandon "14 Limbs" McMandor had served for 24 years before his dismissal.

PARROT

Parrots can repeat nearly any phrase they're taught, but can't repeat most recent songs due to copyright issues.

PASSPORT

From 1967-1971, U.S. passports included the individual's fingerprints. Not copies of them in ink. The actual fingertips.

PATTON, GENERAL GEORGE SNEEDLEMEYER

General Patton insisted his men listen to no music but Wagner to keep them in the mood for a fight. He once slapped a soldier for listening to "My Chemical Romance."

PAVEMENT

Some pavement has pebbles in it. That's called pebblement. If you made a patio out of it you'd have a pebblement patio. But you'd probably not want to eat it.

PEACH

Peaches are delicious and covered in fine fuzz. Generally they're yellow and red or pink. Inside it, around a porous pit, is an edible and popular fruit-flesh that can be consumed raw, or cooked into pie and cobbler, and so on.

But to the Greshami, the peach is far more than a fruit. It's even more than a way of life. To the Greshami, the peach is God.

From the dawn of Greshami culture as recorded in their history (which is written entirely on leather-tanned peach skins), the peach has been revered as the sole source of food for the Greshami people. Limited in trade by their isolation (until recently, see below), the Greshami developed over ages to subsist solely on the peach. Peaches, like potatoes, contain nearly every protein and mineral necessary for human development, with the exception of fatty acids, which the Greshami ingest in minimal portions from the fatty air that surrounds their region.

As the sole food, the peach has long been revered as their god. That they follow the peach harvest with the utmost solemnity is a given, but the more curious nature of the Greshami is how they've incorporated this godly fruit into the rest of their culture:

When the Greshami are born, they are taken from their mothers and immediately given a peach from which to suckle. That peach nectar is always the first flavor to touch their lips, and in their last rites, it is administered again as they die in the same manner. Their mantra, recited each morning and night, and upon the onset of death, translates roughly as "From the Peach we came and to the Peach we go, for the Peach is life, and life is Peachy."

The linguistics of the Greshami also show reverence for the fruit. "Hello" in Greshami is "ZnZni-Zni" which literally means "Peach be upon you." This invocation is a blessing of good fortune. Goodbye is "HuHu-Ha" meaning "Parting is the pits," also a benevolent though melancholy statement.

The peach pit itself is the currency of the Greshami. This has led to extreme class disparity, as those who have the most peaches to eat get the most pits from those peaches and can afford even more peaches. However, charity is also important to the Greshami, and a rich tribesman who ignored the hungry would be ostracized instantly and permanently. To deny a hungry person a peach, among the Greshami, is total anathema because it is to deny them access to God, a religious offense.

Greshami contact with the European world has been fairly problematic. They were first recorded into European history when explorer and ethnographer Richard F. Burton encountered them by chance when one of their peach peeling ceremonies spilled over into his camp. The Greshami run while peeling peaches so that the skin can be scattered and enrich the land. One boy, known only as Znizne (Peach eater) ran into Burton, who he led to the nearest encampment, a village known as Znu-Az-Zni (Peachville). Burton was given the ritual greeting peach, which he consumed on the spot, much to the pleasure of the Greshami. Unfortunately, Burton had no peaches of his own and was unable to reciprocate, leading the Greshami to consider European culture childish, as children were the only ones in their world who did not carry peaches (the concept of an "Adult" or "Child" does not actually exist in Greshami culture, there are simply those who have peaches and those who have yet to carry their own). As such, the Greshami are very kind to visiting Europeans, who they look down upon with a kind condescension. They are quite helpful to anyone they meet, giving them peaches and conferring upon them the blessing to the young or unfortunate, translated, "May you one day eat a peach so delicious that it blows your tits clean off." Note that this is a wholly positive blessing to the Greshami.

The Greshami are a dwindling culture. The Orange-folk of the south and the northern Applemongers (both known to the Greshami as "GuZni" or "Non-Peach people" intermittently declare war on this peaceful tribe. According to Margaret Mead, "The Greshami are a pleasant folk, but a doomed folk. When they are attacked, they merely pelt their attackers with rotten peaches. Their birth rate is low, and they never accept outsiders to replenish their stock. I do not expect they shall live to see the 21st century, no, nor even the 1990s."

The Greshami number only in the hundreds now, but they still thrive. And they have begun to explore the regions outside of their native land (Gresham in Atlanta, GA, near Melvin's Used Appliance Sale and Repair). Recently they stumbled upon the local Wal-Mart SuperCenter and their access to its produce section has provided the "XiZni Unu" or "great Peach feast" weekly, when it was previously only celebrated each season. The manager of the aforementioned Wal-Mart has welcomed the Greshami and is currently learning their language:

"They don't say "I Love You" in Greshami, they say "Znizi zi Zni, Xuzni Hu Zniznu" which means "Your company is as delicious to me as a peach," and I think that's beautiful.

PEANUT BUTTER

Crunchy Peanut Butter is the exact same thing as Smooth Peanut Butter, just 15 weeks later. Unsold Smooth bottles are simply relabeled.

PEARL

Pearls are made from the same substance as tooth enamel, this is why pearls are often used for false teeth.

PELICAN

Pelicans can eat up to 500 pounds of fish a day, assuming one fish costs 500 pounds.

PELICON

For a brief time in 1927, a company called Pelicon had a near total monopoly on manufacturing bookshelves in London. This is widely considered the least interesting fact in all human knowledge.

PENGUIN

Penguins can't fly because they don't believe in themselves.

PENNSYLVANIA

Pennsylvania is where Graphite Dracula is from.

PENTAGRAM

Pentagrams can represent Wicca with their point up, Satanism with their point down, and if on their side between the two, they represent the Prune Juice industry.

PEPPER GRINDER

Though the mechanism is simple, a pepper grinder exerts over 750 teranewtons of force on its contents.

PEPPERONI

The wild pepperoni went extinct in 1981, what we consume now is actually a vegan product made to taste like pepperoni with various spices. The authentic flavor is lost though, and the current flavor may not be accurate.

PERCUSSION

Most couches have about two feet percussion.

PERFUME

A perfume manufacturer in Grasse once killed one of his debtors and turned him into perfume. As neither the amount of money or amount of perfume are recorded, it's uncertain how much the man did actually eau.

PERPETUAL MOTION

DARPA and Raytheon once developed a perpetual motion machine but misplaced the napkin it was written on.

PHILOSOPHY

You are more than the sum of your parts. You are in fact equal to the tangent of your parts squared minus your age.

"Good" and "Evil" are just concepts and do not exist in reality, where "Epic" and "Bummer" are the proper philosophical terms.

Philosophers in the 1820s held a major debate to decide whether or not humans had teeth. They decided that we did not.

Though they appear to be made of different letters at first, the word "Philosophy" is actually an anagram of "Legume."

PHONE

The earliest rotary phones were so large and tough to dial that they came with metal dialing wands. They also only went up to seven digits, as the 4 and 8 were not invented until 1948. Necessity is truly the mother of invention.

The first phone invented by Alexander Graham Bell was vastly inferior to modern smart phones, having under 20 available apps.

PHRASES

To this day we don't know the origins of the phrases "To this day," "We don't know" and "The origins of phrases."

PHYSICS

Among the least understood principles of physics is the "Somethingorother Effect," an occurrence so rare and diverse in manifestation that nobody can agree on what exactly it is, let alone what causes it. It was first recognized by Alfred Somethingorother in 1998.

In addition to an equal and opposite reaction, every action also comes with its own collectible trading card and a kung fu grip.

PIANO

The first piano was invented in 1881. It had only one key and could produce only one note. A modern piano is technically called a "compound piano." Early compound pianos still only had five keys, for the notes "P" "I" "A" "N" and "O", hence its name.

PICCOLO

A piccolo is an oboe that's been soaked in brine.

PIGEON

Pigeons will die if you feed them Mueslix. They will die if you don't, too. They are mortal.

PILL BOMB

1957, the cold war rages on. Nuclear arms miniaturization threatens the globe as the hydrogen bomb becomes capable of fitting on missiles, then in suitcases, and finally, on October 19th, in the unlikeliest place of all.

Professor Morton Isidore Rammwick IV was hired by the US Military to develop the smallest possible nuclear weapon, one that could be implanted within a human body. Like a 10 megaton poison tooth, the "Internal Bomb" was to have been the most vicious weapon in the anticipated nuclear war that loomed over the globe. But Professor Rammwick exceeded even the military's wildest dreams when he succeeded in making a pill, 1cm X 1cm X 4mm, that could be safely swallowed, or naturally hidden just about anywhere in anything. But that swallowable bit- That was the cause of the disaster.

In 1959, 17 pill bombs had been created and were kept in, obviously, a prescription pill box under heavy guard in the pentagon. President Eisenhower was shown the weapons on his routine tour, or a tour that would've been routine had the president not suffered an attack of peripheral neuropathy only days earlier. The treatment was simple, he was prescribed Gabapentin, which caused the attacks to cease. If you have a wild imagination, you probably guessed exactly where this is going.

When the president visited the pentagon, his pills were carried by his aide, Chester Hanswurkinsen, in a small red pillbox with his prescription notes printed on the side, in coincidentally, the same font and size as the details of the nuclear weapons on the small red pillbox containing the pill bombs. What happened on the tour is not yet declassified but the result was that when President Eisenhower emerged from the vaults, he tripped a radiation scan on his way out. Indeed, the president had accidentally ingested not one but two hydrogen bombs.

Surgery was recommended, but the president refused, insisting that nature would take its course. Nature unfortunately worked by means of an acidic digestive system which was quickly dissolving the protective matrix of the bombs. How long they would take to trigger the explosives, and how effective the explosives might be once dissolved, was anyone's guess. Professor Rammwick was rushed in to consult. The president was given heavy stool softeners in order to remove the weapons. But still, he refused surgery. Thus it's a good thing that his stomach acid had tempered the bombs efficiency.

Records show that at 2AM the next day, both bombs detonated at 1/7,000th of their nominal yield. The results, though not fatal and not particularly damaging to any facilities, were still nuclear in nature and thus constitute what sealed records described at the time as "The most extreme bowel movement ever recorded."

According to Eisenhower's doctor, the full force of the nuclear blast was directed from his colon through his pants and underwear onto and through the northern wall of the oval office, annihilating two houseplants, one curtain, and much plaster. The radioactive flatulence made the building uninhabitable for several months, and the odor resulting from the atomic dump could be smelled up to 15 miles away from ground zero. The President was unharmed, save for his dignity which among those present, never recovered. Seismometers in Washington DC recorded a 1.1 Richter scale event at the time, which cannot definitively be linked to the rectal fireworks.

There was, however, a positive result of the event. Russia it seems had been developing a similar pill bomb at the time, but, when their spy network reported the results, Nikita Khrushchev is said to have laughed so hard that he ruptured his left lung, and immediately ordered a stop to the equivalent Soviet nuclear program.

Thus the world was saved, not by the goodwill of politicians, nor by the wisdom of scientists, or even by accident- But by the massive explosive diarrhea of a single man, who shat the single greatest shit ever recorded by an American President.

PILL BUG

Pill Bugs or "Roly Polies" are common insects that many children find adorable and even collectable. But those kids never looked under their head plates, or looked at them this close up. These seemingly innocuous bugs hide fearsome heads with jagged teeth under their armor.

Luckily, Pill Bugs are too small to bite humans. Even the ridge of a fingerprint is too broad for them to bite. But to smaller insects and microscopic mammals such as the humble bumblebee, Pill Bugs are the stuff of nightmares. Their teeth are capable of biting through any exoskeleton or bone, and their series of over 50 stomachs is able to digest any substance fully, even solid uranium, which they consider a delicacy.

Over ten million pill bugs are killed every day to manufacture pills for medical usage.

PILLOW

Though foam pillows were invented to save birds from being plucked for their feathers, it actually takes more birds to make a foam pillow, as foam is made from beaks.

PIMPLE

Pimples are just God's way of telling you that you're too beautiful without them. And pus. They're also full of pus.

PINBALL

The inventor of Pinball only died in 2007. When his coffin was buried, three more popped out of the ground and rolled away.

PINEAPPLE

In 1492 when Columbus was sailing the ocean blue to terrorize and enslave what he thought would be India, he landed in the Americas and among the new fruits he finds was this thing that resembles a spiky apple or maybe a pinecone. He called it a pineapple.

But the story is far from over. When Columbus got back to Europe he showed the thing to the king and queen and some scientists, who gave it the scientific name of "Ananas comosus," from the words Comosus for "tufted" and Ananas for the lead scientist's sister Ana, who had just always really wanted a tufted genus of bromeliad named after her. Most of Europe calls the fruit an Ananas, while Columbus and his British and Spanish admirers still prefer to call it a Pineapple.

Now, in Europe in the late 1400s, they were fighting over literally everything, so the war of the people who called the fruit an Ananas and the people who called it a Pineapple was inevitable.

The war lasted 62 years and was thus called the "13 Year War," as was the style of the time. It ended in 1558 with a decisive victory by Italy, which was at the time like 50 different countries and none of them had actually fought in the war because Italy calls the fruit an "Erbagustosaappuntita." So to this day nobody in most of Europe or America can agree on what to call the thing, but most English speakers call it a pineapple because english speakers refuse to admit they lost any wars.

Oddly enough, this is also why we call the United States by its traditional english name and not its proper name of "Stati Uniti," the country having been surrendered by the president to the Italians after losing a poker game going all in pre-flop on 9-2 offsuit.

PINKERTON AGENCY DETECTIVES UNION

The shortest lived union of all time was the "Pinkerton Agency Detectives Union" which lasted only a few minutes before its own strikebreaking members busted it while breaking its own strike against itself.

PIPE CLEANER

Pipe cleaners are made from the antennae of the aluminum bark weevil.

PIRATES

Piracy in the 1700s was primarily concerned with stealing tobacco and gold, only a small percent of pirates in those days were known for downloading copyrighted music. Children who pretended to be pirates during playtime are 60% likelier to download music illegally as adults.

The first pirate to wear an eyepatch was Blackbill Pete, who has perfect vision in both eyes but wore it because even then, he felt it would make him look more like a pirate.

PIZZA

Little Caesars is the oldest pizza manufacturer, dating back to ancient Rome. They were indeed founded by Julius Caesar himself when he was little.

The world's largest pizza measured 85 feet across and could have fed over 4,200 people had some jerk not ruined it by ordering anchovies on it.

PLATO

Plato was only a philosopher on weekends. During the week he was a popcorn salesman at the Athens arcade.

PLUTO

Pluto is between jobs right now. This refers to both the dog and the planet.

PODS

Pod based movers do not transport your belongings. They grow copies in a new pod that replace the original objects.

POKÉMON

The shape of Pikachu's tail is Ninendo's July 1993 budget graph. Despite its popularity in America, the Pokémon franchise is relatively unknown in its native Japan.

POKER

The history of Poker is the history of the world and its peoples, of cultures across geography and time. Poker has existed far longer than most people realize. Our earliest records of the game date back to the dawn of humankind- To the cave paintings of Höhledieicherfundenhabe which date back to about 40,000 B.C.

The paintings depict the usual animals and handprints, but include one sequence which is unquestionably the record of a loss from a hand holding AJ suited against pocket 3s, which became a full house on the river, knocking out the player-artist.

The ancients seem to have attributed their knowledge of poker to the ox goddess Pough-Kar, who it was said descended from the clouds to teach the Clan of the Northern Gambling Ox how to play her new game. She then challenged the cave people to many hands of the new game. Having superior knowledge, she won all their money and then left.

Despite a vague popularity of lowball in Mesopotamia around 15,000 B.C., the next major poker events happened in Early Dynastic Egypt and play a role in their mythology. According to Western Egyptologist E.E. Wallace Bungie III, who is noted by

Egyptian archaeologists to have been correct about nearly 2% of his claims, ten hands of 7 Card Stud were played heads-up by Horus and Set as they fought for the throne of Osiris.

On the final round, Horus had AAKA showing while Set was drawing blank. Set went all in, but when Horus snap called, Set claimed that he was only joking, resulting in a conflict that lasted ten thousand days and ten thousand nights until Amon-Ra broke it up and banned Set from the Eternal Casino. Poker was banned in the kingdoms of Egypt and was not unearthed until the days of Ptolemaic Pharaohs, namely, Cleopatra.

Cleopatra was a notorious gambler and ordered the seals of the Eternal Casino broken that she might learn the forbidden games within. Playing mostly Blackjack and Baccarat, she ignored Poker and as such it became a peasant game, gaining popularity through Rome and Greece. Julius Caesar is said to have been a strong Badugi player, earning a hand of 3456 against his friend Brutus, who also held a 56-high Badugi, but Caesar's immortal words revealed his downfall, "Ace-2, Bruté?"

Charlemagne took up poker along with Christianity and through the age of the Holy Roman Empire, Poker was played among kings and nobles until the coming of Oliver Cromwell, who banned Poker, along with Christmas and for some reason, puppies. Cromwell was deposed but Poker had to grow back slowly, more in Italy and France than England.

Still, the game lingered and is attested to have been played by monks as far west as Ireland, where the Book of Kells included a section on Omaha Hi/Lo.

But Poker did not come into its modern popularity until the 1800s, in the new world: The Old West.

Poker was a way of life in America of the 1800s. Saloon-Casinos were by far the most profitable business, and their chips were considered legal tender by most businesses. The poker economy of the old west was in fact so much more robust than the printed money of the east, that "minted" money resembling poker chips was invented to be bet more easily.

And so the game continued to grow in popularity, becoming at once more civil and yet more competitive. Being too unpredictable to play outside of home games and casinos, and because no economic system can ever have any element of gambling with finances, Poker left the American economy but persevered as a mode of entertainment, in fact a pastime. Poker is now played in tournaments with thousands of players, and at cash games at bars with some of the most notoriously annoying people ever to live.

The "Hold 'Em" in Texas and Omaha Hold 'Em refers to the earlobes of the player left of the dealer, a tradition no longer practiced outside of Omaha, TX.

POLAND

Poland has more bears than Bearland, an amusement park which had to be shut down in 2001 after its 700th bear related death.

POLAROID

Polaroid once accidentally made a camera that could photograph people's auras. It was seized by the FBI and never seen again.

Cool visual trick: Place a polaroid photo of a piece of clear glass upright on a surface in the sun. The portion that pictures the clear glass will not cast a shadow.

POLITICAL CONVENTION PLAGIARISM

Accusations of a plagiarized speech have been leveled during several Political Conventions. Here are some other examples of suspected speech theft:

"It is a far, far better thing that I do, than I have ever done; it is a far, far better rest that I go to than I have ever known." -Barack Obama, 2012

"Whether you think you can or think you can't, you're right." -George W. Bush, 2004

"Of the million people in Kyle City, there was none so aimless as Violet MacRae." -Richard Nixon, 1968

POLO, MARCO

On his journey to China, Marco Polo discovered India, Cambodia, Greenland, Argentina, Hawaii and Paris. He is thought to have used Priceline.com.

POOL

You can avoid buying a pool permit for your house by installing a flushing mechanism and classifying the pool as a toilet.

The "chlorine taste" of pool water comes not from the chlorine, but from the absence of bacteria the chlorine kills.

The post of lifeguard used to be more involved. Before 1900, every swimmer had their own lifeguard, who would protect them in and out of the pool until their death, at which time the lifeguard would be buried alive by their side.

It was once suggested that Vantablack paint could be used to coat a pool for an interesting visual effect. Because Vantablack absorbs all light, it heats up very fast. If exposed to direct sunlight, it takes in all the UV and heat and contains them, and can reach heats well over 212°F, the boiling point of water. So if one did coat the pool in that material, the water would boil as soon as the sun touched it, killing everyone swimming in it.

But that's not all. The flash boiling of an entire pool of chlorinated water would release the chlorine as gas, which would kill everyone within a 200ft radius of the pool. And it doesn't end there.

The release of chlorine gas combined with the heat of the black tiles would be more than sufficient to fuse the boiled hydrogen ions with the chlorine, creating an explosive reaction with the nitrogen in the air. So shortly after everyone in the pool boils and everyone around the pool dies of chlorine gas poisoning, the region would explode with the force of a small atomic bomb (8kt for a common backyard pool), leveling about 50 city blocks.

Such chemical explosions expel gamma rays. Gamma rays ionize hematite, which is the mineral from which the black material mentioned is made. This creates Scopohyoscpnol, a compound known as "The Zombie Drug" because it essentially erases the brain and induces cannibalistic tendencies in its victim. It can be transmitted through saliva, infecting all who are bitten within hours.

So basically, if you did have Vantablack tiles in your pool, you would boil your friends, poison your neighbors, nuke your city, and condemn the globe to a zombie plague. But to be fair, it would look pretty cool.

POPE

From 1384-1386, a dead eel served as Pope. A frustrated Cardinal had made a joke about the long-lasting election to the effect that they should elect a dead eel and be done with it. He could not have predicted that every cardinal would jokingly write in "a dead eel" on their ballots. The reign of Pope Anguilli is widely believed to have been the most prosperous time in the history of the church.

Several Popes are noted not to have observed the oath of celibacy. These include:

-Pope Alexander VI
-Pope Adrian II
-Pope Don Giovanni
-Pope Harald the Fornicator
-Pope Justus the Hung
-Pope Not-That-Innocent XII
-Pope Ballin' III
-Pope Gene Simmons
-Pope Viagrus XXIII
-Pope Andrew the Often Premature
-Pope Maritus of Vegas
-That pope that nailed Carrie from my Geography class
-Pope Augustin the Virgin*

*His name refers to his unblemished skin. Sexually speaking he is recorded as having mated with 108 women (88 of the nuns), 67 men (43 of them clergy), 19 sheep, 13 goats, 7 oxen, 7 cadavers, 2 turtledoves and claimed to have had a 3-way with God the father, the son, and the holy ghost. Amen.

POPSICLE

The largest popsicle ever remains uneaten, probably because it was grape. Nobody likes grape.

POSEIDON

Poseidon was never pictured in antiquity with a trident, but rather with a large dinner fork with which he ate his favorite mythological dish, asparagus.

POTATO

A potato is a mysterious chthonic being that lurks beneath the surface, growing ever more eyes. These eyes are poisonous to humans and can curse us with wrath of the tuber, or "tuberculosis." Potatoes are directly responsible for the killing of over one million people in Ireland alone. They can also be turned into Vodka, which is directly responsible for the killing of over 45 people in the frat next to my old USC dorm alone.

The true name of the potato grants power to those who master it, but failure can be costly- Merely attempting to write the name of the potato on a blackboard ended the career of Vice President Dan Quayle. Writing the name of the potato in Enochian resulted in the fall of Rome, the collapse of the dollar, and if I did it correctly, the inside-outing of Elon Musk by his own private jet's toilet.

Potatoes contain every known protein and nutrient needed to sustain human life, but they contain no fat and must be augmented with Butter, another eldritch thing. Even alone though, the potato can be boiled, mashed, stuck in a stew, turned into chips, turned into french fries, which some call chips, and chipped and stuffed into fried pancakes, which are for some reason called Latkes. Latkes can only be eaten during the month of Kislev, which means people using the Gregorian calendar are doomed never to taste them.

The song "Forty Six & 2" by the band "Tool" is about the chromosome count of the common potato, it is their first (and only) song with lyrics not solely about butt sex.

POTTY TRAINING

Potty training your child too young can lead to severe mental disorders. This is why it's best to simply force them to hold it in until they turn nine.

POUTINE

Authentic poutine is made without potatoes, gravy or cheese. It's considered a "conceptual dish."

PREFACE

General E. Speaking of the British Armed Forces was often mistaken for a preface.

PRETZEL

The pretzel was invented by mistake when two burglars attempted to tie up a chef with his own dough.

PRESIDENTIAL LIMOUSINE

The U.S. President's car has a special refrigerator that always carries 1.5 gallons of blood matching the president's blood type, and 0.5 gallons of AB positive in case he gets thirsty.

PRIESTHOOD

The "Roman Collar" worn by priests is a folded piece of parchment on which is written "Siccare Mundare Tantum," latin for "Dry Clean Only" as it must be.

PRIMATE

Gorillas are far weaker than humans physically, but they are stronger emotionally. A research team at the San Diego Zoo once performed an experiment to see if monkeys could be taught to drive a car. The experiment was interrupted when the monkeys stole a zoo employee's car and drove away, never to be seen again.

PRINCESS AND THE PEA, THE

The story of the Princess and the Pea was originally about her super-sensitive sense of smell. The word "Pea" was not spelled the same.

PRINGLE

A single Pringle contains as much salt at 30% of the entire Atlantic Ocean.

PRISON

Few modern prisons have bars. Even fewer actually serve alcohol at them.

Despite its name, Sing-Sing Prison does not allow singing within its grounds. It does however encourage yodeling.

PROHIBITION

During prohibition, it was not only illegal to drink alcohol, but to use it for disinfecting medical instruments. Over ten million people died as a result, including President Woodrow Wilson.

PROMETHEUS

It is only in recent tellings of Greek mythology that Prometheus stole fire from the gods. In older tales, Prometheus stole their car stereo.

PROPHECY

The prophecies of Nostradamus are well known for predicting things that they are only ever attributed to once they have already happened. In reality his writings were mostly vague poetry that could be applied to anything.

The same is not true of the very specific predictions of his wife, Henriette d'Encausse, who was ignored by history in favor of her husband, the notion of a female prophet being unacceptable to most contemporary scholars.

Here are just a few of her predictions:

-A man shall walk upon the moon and upon it leave his footprints.

-Plays shall be performed as symphonies of light upon a flat silver skin.

-It is the merchants and their companies that shall rule the world after kings have fallen, their greed shall eclipse even the royalties.

-There shall be an encyclopedia after the millennium with more than five million articles, which takes up not a single volume of paper.

-Many a plague shall become a distant memory, as shall the great pox, owing to the application of hollow needles to the flesh of the population.

-The cannabis plant shall be burned at ceremonies and within the homes of the population, and it shall calm them though it be prohibited by their rulers, and contaminate their clothing and hair with a great stink.

-The orange man shall lead his country astray, and invoke upon it the ire of the rest of the world.

All these prophecies have according to some researchers been fulfilled, but of even more interest are her unfulfilled prophecies:

-Man shall too walk upon Mars, and upon Venus and Mercury, and upon Mercury shall he find the bones of those seven-legged men who died long ago.

-A great comet shall fall upon the Earth, but it shall kill none, for it shall be made of spun sugar and milk.

-Transformers 6 will win the best picture Oscar.

PRURITIS POTESTUM

Pruritus Potestum is the medical term for an itch you can't scratch due to restraint or the spot being covered, like when you have goggles on and feel and itch around your eye, or when you're hanging from a drawbridge shooting at a skeletal demon from the planet Orignarkia and you have an Uzi in each hand and if you scratch the itch you'll drop one but you know the demon won't stop hunting your daughter unless you pump as much lead as possible into the crystal of Zazugog that rests within its rotting skull.

PUDDING

The chocolate and vanilla portions of chocolate-vanilla swirl pudding are the same flavor. Only the mind's color perception makes them taste different. The word "Pudding" comes from the Latin word for "Food Snot."

PUNK, CRUST

"Crust Punk" refers to a type of music so hardcore that the bands will often eat their sandwiches without making their mothers cut the sides off the bread, in contrast to most modern musicians.

PUNK, STEAM

Always steam your punks regularly, lest they wrinkle.

PYTHAGORAS

Pythagoras used to host enormous parties at his home in Samos. This is the origin of the phrase, "Be there or B^2."

-Q-

QUANTUM PHYSICS

Quantum entanglement is naturally permanent, and cannot be undone without the aid of quantum scissors.

Schrödinger's Cat is only one of several animal analogies in quantum physics. Others include Heisenberg's Capybara, Gutzwiller's Parakeet, and the South Paraguayan Spotted Alligator of Wave Function Collapse.

The observer effect states that observing a particle will change its properties. This is why a watched pot never boils.

It is impossible to know both the position and momentum of an electron at the same time, but if you observe one and your friend observes the other, you can likely sort them out by phone, or possibly a Zoom call later.

Like light itself, surfboards also travel on both particles and waves.

QUEUE

The word Queue was originally spelled "Queueueueue" and was pronounced, "Kyoooooo." One had to say the "oooo" for 15 seconds to be correct.

-R-

RABBIT

The largest rabbit ever recorded weighed 2,250 lbs and ate 95 carrots a day. Though smaller, typical rabbits are harmless alone, in swarms they can skeletonize an elephant in under a minute.

RADIO

The original RadioShack was literally a shack that sold radios. It is now partnered with Sprint, which was originally just a guy who ran everywhere to deliver messages.

RAIN

Rain that falls on any given day began to fall almost a week earlier. It takes six days for a raindrop to reach the ground. Snow takes an entire year, and the flakes we see today began to fall in the last year's winter.

Rain can't fall in temperatures over 90 degrees, as warm water rises.

It rained so hard in Seattle in 2008 that the Space Needle washed way and ended up in a drainage ditch.

RAINBOW

A rainbow may appear to be light and ephemeral, but it weighs well over 50,000 tons. The points where it touches down on either side are under immense pressure and can collapse, this is why we sometimes get sinkholes after it rains.

RAINDEER

Despite their name, raindeer are capable of leaving the water even when it's not raining. This makes them one of the largest and most versatile amphibians.

RAISIN

It was thought for centuries that raisins were just dried grapes. The truth of what raisins really are would destroy the raisin industry, and I don't want that to happen as I think the world has too many stink bugs as it is.

RAMBO

Rambo was filmed before a live studio audience. They're not alive anymore.

REALITY TV

The reality show "Child Swap" was cancelled after one episode where a child from a vegetarian family was forced to eat his own siblings by cannibal parents.

REEVES, COL. JACK

Col. Jack was known among the troops for his extraordinary strength and cool composure. Fighting on the German Front for most of WW2, he recorded 72 confirmed kills, almost 7 of them Germans. His aim was said to be sub-par but he remained in the service because of his talent for lifting heavy objects and throwing them at the enemy, or at least in their general direction.

In the midst of battle on May 9th 1945, Reeves threw two Jeeps, one boulder and two riflemen over the Berlin Wall, taking out an entire regiment of the Deutscher Pfadfinderinnenverbände, and he went on fighting for several months after. As the war had ended on May 8th, Reeves was committed to the DCMH where he remained until his escape in 1949, when he threw a water fountain through the window and ran away. He was never seen again.

A memorial to Col. Jack stands in Boston in the United States, because neither Britain nor Germany wanted it.

REVERSIC ACID

Reversic acid is a rare fluid that can reverse the angle of light traveling through it. Science remains unable to completely explain the phenomenon, though it was known to Ancient Egyptians who believed it to be the work of Set.

When light travels through a normal liquid like water, the light simply travels through unaffected. But when light travels through Reversic acid, it gets confused and the photons forget which way to go, an interruption in what scientists call "Quantum Memory". Magnifying glasses are assumed to work on a similar principle, in which the photons forget what size they are and grow larger.

Though practical applications are scarce, experiments have taken place to exchange the vitreous humor (The water inside your eyeballs) with Reversic Acid. The results as reported by the first test subject stated that he could not only see backwards, but backwards in time, thus witnessing his own birth.

Reversic acid only has a Ph of 304,219 so it's perfectly drinkable, but consider the effects if you did: First, your intestines would twist around to flow in the opposite direction. Then your blood would flow backwards. This in turn would cause you to walk, talk and even think in reverse. You would wake up in the evening and then wait to go to sleep in the morning. You would eat with your butt and poop with your mouth. The film "Memento" would make perfect sense to you. That's just not natural.

Don't do R.A. If you see anyone going backwards, report them to your local police or hold an intervention. R.A. spoils lives, but it's never too late for its effects to be… Reversed.

RIVER

The Yukon River used to run through New Mexico until the 60's when it fled to Canada.

Rivers moved slower before humankind evolved and built water wheels to keep them going at a faster pace for boats.

ROBIN HOOD

The legend of Robin Hood has been conclusively traced back to the historical figure Rebyn Hüd, who was not an archer nor a benevolent thief. Mostly he wandered around exposing himself to passersby and shouting obscenities during public events. He is thought to have had the greatest publicist who ever lived.

ROBOTICS

The first android was created by Karel Capec, who was himself an android. Modern science is fully capable of creating a sentient humanoid robot, but does not do so out of respect to Linda Hamilton.

A man in Nebraska once designed an automatic fruit juicer that could detect the type of fruit and mechanically jar and label it with hydraulic arms. After it killed him, it labeled the remains, "Tomato Juice, Chunky."

ROCK

Both the music and the substance are banned in Oklahoma.

RODIN

Rodin was by far the most talented sculptor ever to fight Godzilla.

ROLLING STONES, THE

A Rolling Stones biopic had to be cancelled due to casting problems. Producers were unable to find anyone without sin to cast the first Stone.

ROME (ANCIENT)

The Ancient Romans referred to themselves as "Ancient Romans" back in their own time, knowing that one day Rome would be a thing of the past.

Roman news declarators often spoke with "clickbait" like introductions. One preserved tablet states in Latin, "You won't believe who Brutus just stabbed!"

Ancient Romans had intravenous technology and they could set up IV drips for patients, or as they called the technology, "Four Drips."

In Rome around 440 B.C., Albertus Feces committed a crime so horrible that the very word for poop was named after him.

Among the great oddities of archaeological lore is a simple ancient Roman vase that despite being about 2,000 years old, appears to have been made by a 3D Printer.

The vase was unearthed in 1807 by Ladrón DeTumbas on an expedition to Rome, the same expedition which would discover the long lost Bracelet of Emperor Tiberius, the skeleton of Osseus Sepultus, and the elusive Beads of Nates Obturamentum. The vase was considered unremarkable at first except for its condition, but scientists were unable to classify the material from which it was made. By 1960, they realized it was made of a type of plastic that had not otherwise been invented until 1958.

More interesting still was that the artifact was made in a single long spiral measuring only 400 microns thick- Exactly the same way a modern 3D printer would accomplish the job. The precision of the vase was also astounding. It was perfectly circular within 10 microns, an accomplishment no human could have achieved. With the invention of the 3D printer however, there is little doubt that this vase was indeed printed in the same fashion- Over 2,000 years ago.

Speculation has run rampant. Some say it's proof of an advanced civilization predating Rome. Others claim it proves Earth was visited long ago by aliens. No fully satisfactory explanation has been offered to date, making this one of the greatest archeological mysteries alongside the Circuitboard of Charlemagne, the iPhone 6s of King Solomon, and of course the perplexing Bionic Elbow of Akhenaten. It is also one of just two historical artifacts suspected to have been made by a 3D printer, second only to Hypatia of Alexandria's Fidget Spinner.

ROPE

Rope is called "line" in the Navy, and drawn lines are called "ropes." This has caused much confusion as the difference between slang and mere gibberish is a fine rope.

ROYALTY

The role of a royal food taster was not merely to confirm the food was poison free, but to pre-chew the meal for the royals. It was unthinkable in medieval times that a king or queen would ever chew their own food.

RULER

Much as the King Flarrigan's knuckles were used to measure "one inch" and his feet were used to measure "one foot," his execution by drawing and quartering allowed the creation of the little used measurement "one intestine" which equals about 23 feet.

RUSSIA

Russia invented the automatic sweater dispenser, to date the only invention invented by a country and not a person or people living there.

SAINTS

The Northern Orthodox Museum of Martyrs includes the following Saintly relics:

-The severed head of St. Klaus of Hyboria
-The warts of St. Wilfred
-A pinky bone of St. Slarley of Siberia
-An arrow that pierced St. Sebastian
-The once-missing nose ring of St. Corriander
-The iPod of St. Jones of Michigan
-The shinbones of St. Clarkus of Gaul
-St. Patrick's pet snake
-Both nipples of St. Jourgensen the Evangelist
-The bong of St. Marley
-St. Hildebrandt's silent T
-St. Valentine's heart
-St. Sinatra (All of him, they just took all of him)
-The 14 toed cat of St. Hemmingway of Kiliminjaro
-Eva Marie Saint's hair
-The jet ski of St. Martinez de Acapulco
-The toenails of St. Reggie Von Hedgicide
-And most famously, the chalice that held the blood of St. Gilmore of Orleans that spilled on August 9th, 1432 when he ascended the steps of Numernunk and got a bloody nose upon the 193rd step and then tripped and fell down to the 177th step and cursed the name of our lord and got struck by lightning as a result, praise be upon him.

SALAD

The invention of the salad is credited in myth to Enceladus, the giant child of Gaia and Uranus. In a fight with Athena, Encaladus trampled the Foloi Oak Forest and crushed the trees to smithereens, creating the first salad. This is why traditional Greek salad is still made only with oak trees.

SALIVA

Spit is the tears that our mouth cries for hunger.

SAND BOX

The idea of sandboxes for kids was invented by Mark Marshall in 1902 after losing several children in his scorpionbox.

SAND CASTLE

The biggest sand castle ever constructed was over 30 feet tall, and housed the royal family of Prussia for 17 years.

SANTA CLAUS

Santa Claus is based on St. Klaus of Hyboria, who was martyred in the 12th century when he attempted to sneak in through the chimney of a viking chieftain in hopes of evangelizing.

SATAN

Satan has only one spoken line in the old testament, "And also, Job hath not yet returned thy lawnmower."

SATELLITE

Though Sputnik was the first satellite to enter orbit, the first satellite to stay there permanently was the Bezboznik, a camera designed to take photos of God so that Khrushchev could blackmail him.

SATURN

Saturn's rings are different colors because each is made up of a different flavor of candy. The largest gap in the rings is the Jolly Rancher Quarry, which destabilized the orbit of Phoebe. If mining continues at its present rate, Saturn's rings may disappear completely by 2035, and candy may cease to exist shortly after. Candy has also been discovered orbiting Uranus, but nobody really wants to eat candy from Uranus. Chocolate is safe as it comes from Mars.

SAWDUST

Sawdust is not made of flakes from the saw itself as the name implies, but of the wood cut by the saw. This confusion has resulted in several thousand pages of unnecessary laws in Montana.

SCHOOL

Legend has it that if a kid ever swings 360 degrees around the swing set, they will be crowned as the Coolest Kid In School, and usher in a time known as the "Eternal Recess."

Though there is no such thing as an "F+" grade, there is a possible "A++" grade, as well as a "D-+" grade and the elusive and mysterious "ə" grade.

300 jungle gyms are torn down every year to make space for free range children to graze.

SCIENCE

Science was invented in 1402 by George C. Science of Oxford University, but its means of progress were not invented until much later.

Augustin Thierry Theory was the first innovator, who in 1574 introduced his theory of "Theories," which had never before been theorized. This resulted in the 1578 invention of the Hypothesis by Harry H. Hypothes, after whom the proposed explanation was named. Having theorized the theory before the hypothesis, A. Thierry Theory was desperate to prove his theory forthwith and joined forces with Hypothes to form a hypothesis that could be tested and proven, with Arnold Test and Claire Proof donating their concepts of the Test and Proof, which were invented by Proof and Test respectively.

So Thierry Theory's theory was tested with Proof's test after Hypothes hypothesized Theory's theory could be proven with Tests proof. Hypothes's hypothesis was that Theory's "theory" theory proved Test's proof of Hypothes's theory, developed in 1591 to reflect the conclusion theory of Conclusion J. Concludermeyer (Known as The Great Concluder), which theorized using Thierry Theory's "theory" theory hypothesis Hypothes's hypothesis tested Test's proof with Proof's test proving Proof's hypothesis theorizing theory's "theory" theory theorized Proof's proof test Test proved concluding Conclusion's conclusion proved Theory's hypothesis hypothesis, thus proving Theory's theory definitively, with Delwin Definitely having contributed the definition of "definite" definitively in 1613.

Science was coincidentally invented shortly before the invention of the tongue twister, for some reason that we have yet to hypothesize, theorize, test, conclude or definitively prove.

SCOOBY-DOO

Scooby-Doo was named for Skubidu, a mythic Polish dog that solved crimes in 790 A.D.

An unaired Scooby-Doo episode ended with the gang pulling off a villain's mask to reveal a horrifying demonic face covered in maggots and pus. It remains unaired due to Shaggy's use of the word "Crap."

SCORPION

Many insects can make musical chirping sounds, but only Scorpions can rock.

SCOTLAND

Most animals native to Scotland were designed by Jim Henson.

SCUBA

SCUBA stands for Self-Contained Breathing Apparatus. The origin and meaning of the U is a subject of debate among scholars everywhere.

SEA LION

Sea lions are just seals with an extra electron.

SEASONS

While there are four seasons a year in America, England often has only one season every three years or less.

SEX

Archaeologist Sue J. Westheimer discovered a position previously unknown to modern sexual science. Practiced previously in ancient Mesopotamia, the position was called "Gordinoktu," in cuneiform script, which translated roughly as "The Tangled Knot".

The position was discovered by Westheimer in late 2019 on a dig on the site of the Great Sorority of Eridu, which once served as a veritable library of romantic acts. Previously discovered at the same site were early forms of the Kama Sutra and Perfumed Garden, as well as the Ananga Ranga. The site also housed figurines depicting various acts, some of which only became popular in modern culture as recently as the 1990s.

But the Tangled Knot position is unique. Said Westheimer, "The Knot is unusual in that it seems to have been lost even by the time of the Pharaohs. There is no known record of it in the Ancient Egyptian Papyrus of Pornotep, the Greek Erotonomicon, the Roman Ars Amatoria, or even the 1611 King James Penthouse." Furthermore, no modern publications nor learned lechers seem to have discovered the position independently. According to renowned and prolific love master C.C. Lothario, "I ain't never seen this shit."

The stele depicting the act gave detailed instructions on how to engage in the position, which was reserved only for members of the high priesthood and royalty. The instructions are duplicated here in their entirety, but we warn readers not to try the following without first consulting a chiropractor:

1. Place thy left foot by the tailbone of thy lover.
2. Place thy right arm upon the lover's right thigh.
3. Fold thy right arm backward toward step #2, and crease.
4. Twist thy pelvis northward, though thou faceth the sun.
5. Applying generous ointment to thy feet, push them crossways nearest the elbow.
6. With the tools provided, affix thy legs to the underside of thy lover's thorax, making a gap between.
7. Put thine left arm in, take thine left arm out, put thine left arm in, and shaketh it all about.
8. Tie the end of thy (untranslatable) around the length of the right pinky.
9. The significant organs should now be in place, conjoin them according to anatomical feasibility.
10. For best results, thrust in a circular motion counter-clockwise thrice per twelve seconds.
11. Notes on disconnection may be found on the opposite side of this stele.

Unfortunately no such opposite side has been found, so lovers intending to perform the feat may not be able to disconnect themselves.

Still, the discovery is one of the most significant finds of erotic science since the invention of the dildo by Albert Dildeaux, the vibrator by Ernesto Vibrador, or even the invention of the blow job by B.J. Fellatrix in 1669.

SEX, POSTMARITAL

The religious order of St. Nyarlathus abstains from post-marital sex and reproduces exclusively by mitosis.

SHAKESPEARE, WILLIAM

William Shakespeare wrote his plays Henry IV, V and VI with the intent of revisiting the subject with a prequel trilogy about Henry I, II and III.

Shakespeare based another one of his plays on a dream that he had on a mid-summer night. That play is titled "Hamlet."

Juliet from "Romeo and Juliet" is stated in the opening text to be an orangutan, but no known production of the play has adapted this element from the original.

The phrase "Horny On Main" dates back to Shakespeare, who used it in its literal sense of growing horns on one's head.

The witches line from Macbeth, "Oddish gloom and vile plume" inspired three Pokemon.

Executions by beheading in Shakespeare's time were a daily occurrence. As MacBeth required a prop severed head for its finale, Shakespeare would run to the gallows and procure a fresh head each night. Once word got out attendance to his plays quintupled, as patrons were always eager to see the criminal of the day make his final appearance.

SHARK

A shark will produce and lose over 7,500 teeth in its lifetime, mostly stuck in Starburst candies.

Despite their fearsome appearance, there still has yet to be a single movie about sharks attacking people.

More people are killed every year by rabid pigeons than by sharks, but more rabid pigeons are killed by sharks every year than people. In science this is known as the "Rabid-Pigeon-Shark-People Cycle."

SHAVING

Humans are one of only five mammals that shave regularly.

SHEEP

Sheep as we see them are mostly wool. Their bodies beneath the wool are said to resemble greyhounds, but no one has seen one shorn and lived to record the appearance.

SHELLEY, MARY

A lawyer from Prague publicly confronted Mary Shelley after the publication of Frankenstein claiming that a woman could not have written such gruesome literature. He challenged her to write a horror story on the spot to prove her worth. Instead, she stabbed him in both eyes with a salad fork. He later admitted that she might have been capable of writing gruesome literature.

SHIP

The world's largest cruise ship uses normal sized cruise ships as lifeboats. At 39 decks tall, the USS Compensation is the worlds largest cruise ship. It's so large that is uses normal cruise ships as life boats, and each of these cruise ships has conventional life boats.

The Compensation was commissioned by Gordon Gila in the 1980s when he was at the height of his riches, and cost 17 billion dollars (560 Billion adjusted for 2015). That means it cost more than the GNPs of the smallest 55 nations on Earth combined. It can house more than those countries as well, able to carry 150,000 people plus a crew of 18,000.

The great ship no longer sails however, as when it's placed in the ocean the water displacement floods most coastlines, killing thousands. It is currently stored in a dry-dock on the coast of Wyoming where locals worship the great ship as a god.

Using patented "Matryoshka" technology adopted from the Soviets, the great ship's smaller life-cruise-ships each have smaller lifeboats in the shape of cruise ships, which in turn have even smaller cruise lifeboats, and these cruise lifeboats have cruiserafts, which in turn have smaller cruise lifesavers. These lifesavers also have cruise lifevests, and those vests have lifebuttons. Which have life-molecules containing life neutrons. With lifequarks.

The keel of the ship goes well over 4 inches deep.

SHIT

The phrase "Don't shit where you eat," may be the oldest human statement. It has a literal translation in every known language, and appears in literature through the ages all the way back to Proto-Mesopotamian texts, including the Sumerian Excrementicon.

SHOES

Though shoes were invented before antiquity, the idea of wearing two at a time only originated in the late 1800s.

SHOVEL

The shovel was only invented in 1930. Before then, holes had to be dug by hand or by dog. This may be why dogs were originally domesticated.

SHOWER

Though showers in the USA send water down onto the person, most across the globe spray up like fountains.

If everyone in the world took a shower at the same time it would raise the humidity enough to start a new ice age.

SHRIMP

Shrimp as we know them are not animals, but limbs of a larger animal called the "Shrump," which sheds them frequently as it grows. Thus they can be collected from the sea (or aquarium) floor and sold as food. The common Shrump is over 20ft long, eats octopi and squid, and can speak whale fluently.

SICKNESS

Sickness is the use of the correction "[sic]" in quotes and literature to denote when the original was in error.

Some will claim that the term originated in Latin but this is in error. According to Alvin Sech, quoted in the Sixth Edition of Cyclopedia Litterati as Alvin Sekh [sic], "Sich [sic] is Latin for "Thus" and thus it stands as a notice of an original eror [sic]" That second sic being a sic from the Cyclopedia, or a "Cyc Sic."

The truth is far more bizarre. Sech, who had his own difficulties in spelling, didn't know in his time that Sic was actually a cyclical sequence of secondary suffixes, such as "Sik," "Sak," and "Sac," which were added in Greek times to errors made by philosophers (Such as Socrates) in logical disagreements as a challenge to correct. Most peculiar of all is that these seem to have been added first by Hippocrates, who was according to Sech a "Healer of the Sik [sic]."

So if Sekh [sic] said Sich [sic, (sic)] were said by a healer of the sik [sic] then the sic, said Sech (Sekh in the sixth Cyc's sic [sic]) was not sick [sic] but sik [sic] and not in fact sic (Sech). This caused a heated scholarly debate, likely due to Sech's claim that "the pronunciation of all variants in the same maner [sic]." In semantic circles this was humorously called "The Sic-ness," and referred to as the "C Sickness" due to the C in sic, which Seck naturally confused himself for Sea Sickness, or as he called it, "C Sicness [sic]." So, if one had C Sickness [sic] or Sea Sic-ness [sic] one had to see the sic to know they were sick, and were thus sacked by Sack [sic] who had no tolerance for such confusion.

All that is to say that the [sic] community grew sick of Sech, and sought to sic their dogs on his original error, which to this day is noted by the use of his name, 'Sech' [sic].

SEE ALSO: ILLNESS

SILLY PUTTY

Silly Putty is illegal in every country that knows what it's really made of.

SIMPSONS, THE

"The Simpsons" was cancelled in 1998. Nobody knows where the new episodes are coming from or how they make it to TV. In all years of the show to date, never once has the family name been mentioned within an episode.

SIN

There were originally 11 deadly sins, but theologians decided backseat driving and wiping your nose on your sleeve weren't that bad, while shoes and socks have since been reclassified as clothing.

Though the "Sin of Sodom" is well known, it is believed that the "Sin of Gomorrah" involved removing those tags on your pillows and blankets that say "Do Not Remove."

SINKHOLE

A sinkhole in downtown Colorado Springs opened up to reveal a spectacular underground jungle located beneath the city.

"This ecosystem has been here since long before the city began, over five thousand years at an absolute minimum," said Colorado ecologist Dr. Dwayne Dana Dehane. The ecosystem features at least two species of plant and ten species of weevil never before recorded by modern science.

According to Professor Preston Praster Pesterson the opening of the region could pose severe threats to the city, many of whose buildings are positioned on no more than one meter of rock over the great chasm. The city's extreme pothole problem may also prove dangerous, as any pothole could now lead to this lost world below.

Said Mayor May Major Maher, "If this thing doesn't have at least one dinosaur I'm filling it in. We need more landfill space you know."

SIXTIES (20TH CENTURY DECADE)

It is widely suspected that the 1960s did not really exist, but were invented as a gimmick to sell tie-dye shirts.

SKULL

The human skull is composed of over 18 fused bones, 12 pockets of red and yellow bone marrow, and 8 metal rivets.

The human skull can hold up to 3 quarts of marmalade. Why this information was on the Paddington 2 call sheets remains a troublesome mystery.

SKY

It's a common misconception that the sky is blue. It merely looks blue because human eyes cannot understand its true color, magenturple-chartreullow.

SKYSCRAPER

The first skyscrapers earned their name literally, doing damage to the sky that's only now beginning to scab over. That's what clouds are, sky scabs, and they didn't exist until the Empire State Building.

The Empire State Building itself used to have a large swimming pool on its roof, but it kept leaking water due to having no sides.

Construction on a tower twice the size of Burj Khalifa was planned for 2016 in Los Angeles, but it was cancelled after the digging of its 14 floor underground parking structure, making it the world's lowest skyscraper at negative 14 floors.

The tallest building in history no longer stands, it was built in the 1400s in Mongolia and its bricks were later taken down to build most of Ulaanbaatar. The tower would have been about twice the size of Burj Khalifa, and seems to have been home to a single man. Nobody knows his name, as nobody ever managed to climb all the stairs to meet him during his lifetime.

SLEEP

When part of you falls asleep, it actually dies off briefly. The tingling you feel are the maggots beginning to eat you. Don't worry though, this is completely natural and they all drown when blood returns to the area. By the age of 20, nearly everyone has about 70,000 tiny dead maggots in their body. Think about that next time you kiss someone. I always do.

SLEEPING BEAUTY

The fairy tale of Sleeping Beauty originally ended with the title character waking up in a post-apocalyptic landscape after ten thousand years.

SLINKY

The Slinky is actually an incredibly complex piece of engineering. It was developed by a team of 400 top scientists in 1989, operating with a budget of over 2 billion dollars. It became a toy when it failed its original intended purpose: DNA for giant living robots.

SLOTH

Humans are the only known species to shed tears when upset. Sloths are the only unknown species to do so.

SLUG

Slugs are the largest member of the Proboscidea order. They secrete mucus the same way humans do, with their noses. Their tiny slug noses can output up to two gallons of the substance daily.

Slugs do not have a front end. They have eyes and mouths at both ends and brains along their spines, making them able to move in either direction as easily as the other.

Slugs have hands, but they are internal like those of the snake or whale. These hands however can move within the slug, manipulating organs and massaging muscles for relaxation and pleasure.

The fastest slugs can slide over 77mph, making it slightly faster than the Cheetah. They rarely travel so fast though as it violates the Slug-Cheetah accords of 1983.

Slugs can speak to each other by shooting each other with small encoded darts that contain genetic information. Most of these messages are simply mating calls, but the longest message intercepted from a slug came in 1968, reading, "Marty, please bring cups to tonights party. We have the cups from yesterday but they smell, and I think Jesse may have done something inappropriate with them."

Slugs and snails are more distantly related than humans and plants, as proven by fossilized slug skeletons from the Cretaceous period.

SMOG

New York was once thought to have been covered in a smog so thick people couldn't see their own hands. It turned out this was merely the start of the reign of the Hand Thief and his terrible crime spree.

J.R.R. Tolkien named his dragon Smaug after the smog in Los Angeles when he visited in 1936. While he was in the city, he was granted a star on the Hollywood Walk of Fame for his work on Peter Jackson's Lord of the Rings movies.

SMOKE

Smoke is composed of the skeletons of fire molecules that have burned out and died.

SMOKE DETECTOR

Smoke detectors contain not only small amounts of plutonium, but also uranium, sulfur, vanadium, and a small copy of the bible.

SMOKING

Within a week of a smoker quitting, lung fairies will begin returning to their homes in the alveoli. Smoking affects not only your lungs, but the lungs of anyone who eats or inhales your lungs.

SMOKESTACK

Smokestacks serve no actual purpose as smoke inevitably rises anyway. They were originally phallic symbols with which energy moguls tried to prove their superior masculinity.

SNAIL

Most snails have one lung with which they can articulate a very quiet (0.006db) voice. Amplified, it sounds very much like yodeling. The foot of a snail is not only its foot, but also its arms, legs, hips, and arguably, its legal counsel.

SNAKE

The deadliest known snake is the Hairy Bush Viper. Thousands have died laughing at its name.

Most snakes can make more sounds than a simple hiss. Several can sing, but refuse to do so in human presence and have never been heard. Thus, we are unaware of this fact and it is absent from this book.

SNEEZE

Every time you try to sneeze but can't, the sneeze retreats into the back of your head and carves another tally mark in the wall of your skull.

SNOW

Snow flakes have the same structure as human neurons. Some scientists have suggested that, water being conductive, large snow banks may be able to function as intelligent brains.

Snow can be set on fire. Lighting a flame during a blizzard can turn the entire storm into a firestorm.

SNOW GLOBE

The white flakes in snow globes are usually rhino dandruff.

SNOW WHITE AND THE SEVEN DWARFS

Each of Disney's Seven Dwarfs is based on a deadly sin:

Grumpy - Wrath
Sleepy - Sloth
Happy - Pride
Sneezy - Allergies
Thorin - Greed
Alberich - Music Piracy
Doc - Making unskippable DVD menu intros over 2 minutes

SOAP

Soap doesn't exist. The idea of it is merely an advertising ploy by the soap companies to raise stock values. But there is no soap. Not in this Wal-Mart bathroom at least.

SOCIAL MEDIA

Twitter was invented long before the internet, about the same time as the first television. Offline, it resembled a long roll of thin paper with tweets. This format was often disposed of as toilet paper, and thus the toilet paper roll was invented too. The British phrase for wiping is still "To twitter one's bum."

Jack Kerouac's "On The Road" is comprised entirely of his tweets while driving.

SOCKS

Socks disappear not randomly, but after making a life decision to leave owners who have stepped all over them.

The phrase "on their last legs" originally referred to socks, which would be shared by the community until they wore out.

SOLAR SYSTEM

In the Chipirundi cosmological myth, the only creation myth to include a heliocentric solar system, planets are the sun's testicles.

According to the Chipirundi bible, the Chichaplikaksizak, stars are living beings akin to gods that wander the skies in a great spiral, making circles around their conception of hell, the Ludglub, described as a vast black hole in space. These stars can be any of seven sexes and twenty-one genders, but all have at least one testicle. These testicles swing in orbits as the stars walk.

The Chipirundi recognized six planets around our own sun, which they named Gorlin. The testicles of Gorlin include Nuz (Mercury), Nuzin (Venus), Orliz (Earth), Forlizin (Mars), Zlax (Jupiter) and Vinzi (Saturn). Saturn's ring was thought to be a testicle piercing.

The testicle piercing of Saturn is sadly not enough to have earned the sun a spouse (binary star). Alpha Centauri however is recognized by the Chipirundi to be in a polyamorous relationship with two other stars, and is known to have a very happy sex life. Our sun's name, "Gorlin," means "The Virgin Star," and it is predicted by the Chipirundi to live alone forever.

SOUL, HUMAN

It has long been thought that the human soul weights 21 grams. This is based on faulty evidence however, as the soul that was weighed was covered in dust and lint.

SOUND

An international vote was once held to determine people's favorite sounds. The results are as follows:

1. A cat's purr
2. Cutting into construction paper
3. The sound of a cracking egg
4. Zippers and velcro
5. Crunching soda cans
6. Sizzling bacon
7. The screams of the innocent upon the gloom altar as their blood summons the demonic lord Morvor-Shelak-Skilfizzle who shall burn the forests and boil the oceans as harbinger of the end of days when evil incarnate shall reign at the right hand of the one true ruler of the universe Hagul-Hazulful-Wigglepimple-Kor-Denimshorts and partake of the devoured souls of the world's children under a blood red moon and blackened day sky
8. Crunching leaves
9. Flipping through book pages
10. The click of an old camera shutter

SOUND BARRIER

The original sound barrier was made of solid concrete. It was broken by Chuck Yeager in a car accident, making supersonic motion possible at last.

SOY SAUCE

Soy Sauce is only 3% soy, the rest is 1% water and 89,374,502,746,408,750% salt.

SPACE

Space, though mostly vacuum, also contains 0.00001% broom. Space isn't really black, it's clear because it's see-through and the wall behind it is black.

SPAGHETTI

All spaghetti comes from cuts of the same original spaghetti strand. The original strand grows at about 2ft per week and is kept safe in the Vatican's main vault.

You can tell if spaghetti is ready by throwing it against a wall to see if it sticks. The same technique can tell if a fetus is ready to be born but this won't stop them from having you forcibly escorted out of the maternity ward.

SPAGHETTI WESTERN

The term Spaghetti Western is actually short for "SpaghettiO" Western. When traveling to remote locations like those depicted in most Westerns, eating the local cuisine can wreak havoc on the inexperienced bowels of L.A.-centric movie crews. Sam Peckinpah began the tradition of spending 10% of his budgets on SpaghettiOs which he and the crew would eat exclusively on location. The SpaghettiOs also served as his gory blood effects.

The experience wasn't altogether pleasant though. When you eat nothing but SpaghettiOs for over a month, your body begins a process called "SpaghettiOsis," which I'd describe in detail but children might read this book and they just don't need to know that an esophagus can do that.

SPAIN

The bearded telephone pole is endemic to Spain, owing its growth to the high precipitation rates of the Iberian plains. Spam was invented in Spain back when it was called "Spaim."

SPEECH

The phrase "Some things are better left unsaid," actually finishes, "much as some foods are better left uncooked, and some video games are better left unbeaten." Curiously the full phrase is from 1840 by Charles Dickens, who never heard of video nor video games. This is thought to be why he never beat one.

SPEED EATING

The world speed eating record by mass went to Billy Kalman, who consumed ten large deep dish pizzas in two minutes. He also achieved the records for loudest diarrhea and most soiled blue jeans later that same day.

SPERM

Sitting cross legged for one minute decreases your sperm count more than two consecutive vasectomies.

SPLIT LEVEL HOME

Most split level homes are constructed as single floor buildings then split once complete.

SPOON

Spoons are more efficient if you hold them upside-down.

SPORK

The most grievous and recurrent misconception about the spork is that its name is a portmanteau of "spoon" and "fork." Being part spoon and part fork this seems like the most obvious origin, but in fact the spork was invented by Edwin C. Sporke in New Orleans. Sporke invented the Spork in 1776, and the year is no coincidence. The story of the Spork is in fact, the story of the United States of America.

The year was 1773 and the industrial revolution was in its first decades. The colonists that would form the government of the United States were just arriving in the 13 colonies. At the age of 21, Thomas Jefferson had just been fired from his job in tech support at the University of Oxford. The only record of his duties there suggests that he mostly cleaned the old valuable globes, clocks, compasses, and the Ancient Abacus of Ankh-Ent-Ah-Baccus. With no job and no prospects in England, Jefferson moved on up to the colonies in America, where he could begin a new life.

Jefferson came to America with only $7 to his name, and those dollars were worthless as the U.S. Treasury would not be formed for another 25 years. He arrived at the port of New Orleans, which was at the time called "The-Orleans-To-Be." He had at the time no interest in politics, and applied to work at the only English-speaking establishment in the town. His days at McDonalds were unproductive. He slaughtered the cattle for beef, he peeled the potatoes for french fries, and he ground the bones for bread, which was made from bone powder before the evolution of wheat. But one important thing happened in his years at the restaurant: He met Edwin C. Sporke.

Sporke had arrived from Norway the year prior, and changed his name from Edvald Cornelius Sporkbeklagerdetfalskenorske to Edwin C. Sporke. Jefferson first saw him when he picked up his order for a Mutton McGruelbowl. Sporke sat down and, to Jefferson's dismay, began trying to eat the liquid gruel with a fork. Curious, he brought the man a spoon and asked why he wasn't using it instead. Sporke explained that spoons had been banned in Norway for hundreds of years owing to the infamous "Blood Spooning" of Vikings, from whom the Christian monarchy wanted to distance themselves. Jefferson encouraged Sporke to try, but he was hesitant. Finally, he agreed to eat the gruel with both at the same time, overlapping. The spork was born.

Because it could eat gruel more efficiently than a spoon or fork on their own, Raymond McDonald immediately began producing the utensil. This was done at first by having Jefferson weld spoons to forks, a job he so detested that he left for the east coast, taking the idea with him and keeping (most of) Sporke's name attached, promising him royalties. Upon his arrival, Jefferson saw the next thing that would revolutionize the way we eat: The assembly line.

Famous businessman Henry Ford was living in New York, growing very rich with his mass constructed horse drawn carriages. Jefferson was impressed with the method, and immediately endeavored to accomplish a mass produced spork by means of his diligence, hard work, and persistence in buying slaves to do his real work for him. Among his early customers was Benjamin Franklin, who would go on to play so an integral role in the founding of the United States that well over 0.04% of Americans can tell you his role even today. Franklin loved the idea of the spork and showed it to George Washington, who could only eat gruel owing to the loss of his teeth in a bad poker game in 1771. The men got along splendidly, and the rest, as they say, is history.

For Jefferson and the country at least. Records of Edwin Sporke are fewer and less revolutionary. Sporke never got any royalties. Whether Jefferson never sent them or whether they were stolen by railroad bandits en route will never be known, but as railroads only began delivering mail after 1804, most historians suspect Jefferson cheated Sporke out of his share of the profits. The only thing we now know for certain about Sporke is that he died in 1779, stabbed to death with his own invention during an argument over whether zebras were striped or spotted. Sporke not only died in the encounter, but made a fool of himself by claiming that the animals were spotted, having been tricked at a local zoo that displayed a dalmatian claimed to be the elusive African zebra.

But thankfully we now know his name, and his fate, and his integral role in the building of both the U.S.A. and the spork that bears his name. In this respect he remains far more fortunate than Muhammad ibn Muhammad al-Nafzawi, who invented the spork in 1211 in Tunisia and is not remembered in any European history books at all for obvious reasons.

SPRINKLER

We do not fully understand how sprinklers work. If you look at them in the sunlight they can make a rainbow, but we don't know where that rainbow is stored within the sprinkler before it is deployed.

SPY

Spies did not exist before spy films. The first spies were only trained after governments around the world saw the earliest spy thrillers and thought every other country already had them, so they needed to as well.

SPYCRAFT

Nothing to see here.

SQUARE

The square is often called "The King of the Triangles" because of its extra corner.

SQUID

Squids and Octopi are the same animal, they just have different evolutions depending on what kind of rock they're hatched on.

The proper plural of "Squid" is "Squeed."

SQUIRREL

The squirrel is the only known animal with a Q in its name.

SR-71

When the SR-71 feels threatened, it will perform a "deimatic display" in which it spreads out its frill, making it appear larger to its natural predators, such as the Air Force Budgetary Committee.

SRIRACHA SAUCE

Sriracha Sauce is named after a city in Thailand, which has become famous as a result and seen a massive influx of tourists. As a result, the town of Sauce has become the seventh largest city in Asia.

Sriracha Sauce features a picture of a rooster on its bottle in America in honor of traveler John James Kelsinger, who introduced the sauce to the United States and was himself a rooster.

Sriracha Sauce was prominently featured in the film 9 ½ Weeks during an erotically charged food scene. It was the origin of the use of the word "spicy" to refer to kinky sexuality.

Sriracha Sauce is one of the safest condiments to eat, owing to the antiseptic ingredients that make up its signature taste. Many hospitals use it in place of rubbing alcohol.

STALKING

The term "stalking" comes from the ancient practice of covertly monitoring the corn stalks of a neighbor. Why these stalkers stalked stalks is unknown.

STANFORD PRISON EXPERIMENT

After the Stanford Prison Experiment, a prison in Oklahoma simulated a college with their inmates. The Prison Stanford Experiment went better than its predecessor, with 14 of the 16 inmates gaining degrees, a higher completion rate than Stanford itself.

STAR

There was a star near the center of the galaxy that gave off amazing and unique radio emissions until 1979, when it was killed by video.

When you wish upon a star, you should wish for thermal shielding because it's hot there.

STAR TREK

The "Phasers" in Star Trek are based on real phased array pulsed energy projectile technology, but the "Photon Torpedoes" are purely fictional, as neither photons nor torpedoes exist.

In the original pilot for Star Trek, the warp engines were powered by coal. Warp speed is based on the average flight speed of the swallow, with warp one being the average speed of an unladen swallow and warp nine being nine times the speed of nine swallows.

Most time travel episodes of Star Trek have not been filmed yet.

STAR WARS

According to the original Star Wars screenplay, "Jedi" is plural. The singular form is "Jed."

With all the Special Edition changes, few Star Wars fans realize that the character of Luke was not in the original film.

STARGATE

In the original Stargate film, symbols barely visible on the gate include an anarchy sign, the Rolling Stones logo, and a simple caricature of Bob Hope.

STARSHIP TROOPERS

Paul Verhoeven didn't read the novel "Starship Troopers" before making the first movie based on it, he merely watched the movie.

STATUE OF LIBERTY

There were many Statues of Liberty once, but they fought in epic battles until there was only one. And the other one in France but we don't talk about that one.

STEEL WOOL

Steel wool is extremely hard to shear from steel sheep owing to its steely nature.

STOMACH

Most people are born with two stomachs, but the unused stomach withers before puberty unless it's selected on the starting screen.

The interior of your stomach is full of folds. If flattened out, your stomach lining would cover three football fields. It would however be too slippery to play football on.

STROP

Though many words begin to sound funny if you say them over and over, the word "Strop" starts off funny and gets boring and sensible instead.

STUDIES

Studies show that if you begin a sentence with "Studies Show" then everyone will believe you.

STYROFOAM

Styrofoam was invented in 1997 by Jorge Styro as a means to pollute the Earth more permanently. By combining yeast, sea foam, cloud snot and elk hair and putting it all in a taffy puller with some gasoline, he made the first "styrofoam."

Styrofoam was not used for packaging until 2001, when the Bush administration demanded it be used for packing everything from food to electronics. This had nothing whatsoever to do with him buying 30 million dollars of stock in styrofoam the previous week, which was suddenly worth over 2 billion dollars.

Styrofoam has a great future ahead as it's the only thing that will be left of humankind after it destroys the environment and makes the planet uninhabitable by anything but deep sea shrimp, leading many scientists to believe that humanity's only purpose in the global ecosystem was in fact to allow for the evolution of styrofoam-eating deep sea shrimp.

Styrofoam also goes squickity-squeak when handled. Try it at home!

SUBMARINE

Submarines rise and sink using a system called "The Billboard Top 40" in which ballast is expelled according to its popularity among teenagers.

SUN

The sun is not a nuclear fire like most stars, but a grease fire like the one at McDonalds.

Direct sunlight in space would kill you instantly. We can only enjoy it here on Earth because our atmosphere filters out the grizzly bears.

Sunrise and sunset used to be different, but for budget reasons sunset is now just sunrise but backwards on the other side.

SUNBLOCK

The thickest sunblock available is SPF 14,000. It reflects all light that hits it and thus it gives anyone who wears it a mirror reflectivity. It was used for the alien's camouflage in Predator.

SUNGLASSES

Sunglasses do not allow you to look directly into the sun. Only Sungazing Form 27B-6 can give you that right.

SUPERSTITION

Four leaf clovers are considered lucky because their shape is similar to the Ugraxion, an ancient symbol of fortune from the Grimoire of the Brain Eating Imp.

SUPPER, LAST

Before synthetic dyes, paints were made with organic materials. The paint comprising The Last Supper includes blood, feces, rabbit eyes, tree bark, gym sock mold, and martian dust samples.

SUPPER, FIRST

The first supper after Jesus was weaned from breast milk was Gerberus Strained Chickpeas. It is not often painted because he got that shit got everywhere. Spoons were sadly only invented in 34 AD.

SUPREME COURT

In 1907, four supreme court justices were appointed and they all shared the same three names: Justices Carter Friedrich Lawson, Lawson Carter Friedrich, and Friedrich Lawson Carter.

SWAN

When fed the same shrimp as flamingos, swans will turn bright pink. This is the plot of Tchaikovsky's "The Pink Swan."

SWEATER

Sweaters are so named because they sweat. A sweater without sweat glands is technically a cardigan.

SWEDEN

Sweden is not actually a distinct country, but rather a copy of Norway produced as a location by location duplicate of Norway for rental when Norway got demagnetized.

SWEET NOTHING

A "sweet nothing" is a phrase or word used to express intimacy to a loved one. Traditionally, such vocalizations are whispered but can be expressed at any volume for different results:

If one were to hold their lover close and caress their neck and whisper softly, "You make me so happy," the partner may well simply smile and hold them closer.

If however, one were to grab them by the hair and growl loudly at them, "You hot slut, I'm gonna make you moan like a walrus with sleep apnea," then their reaction may be very different.

Please also note that walrus apnea is no joke as CPAP masks cannot fit their tusks.

SWORD

Sword fights looked nothing like how they're depicted in movies. Movies use fencing moves to look exciting. Real sword fights of yore were fought with guns.

The sharpest sword in the world belonged to Hiram "Sharpie" Snogloggindoggett, who sharpened it every five minutes. By the time of his death, the entire sword was thinner than a tenth of a millimeter. An even more sharp sword is in development at CERN, which will be only one hydrogen nucleus thick. It is exclusively to be used for cleaning the fingernails of one intern who frankly really needs it, they're utterly gross. Seriously.

Most swords manufactured were made for decoration, not fighting. Conversely, most Christmas Ornaments through history were made for battle.

Many decorative swords are the biggest of their kind:

The heaviest sword of all time is the 468lb "Le Glaive Chungeuse" of King Louis LXIX, so heavy nobody could wield it.

The longest sword ever made was the Gobai-nodachi, or "quintuple length longsword" forged by Masayoshi Johnson for a ceremony said to have resulted in the deaths of everyone present.

The thickest sword, three feet thick but only six inches long, was the Hungarian Chodesaber, which was used mostly for flattening dough.

The widest sword is currently the Grand Coronation Stub of King Charles, ruler of England as of March 2024. Shaped like a shallow isosceles triangle, its tip is almost 165 degrees.

The most expensive sword ever forged was the Diamond Sprinklesword of Muffy von Fitzwiggle-Plumnugget, which a rich Californian gave to his chihuahua for its third birthday. It could have paid to feed 30 billion people for five lifetimes.

The "biggest" sword in terms of fame and notoriety is the Sword of Damocles, which metaphorically hangs over the head of those with power as a reminder to be responsible lest they grow greedy or despotic. It has not been seen since around November of 2016.

If spelled with a hyphen, S-word can refer to the word "Shit."

SYNTHPOP

Synthpop is what the Rice Krispies had to add when one elf died and Snap and Crackle got lonely.

SYRUP

Syrup can refer to any kind of liquid made by boiling sugar or proteins into a thick, usually sweet flavored and edible substance. Most often, plant products (especially fruits) are boiled into syrup, but syrups can also be made from vegetables, tree saps, meats, and as one Brony on 4chan learned, from a Rainbow Dash figure boiled in-

-T-

TANK

Tanks had wheels until 1913 when treads were invented, originally as a decorative component. Even still the main purpose of treads is to look cool.

Many people think tanks fought by firing their guns at each other. This was never true. In reality, most tank fights were up close and personal, using the large turrets very much like swords.

Tank fights often consisted of parking the big metal beasts next to each other, evacuating them of all but one operator, and then whacking the hell out of each other until one tank's gun broke. The strongest tank would be declared the victor. Meanwhile, the tank crews would generally sit together and watch, with Allied and Axis personnel often making bets on who would win.

This resulted in the construction of larger and larger tanks. The Panzer Landstampfer P. 9000 was by far the largest tank ever built. Weighing 8950 tons and measuring 70 meters in length, the behemoth was to have been the crown jewel of the German army. Thankfully several flaws prevented its use in war:

-It was impossible to repair in the field, as even a single tread plate weighed as much as a common tank.

-The tank was too heavy to travel on most terrain. It sank in swamps, crushed any road it traveled, and was unable to move efficiently on anything but solid granite. Oddly enough, it could float in water without difficulty.

-Despite its size, the tank was relatively weak. Its massive engine required a thermal exhaust port so wide that a smaller tank would have been able to travel down its meridian trench and fire into the engine itself, causing a chain reaction that could destroy the entire tank.

-The tank required a crew of 78 men to operate, and featured internal dormitories to house them. Unfortunately, a design flaw left it with only one functional bathroom. The results were the last nail in the coffin: Within its first day of prototype trials, the toilet became clogged and sewage slowly backed up, flooding the lower 3 decks. Command quickly arranged for a compliment of "scheißeschlepper" tanks to pump and remove the offending material, but the damage was done when Heinz Guderian declared the tank's element of surprise would be ruined when opposing troops smelled it coming.

-Additionally, the cannon was so large that were it ever fired, it would drive the entire tank 50ft into rock solid ground and cause an earthquake that would have annihilated most of Europe.

The only working prototype of the tank was literally scrapped, and its metal was used to build the entire Berlin, Munich and Hamburg subway systems. But the story doesn't end there. In 2016, historians uncovered plans for the Panzer XXVI Walross, a 250,000 ton tank the size of an entire city, which would have traveled on treads five miles long and fired hydrogen bombs from its 4,000mm cannon.

It was cancelled, apparently, because it would've required more metal than exists in the entire solar system.

TAPE

Duct tape uses organic adhesives, oddly enough, made from liquefied ducks. They are usually liquefied by a reducktive agent.

TARDIS

The original TARDIS police box was a real police box stolen from the street outside of the BBC studio only minutes before filming began on the first episode of Doctor Who. The crime was

256

never reported because the police box was gone and nobody could call in to report it missing.

TASTE

Flavor exists as a spectrum like light, with bitter on one end and sweet on the other. Like ROY G BIV, you can remember the flavors by the name BOB C SWISS.

TAXI

The term "Taxi" comes from Taxidermy, the art of stuffing dead animals. Taxis took the name because they were originally stuffed horses before cars were invented.

TEA, EARL GREY (HOT)

Earl Grey tea hasn't been authentic since 1905, when Twinnings ran out of the Earl's ashes.

TEARS

It was once believed that if you collected your tears and dried them for the salt, and salted potato chips with that salt, and fed those chips to the person who was the cause of your tears, that they would say, "Eww, that's gross, and possibly illegal."

TEDDY BEAR

It takes the fur of five grizzly bears to make one teddy bear.

TEETH

Before modern dentistry, nearly everyone from every social class across the globe had lost all their teeth by the age of 20. All the teeth everyone lost were found in 1966 in a valley in Paraguay and nobody can figure out how they got there.

The phrase "Like Pulling Teeth" does not refer to dental extraction but to dental transportation. Back in the olden days, human teeth could weigh up to 50 tons each, thus pulling them along the roads was an arduous task.

TELESCOPE

The sharpest telescope ever designed was first used in 2015 to look at the lunar landers left on the moon. Most were present as they were left, but that of Apollo 14 was covered in 76 parking tickets and had a boot. It had managed to land next to one of the only four fire hydrants on the entire moon.

A child visiting Palomar Observitory in 1986 asked to use the big telescope to hunt for flying saucers. Though she found none, she did discover 18 comets, 2 exoplanets and evidence of rings around Pluto and Ceres.

TELEVISION

Before the invention of television, most schools had their own acting troupes to demonstrate scientific shorts. They too were wheeled into classrooms on small square carts.

There is no standard for what resolution qualifies as HD. Broadcasts labeled as such range from 4096 pixels across to a single giant pixel that takes up the whole screen.

Cathode Ray TVs were named for their inventor, Cathode Ray.

TEN COMMANDMENTS

The ten commandments as we know them today are the result of an English translation of a Latin translation of a Hebrew translation of an early Semitic language, and due to the thousands of years and many translations, these immortal words have been a bit skewed from their original meanings. Here are their true wordings:

Honor thy father and mother.
In the original text, this actually says "Honor all of your elders."

Thou shalt not steal.
More accurately and fully, "Do not take that which does not belong to you unless it is a burden to the other person and he cries out to be relieved."

Thou shalt not kill.
This one was more specific in the first texts, explaining, "Never kill another human being, unless they really, *really* deserve it."

Thou shalt have no other gods before me.
Properly translated, this commandment says simply, "No cutting in line in front of God."

Thou shalt not bear false witness against thy neighbor.
Oddly, this one accurately translated means, "Bears are not sufficient witnesses in court, but neighbors are."

Thou shalt not take the name of the Lord thy God in vain.
Literally translated, "That's my name, don't wear it out."

Thou shalt not commit adultery.
Often completely altered to fit the morals of the times, this commandment was originally, "Do not leave your spoons right side up in the dishwasher or they will collect water and stain with minerals."

Thou shalt not make unto thee any graven image.
Originally, "Do not reblog God's selfies."

Remember the sabbath day, to keep it holy.
Originally, "Thank God it's Friday."

Thou shalt not covet thy neighbor's house, wife, or donkey.
The original list of uncovetables in the first copies of the bible was far more exhaustive, stating, "Thou shalt not covet thy neighbors house, nor his wife or donkey, or horses or mule, or camel, nor his chimney, roofing or tile floor, nor shalt thou covet him his money or pottery,

or milk cow, or his job or parentage or even his wristwatch, though it be gold and ivory, nor shalt thou ever covet his music collection or his familiarity with Jessica the check-out lady at the Barnes and Noble even though she's seriously hot and he doesn't even treat her right, I mean seriously, he's being a dick to her and you always ask how she's doing but she still digs him more and smiles really big and what's up with that because you see her more often, you read way more than Josh does and he only ever reads like self-help crap and she literally saw you reading Dostoyevsky after she was wearing a Brothers Karamazov shirt that one time but he's the good looking one with his big thick mustache so she's totally into him not to mention that he's fucking MARRIED. Nor shall you envy his boat."

Modern copies of the bible also generally leave off the mysterious and rarely understood eleventh commandment, "Wrap it before you tap it."

TENNIS

The fluffy stuff on Tennis balls is the same stuff that makes milkshakes thicken.

TESLA, NIKOLA

Nikola Tesla theorized that if someone misweighted their washing machine in a very specific way, its vibrations could destroy the planet. He was wrong of course, it doesn't have to be specific at all.

Late in his career, Tesla invented a working digital camera. He destroyed it himself though, having foreseen the coming of "Alvin and the Chipmunks: The Squeakquel."

TEST TUBE

Test tubes are quite large. For small samples, scientists use quiz tubes.

TEXAS

Texas is the state equivalent of what happens when you leave a pizza in the oven over vacation and it grows so much mold you have to buy a new oven. It also contains the "Alamo," which is best remembered for being urinated upon by Ozzy Osbourne.

THEATER

Improv theater was considered witchcraft until 1930. In some states it is still punishable by burning at the stake, or another method of death that the audience shouts out.

Before Samuel Beckett became the Archbishop of Canterbury, he wrote absurdist theater plays, having traveled from the distant future to do so and hoping his next leap would be the leap home.

The term "Audition" comes from the Greek deity Auditios, the god of embarrassing yourself publicly.

Most backstage doors are locked from the outside to prevent actors from escaping.

THIS TOO SHALL PASS

A phrase often attributed to King Solomon, it was in fact just the slogan of the Fec-Ease Constipation Treatment Company.

TILE FLOORING

Tile floors are illegal in two states: Liquid and Gas. Most tile floors installed before 1930 use a paste made from dog hair instead of grout. It takes the spleens of 20 grouts to secure a single tile.

TIME

8:00PM-8:01PM is not technically part of the eighth hour, but is properly known as the end of the seventh hour.

Like Russia, Luxembourg covers nine time zones. Unlike Russia, in Luxembourg they are all within one city block of each other.

TIME TRAVEL

In January of 1709 during the War of Spanish Succession and a notoriously harsh winter, a man was found just east of Tours walking on the frozen Loire river. Naked and covered in burns that took the shape of vertical stripes all over his torso and legs, the man was found to speak only English and a bit of an unidentifiable dialect of French or Italian. Believed to be an opposing soldier, he was held in a military prison until 1714.

During his time in the Tours prison, he made numerous bizarre claims. The man, who accounts record as calling himself "Alexandre Ramieresse" stated that he was from the future, coming from a city called "Baz-Dan." He stated that he was a university professor and scientist and that he had accidentally thrown himself back in time about 300 years while developing a type of vehicle, which he claimed was supposed to send people across great distances in a second. His accounts of how it worked were stated to be gibberish by his captors.

On February 18th 2016, Professor Alexander Ramirez of Boston University disappeared from François Rabelais University near Tours while working on a quantum entanglement study.

The description of "Alexandre Ramieresse" does indeed match Alexander Ramirez, bald with a thick black mustache is all that the historical records say about his appearance. But they do list a good number of his rantings and prophecies. Among them are claims that France and Germany would have two great battles in the 20th century, one of them due to a German Tyrant whose name was stated but not recorded; a claim that he flew to Tours in a large metal object with wings; a claim that people across the globe would one day be obsessed with a play called "La Guerre des Étoiles" (Roughly translated "the war of stars"), and that they would spend most of their time writing words on communication devices called "His Salt" ("his salt" in French would be "sel fon").

Alexandre Ramieresse died in 1716 and was buried in the Holy Innocents' Cemetery in Paris, but his grave marker has never been positively identified. Notably though, in 1987, a geiger counter located a heavily radioactive corpse buried in the cemetery, which was removed for public safety. The corpse, unidentified, bore several anomalies, including a fatally high polonium levels and evidence of advanced dental surgery. Suggesting a further connection, individuals who had extended contact with Ramieresse were said to have gone bald and suffered from tumors. Alexandre Ramieresse himself was not stated to have had any deformities, but the bones of the removed corpse did bear signs of internal cancerous growth.

Most alarming of all though, is the will of Alexandre Ramieresse. Dictated to an avocet in 1715, the will is in English and though it does not definitively state that he had traveled in time, its actual contents are quite suggestive of the phenomenon. It reads in its entirety:

"To Monica I leave my home and its furnishings. To Maurice I leave my accounts at Banque Courtois and my cat, Frodo. To Marie I leave one hundred livres on the condition that she pass on my letter to be delivered to the François Rabelais University on February 15th, 2016."

Upon reading this bizarre will, investigators checked with the University to see if any letters had been delivered. Indeed, one had been received on the 15th but had been stowed in a sorting pile due to its faded address through the 18th and was only opened after the discovery. The letter read:

"Alex- It's you from the past. For the love of fuck don't use a resistor on B-13 or B-15. It will send you back in time and hurt like a mother fucker. Also I think you forgot to throw out the expired eggs in the fridge. Have Marty toss them fast or it will stink up the house like one of Larry's farts."

The final evidence came when investigators contacted Ramriez's T.A., Martin Salandor Essex and sent him to the refrigerator in question. Upon opening it he reported a smell that he confirmed was indeed nearly identical to the farts of student Larry Perspex.

Upon learning the near incontrovertible evidence that time travel is real, Martin stated for the record: "It's true. It's all absolutely true: Larry farts like a fucking skunk on Taco Bell."

TIRE

Early car tires were made from cake, and would be consumed nightly by the car's family. Only recently have rubber tires been used as semi-permanent, inedible tires.

TITANIC

More people died from accidents on the set of James Cameron's "Titanic" than died on the actual Titanic.

TOAST

We can't be certain where toast comes from, but some suggest it had something to do with the great bread fire of Toaston, England in 844, three miles from the shore of Butterlump.

TOE

The human pinky toe is the strongest toe in the animal kingdom, even stronger than the toes of the iron grip turtle.

Pasithimeliophobia is the suspicion that your toes belong to someone else.

TOENAILS

Most toenail clippings form a perfect geometric crescent, and can be used to measure longitude.

Toenails are the only body part that grows back double when trimmed. We usually trim out toenails often enough that we don't see them double, but if anyone who has trimmed their nails regularly were to stop, they would in fact grow well over 96 new toenails at once.

TOILET

Most medieval thrones were also toilets, as royalty had to sit for up to 12 hours at a time. You don't even want to know what the royal scrolls were used for.

Toilets north of the equator flush with the water in a spiral to the left, and those south of the equator spin to the right. It is theorized that a toilet exactly on the equator could damage the planetary orbit if flushed.

Modern toilets are ceramic because wool ones stank after a while.

TOILET PLUNGER

The toilet plunger was originally invented as a surgical tool.

TOMATO

Tomato seeds differ from all other seeds in that they will grow into tomato plants. Also they explode when crushed. Tomatoes and Potatoes share a common ancestor, the Saber Toothed Turnip.

TORNADO

When tornadoes destroy fruit groves, their force crushes the fruit and causes it to rain juice up to 15 miles away from the funnel.

TOTORO

Totoro was Mr. Rodgers' first neighbor, before the Yamadas moved in.

TOWEL

A towel is just about the most massively tempting place for me to commit plagiarism upon Douglas Adams.

TRAINS

The longest train ever assembled stretched 145 miles, entirely from its origin to its destination. Thus it is also the fastest train ever recorded, having made its 145 mile journey in 0.00 seconds.

Steam powered locomotives were received poorly in their day because of region locking and downloadable content issues.

TRANSISTOR

The Papyrus of Djer-Djet Hotepsekhemenedji Nefer VI, also known as Papyrus DD17c in the British Museum, is just over 4000 years old but was not considered significant until recently, when an intern at the museum noticed that it resembles the circuit diagram for a transistor.

Transistors are critical electronic "switches" that form the basis of most modern technology, including computers and phones. The hieroglyphics around the center read, "base," "collector," and "emitter" in Ancient Egyptian, further suggesting that the ancients may have had an understanding of basic computing.

According to Egyptologist Robert Hawa, "This is surprising but not entirely unexpected. We knew that the ancients had used something like a battery to electroplate gold onto ritual objects, but this is quite a bit more advanced than we had previously assumed. I'm hesitant to say that this was a transistor diagram yet, but the evidence is building."

With the recognition of the diagram, other papyri from the same expedition are currently under heavy analysis. According to Hawa, three other significant illustrations have been identified: One resembles the circuit diagram for a cathode ray tube, one resembles a keyboard, and the third is hieroglyphs only but seems to read, "Change thy provider to Timit-Warnotep Cable for $35 off your first month."

If true, this would be the most significant archaeological find since the Carburetor of Nejed-Nefer Hedjkheperresetepenre, or the Antibiotic Pills of Khepermaatre-setpenptah Ramesses XII.

TRAVEL

Depending on the location and mode of transportation, getting there can account for 37-72% of the fun.

TREE

Trees make a lot of noise during photosynthesis, but it's all over 29kHz so humans can't hear it. When toned down to an audible range, it sounds oddly like Vangelis.

When a tree molts its first bark, it departs the larval or "sapling" stage and becomes a fully grown tree, capable of reproduction. A tree only ingests nutrients from the roots during the larval phase and will have to subsist on this food long enough to fruit before dying. When given "Royal Sap" as a larva, a tree gains the potential to grow into a Queen Tree.

The tree whose flowers become venus fly traps is also toxic to the touch, while the traps themselves can only consume flies. For humans, its bark is worse than its bite.

TRIVIA

The first trivia contest ever held occurred in 47,000 B.C., and consisted of only two questions, as the total of human knowledge at the time was only two things.

TUMBLR

A check back to post 0000000000000001 on the Tumblr timeline reveals it to have been posted by "Anak-Sut-Num" in Egypt, 4,000 years ago. Unsurprisingly it's a cat photo.

TUNA

The food commonly called "tuna" is not made from the tuna fish, but the tuna rat. Don't worry though it's still dolphin safe.

TURKEY

The turkey bird and the country of Turkey are not related. The country is really called Türkiye, and the bird is really called a Meleagris. The weird thing is that the common name for both being Turkey, they were confused for each other by former vice president Dan Quayle, who was himself often mistaken for a bird.

TURTLE

The turtle is the largest insect known to biological science. For centuries it was mistaken for a reptile until Charles Darwin finally caught one of the elusive creatures in the Callipygous Islands and was able to study it up close.

Darwin's description of the turtle reads as follows:

"Turtle, clade Testudinata of the class Insecta. Hyperdeveloped shell with retractable appendages. Biology mimics reptilian, including rudimentary structure mistaken previously for spinal column. Delicious in soup, coarsely ground with traditional Creole seasoning and minced garlic."

Trutles are also unique in that mated pairs share their shells. Not always but often when a pair of turtles mates, the male will leave his own shell and move in with the female. After doing so the couple will coordinate their arm and leg movements to walk and even swim.

TWAIN, MARK

Samuel Clemens was the real name of Tom Sawyer, who wrote about a character named Mark Twain, who was the author of Huckleberry Finn. Huck Finn in turn wrote about Samuel Clemens. This is why their works are all considered circular narratives.

TWELVE DAYS OF CHRISTMAS, THE

Every gift in "The Twelve Days of Christmas" involves birds. This is because the song was written in the 1780s under the reign of George III, when birds were extremely scarce in England due to over-hunting. The specific birds listed were the most hunted, thus the song is about the singer's true love finding the rarest things in the country to give for Christmas. The birds included were:

A Partridge in a Pear Tree- Both things uncommon in the country, partridges having gone extinct in the region due to hunting in 1763, when the last of its kind was shot down by The Duke Of Ellingsby and left for his dogs. Pear trees cannot grow in the region at all.

Two Turtle Doves- The rarest known dove, now completely extinct as it was hunted for its precious shell, which was often used to make frames for glasses. As the only shelled bird, the Turtle Dove died out around 1850.

Three French Hens- The French Hen was not technically a hen, but a species of vulture which resembled a chicken. This species was farmed, not hunted, but was exceedingly scarce as the breed was closely controlled by its farmers, the French family who would go on to introduce "Bird Mustard," a type of mustard meant specifically for the breed. French's Mustard is still made today.

Four Calling Birds- A "Calling Bird" refers to a Aves Cornelius, Or the Calling Cornish Grouse as it's known today. It exists now only in zoos. The bird is notable for its male having a corkscrew shaped 14 inch penis, which was dried and turned to powder for use as an aphrodisiac at the time.

Five Golden Rings- Referring to the Gold Ringed Pheasant, a delicacy which was over-hunted to extinction, the last known specimen being eaten by Gerald Geraldson Esq. who consumed the bird with a dollop of French's Bird Mustard.

Six Geese-a-Laying- This does not refer to Geese laying eggs but to Alayin Geese, golden geese which were likely the inspiration for a goose that could lay a golden egg. They were already extinct by the time the song was written, but this fact was not known until around 1830.

Seven Swans a-Swimming- Swans are common today but only because of an intensive breeding program. They were as rare in the 1780s in England as Astatine is today. This is why the duck in "The Ugly Duckling" is so remarkable, not for its beauty but for its rarity.

269

Eight Maids-a-Milking- The Maidenbird was the only known bird to have live birth and nurse its young with milk. "Maiden's Milk" was used to make the original egg-nog, which was a royal delicacy reserved only for the children of the king and queen and even to them it was only served on Christmas. The bird is now extinct.

Nine Ladies Dancing- Seems an odd gift to give a lover doesn't it? Unless you know that the Dancing Lady Eagle was the only eagle to live in England at the time. It was named for its habit of shaking violently to rid itself of Eagle Ticks, which resembled a frenzied dance. It was trophy hunted to near extinction, and lives only in captivity now. As the tick has gone extinct, it no longer dances.

Ten Lordes-a-Leaping (To use the spelling of the time)- The Lorde Heron still exists today, though it is no longer called the "Leaping Lorde" as it was in the time of the song. Identical visually to the Royal Heron, the only way to tell if a Lorde is a Royal is whether the genome runs in its blood. The Royal gene being extremely rare, that kind of luxury was not for most people, who could only afford a different buzzard.

Eleven Pipers Piping- The Piper Finch is still rare though it's sold today at some pet shops and bird markets. Its voice was said once to be the most beautiful sound in the world, but is now considered a nuisance by most. The Piper Finch is most famous as the type of bird seen adorning the tip of the Washington Monument, as George Washington raised the animals. The British Piper Tax was one of the reasons the colonies split off to form the modern country of New England.

Twelve Drummers Drumming- The Drumming Magpie. Immortalized by Gioachino Rossini in his opera "La Gazza Tamburo." The rarest bird in England by far, only three were known to exist at the time of the song's writing. This would make twelve of them an exceptional rarity and near impossibility to crown the parade of gift birds. The drumming Magpie is named for its habit of tapping on trees to drive out maggots and grubs for it to eat.

So there you have it, the song is a love song about finding the rarest birds in England for the one you love. This stands in stark contrast to "The Eight Days of Hanukkah" in which the gifts include horseradish, cement, hair dye, a basketball, and lint.

Bonus trivia- Christmas was never celebrated as a 12 day holiday until after the song was written. The song likely inspired the tradition.

TWENTY THOUSAND LEAGUES UNDER THE SEA

Disney's 1954 production of Jules Verne's 20,000 Leagues by Richard Fleischer has long been the definitive cinematic version of the story. But it was not the first to enter production. In 1946, famous billionaire Howard Hughes attempted to make the film, following "The Outlaw" which would become his final completed film as director. The production would become one of Hollywood's greatest disasters, taking the lives of over 90 actors and crew, costing nearly half a billion dollars (adjusted for inflation), destroying an entire island, and almost causing a third world war.

As the second world war drew to a close, Hughes was setting his sights on what he intended to be his magnum opus. Verne's book had long been an inspiration to Hughes, in part inspiring his ventures into nautical enterprises, including the construction of the "Mahogany Mackerel," one of the largest ships ever to sail. A party was held to mark the start of production at one of Hughes' seaside homes outside of San Francisco, and was sadly marred when a drunken Hughes began shooting into the air with his crossbow and killed an albatross, which fell into the punch bowl.

The party featured the intended stars of the film, actors Gene Kelly, Gregory Peck, and Orson Welles who would portray Captain Nemo. It was an early blow to the film when all three actors departed the production on its first day due to infighting over an unsuccessful orgy the prior week. This caused a massive production delay during which Hughes bought up over 50 warehouses (including the world's largest building at the time) to hold the sets and specially built water tanks until casting was replenished.

Two of these warehouses burned down (including the world's largest building fire at the time), destroying the sets which then had to be rebuilt. By the time Hughes decided to cast unknown actors in the lead roles, ten more major set pieces had rotted away delaying the production further. Finally in October of 1948 the new sets and all actors were in place on the luxurious island of Bikini Atoll. The crew was to arrive at the shooting location on October 26th but was delayed by weather. This turned out to be a good thing as the United States conducted an unannounced nuclear test on October 27th, annihilating the island and the sets completely. The island is still not habitable to this day, and Howard Hughes, who owned the island, was compensated only $212 (adjusted for inflation) for his losses by the government.

Undeterred, Hughes began again with fresh sets, and new actors as the previous group had long since departed by 1950. This time, production finally began and footage was shot. It was never developed however because despite the expenditure of $800,000 (adjusted for inflation) on pyrotechnics for the first scenes shot, nobody had thought to temperature-protect the film canisters, which were opened at the lab and found to have melted completely into what amounted to large plastic hockey pucks. Hughes filmed the scene again, at the same cost, and then a third time when he was not satisfied with a background extra's hair. This new footage too was lost when it was captured by rebellious 1950s teenagers who held it for ransom. They asked only $50 (adjusted for inflation) but Hughes refused to pay on principle.

The actors and crew were even more upset than Hughes that their work had been for nothing and so began the "Leagues Riots" of 1951. What sets remained were once more burned down, this time in protest. The lead actors were rehearsing in the sets at the time and all died of smoke inhalation. Hughes was also injured in an unrelated accident on the same day when he flew an experimental plane on its first test flight. He managed to steer the wayward jet back to his own property but missed the runway and instead crashed into another set, which had already been rigged for pyrotechnics the previous night, resulting in the loss of the set, pyro, plane, Hughes left pinky toe, and over 30 million dollars in production costs (adjusted for inflation).

Then the real problems began.

Hughes replaced the lead actor with Sam Normanjensen, once thought to be a great star on the rise. Unfortunately he was also a serial killer known then as the Sherman Oaks Ripper. He had killed 17 actors before he was cast, and filmed for only two weeks before he slaughtered and ate the spleen of one of his co-stars. Hughes was exonerated of any negligence but only after 50 million dollars (adjusted for inflation) in court fees and settlements with the actors family, one member of which visited the set on a later filming day to fire his pistol randomly at the remaining cast in anger, killing two more, wounding Hughes who lost his right testicle, and destroying a filming balloon that was the largest air vehicle ever built at the time (adjusted for inflation).

It was then that the Verne family withdrew their rights from the plagued production. Another legal battle cost in the millions, and by the time it was over in 1952, the sets had once again rotted away and had to be rebuilt. By that time, the Disney production was under way and Hughes spent millions more to spy on and sabotage the rival production. Several Disney employees fell victims to car bombs, others to arsenic poisoning, and one to auto-erotic asphyxiation, but Hughes was not considered responsible for that particular event. Walt Disney, of course, declared war.

The "War Between The Sets" began in 1953 as Hughes forces were driven off by Disney's hired guns, the Mouseketeers which in those days were a fully armed paramilitary force. This skirmish took seven lives, but it was only the beginning. Hughes used his government contracts to secure two bombers and arms weighing in excess of 500 tons, all of which were dropped on Disney owned installations. Disney's retaliation was severe. Hughes hotels burned days after, there were so many fires that Vegas and LA were both lit as bright as daylight even at midnight from the blazes. Hughes responded with bombings and drone strikes, with "drone strikes" in 1953 referring to dropping bees on ones enemy. One such strike which killed Disney's allergic son, Walt Disney III (There was no Walt Disney II as Walt felt that talent skipped a generation). The conflict at one point threatened to spill over into Russia's South American interests, leading the president to demand Hughes back down before turning the cold war into a nuclear conflict.

By the time a truce was called, Disney's film was in theaters and Hughes was ready to call it a loss. He became reclusive and wasn't seen much in public from that time on. Disney continued to be one of the largest entertainment companies in the world, and remains the producer of the most definitive adaptation of 20,000 Leagues Under The Sea.

TYPOGRAPHY

The number 9 was originally a shape close to a diamond, but was changed by Gutenberg to resemble an upside-down 6 because he had no 9 shaped type sorts but a surplus of 6s.

UMBRELLA

The earliest known umbrella dates back to 320 B.C., a full 500 years before the first rain.

UNCANNY VALLEY

The "Uncanny Valley" is an effect in which a computer generated character looks too human to accept as a cartoon, but too cartoony to accept as a real human.

The effect is named after the Uncanny Valley near Silicon Valley in California. In the early days of computer animation, Silicon Valley programmers would wander the Uncanny Valley between work shifts, discussing their projects and looking for inspiration in nature.

It was on such a walk that the programmers encountered Wally Urundak. Wally was a hermit who lived in the valley and he often invited programmers in for tea or lemonade, depending on the temperature outside. Wally was a friend to many, though many also recognized something was awry. Wally seemed normal, perhaps even too normal. He was always happy, he was always polite, he always spoke clearly and enunciated well, and his expressions were always crystal clear.

One day, a programmer named Vig Ruskin noticed what appeared to be a wire running out of Wally's left pant leg. He didn't want to be rude so he didn't ask about it, but he mentioned it to other programmers and word slowly traveled about the suspicion that the seemingly perfect Wally was a robot. It would make sense, they were in the computer capital of the world and many suspected that this strange fellow was an experiment, perhaps of Bill Gates or another famed computer wizard. So on a cold Tuesday afternoon as Vig and his friends ventured to the Uncanny Valley to visit Wally, they brought a pair of wire cutters.

They met Wally and sat down and had a chat, speaking in ad hoc Turing tests to see if they could trick Wally into admitting he was run by a computer mind. He passed them all. Then, Vig had his friend Martin trick Wally into looking out the window while Vig himself jumped down and cut the wire. Wally fell over immediately. They thought it was proven.

But then- The wire started bleeding.

Wally began to smell bad, rotten almost immediately. He deflated and decomposed as they watched. And a horrible groaning sound emerged from deep within the house's basement.

It turned out that Wally was like the bait at the end of an anglerfish's lure, and was only part of the house itself, which was a massive underground life-form that had been eating the brains of several missing Silicon Valley programmers. The police and animal control were called and eventually for the safety of the neighborhood they had to kill the creature with poison. It decomposed quickly and deflated leaving little but an organic slime that contained no viable DNA to study.

The Uncanny Valley effect is named for this strange beast and the human lure it presented.

UNDERSTANDING

The word "Understand" has no known etymology or agreed-upon definition, and is thus not at all understood.

UNIVERSE

Here's the thing about the universe- You cannot escape the universe because if you go beyond it, you are by definition still in it. Therefore its escape velocity exceeds infinity, and because nothing can escape it, the universe is by definition a black hole. If the universe is a black hole, then its gravity also approaches infinity and if it has near infinite gravity, every element of that gravity is infinitesimal, making any specific thing in the universe, no matter how massive, tantamount to nothing. So if the universe is a black hole full of large amounts of nothing at all, I was absolutely correct in asserting that the "F" I got in astronomy is meaningless. But did the academic probation officer listen? Nooo.

-V-

VACCINATION

Between 1914 and 1972, most vaccines contained a dash of lemon or lime juice for color.

VALEDICTORIAN

There used to be an even higher accomplishment, that of hyperdictorian, for which one had to achieve higher grades than were possible even with extra credit. As this was impossible, the title fell out of use.

VALENTINE'S DAY

Valentine's Day didn't exist before 1988, when it was invented by Hallmark to sell greeting cards. They picked the date and associated saint randomly by throwing darts at a Catholic altar.

VAMPIRES

Vampires needn't be killed with a stake made specifically of wood. They needn't be killed at all. Live in peace, be happy.

VAN GOGH, VINCENT

Vincent van Gogh was virtually unknown until the 2011 Doctor Who episode that featured him.

Van Gogh never used conventional paints. All his most famous paintings are made with a mixture of pigment and snot. DNA analysis suggests the snot was not his own.

If you think that's bad you definitely don't want to hear about Picasso's "Brown" period.

VANILLA ICE

The song "Ice Ice Baby" is about the science of fetal cryogenics.

VANILLA SKY

Vanilla Sky is named after an ice cream manufacturing accident in 1890 that killed over 400 workers in the most delicious possible way.

VEGETABLES

Radishes only grow from animal fat. When planting radish seeds, farmers must bury at least one slice of bacon per seed.

VEGETARIANISM

Vegetarian plants are shunned by their community for cannibalism.

VELVET

Most velvet is considered a normal fabric because the direction of the fibers is uniform. Blue Velvet however is considered abnormal because it was directed by David Lynch.

VENUS (PLANET)

Venus is the closest planet to the sun. Images taken by the Pathfinder probe were taken from the exact equator of the planet, thus its famous rings were not at first visible. The planet was first discovered by Clyde Tombaugh in 1781, and has yet to complete a single revolution around our sun, Proxima Centauri.

It snows shards of metal on Venus, making Venusian snow-men among the most dangerous in the solar system.

VIDEO GAMES

The complete* history of Video Games is as follows:

1972- Pong is invented
1985- Super Mario Bros. is released for the NES
2013- Plants vs. Zombies 2 comes out on the App Store

*slightly abridged

VIRGINIA

Virginia is where the movie Tron was filmed, owing to its many flat computer generated surfaces, whimsical lighting scheme, and local fashion.

VIRGINIA, WEST

Due to a constitutional oversight, cannibalism is legal in West Virginia. Luckily "cannibalism" in West Virginia is classified as "Playing baseball without a helmet."

VIRGINIA, SOUTH

South Virginia is thought to exist south of Virginia, but none have seen it and returned.

VIRGINITY

Many ancient cultures valued virginity above all, not only in maidens but in virgin snow, virgin olive oil, and Virgin Airlines, which served 86% of ancient airports.

VOLLEYBALL

Only 7% of volleyball tournaments end without the death of at least one player.

VOODOO

If you make a voodoo doll of yourself and put it among other dolls, you won't feel lonely.

VOWEL

Vowels were once considered "dirty" letters and it was impolite to use them in public words.

WAFFLE

The waffle was originally invented by Werner von Braun as a rocket component, but astronauts kept eating them and ruining the rockets so they began making extras just for them to eat.

Eggo once had a contest to visit the Eggo Waffle factory in which a golden ticket was hidden in five waffles. Everyone who got one choked to death on it, not having expected to find a solid gold ticket in their waffles.

WALES

Wales are large marine mammals, some of the worlds most amazing creatures that are sadly becoming endangered. Thankfully a protective zone is being created off the coast of Great Britain, near Whales.

WALLET

Much as cigarettes are smaller versions of cigars, wallets are smaller versions of walls, which proved too heavy for pants.

WALNUT

Walnuts are a genetically modified food, having been engineered by Wal-Mart.

WALRUS

A walrus lurched into Middle High School on the day of the SAT tests and ransacked the building trying to escape. It outperformed 85% of the students and was accepted into its first choice of collages.

WAR

The war of 1812 was actually fought from 1936 to 2147.

WAR, TUG OF

Tug of war games were originally played not with rope, but with razor wire. This is why the 1600s were called "The Handless Era."

WASHINGTON, GEORGE

Few portraits of George Washington painted during his lifetime accurately depict the birthmark on his forehead, which was shaped exactly like the "M" from the Metallica logo. The M is said to have stood for "Freedom."

The most famous portrait of George Washington is also the first illustration done in crayon, which had just been invented in the year 1776.

For all his political and military skills, Washington never learned to operate a computer. It was his greatest regret.

WASHINGTON (D.C.)

The sewers of Washington D.C. are rumored to have huge caches of wildfire under all the critical government buildings.

WASHINGTON (STATE)

Washington is the fifth state of matter after gas, solid, liquid and plasma.

WATER

Water is the only element not commonly listed on the periodic table, owing to it being clear and therefore impossible to depict.

The expiration date on bottled water is actually the water's "half-life" on which half the water within will have decayed into thorium.

There's a 15 foot incline in Peru where the water flows uphill. Scientists have yet to explain the phenomenon, but suspect it may have something to do with the giant slide whistle nearby.

When steam cools, it turns to water. When water cools it turns to ice. When ice cools, it turns back into steam. This is what scientists call "The Circle of No Not Really."

WATERFALL

The upward waterfalls of Cucamonga do not actually flow uphill, rather the hills around them are upside down making it look like they flow uphill.

WATERMELON

Watermelons and Pumpkins are the same plant, they differ in appearance and flavor depending on whether they're grown by day or by night.

Three historical figures are now known to have really been watermelons:

-President Benjamin Harrison was the 23rd president of the United States, but recent documents reveal that he never spoke, nor moved of his own volition. This in combination with his green complexion and subtle, refreshing flavor suggest he was in fact a watermelon.

-Jane Austen. Though her body of work suggests she was an author, new genetic evidence from her grave reveals that she was in fact a specimen of Citrullus lanatus. Records of her autopsy revealing many small black seeds also confirms the suspicion.

-Neil Armstrong is considered the first man to walk on the moon, but he may not have been a man at all. Buzz Aldrin may have been the first man to walk on the lunar surface if allegations of Armstrong's watermelonhood ever prove correct. The most telling evidence is his famous quote, of which clearer radio recordings show he said, "One small step for a Watermel- I mean MAN, one giant leap for waterm- Er, MANkind."

WATERWORLD

Much of the budget of the film Waterworld came from the need for fake water. As real water is difficult to film with, producers paid several hundred million dollars to film with "stage-water," which is liquid diamond.

WAX

There is only one source of wax- Earwax. You may be thinking, "That's not true, there's also bee's wax," but this is in error, as bee's wax comes from their tiny bee ears.

WEAPONS

Cannons and early guns did not kill with bullets, rather it was the directed explosion itself that did the damage. The addition of bullets and cannonballs was purely aesthetic.

The Russian Special Forces invented a type of knife that can shoot the blade as a projectile. Such "Ballistic" knives are banned in America because of the actions of Jimmy Moore, age 12, whose parents warned him what would happen.

It's scientifically impossible to fire a flaming arrow because the wind will extinguish it as soon as it's fired, unless of course the flaming arrow is fired in a vacuum, then it will work.

Battle Axes are so named to differentiate them from Cake Axes and Circumcision Axes.

The safest place to keep weapons needs to be both padded and surrounded by protective bars, so it's best to keep them in the baby crib.

Needless to say, not with the baby still in there. Keep the baby somewhere safer, like the wing of a jet airplane. Then the airport security will protect them.

WEASEL

Despite its name, the weasel is a highly moral animal, the only one other than humans that says grace before meals.

WEATHER

The record of the invention of meteorology is very precise despite its antiquity, having been written down in cuneiform by Darnaval of Crosofos, who oddly enough begins the chronicle, "It was a dark and stormy night."

WEIGHT LOSS

One can avoid weight gain by not eating foods high in higgs bosons. Instead, focus on photon based foods for a light meal.

WENDY'S

"Wendy's" was originally called "Ohio State Snot & Vomit" but changed its name to become more popular. It did not change its menu.

WHALE

The whale is by far the largest breed of horse, and is one of the most capable of swimming underwater.

The whale's ability to swim owes itself to several traits that differentiate it from the common horse, including fins instead of legs, baleen instead of teeth, and a layer of fat called "blubber" which most horses lack.

Several types of whale swim the oceans today. There is the blue whale or "Budweiser Whale" which can survive cold temperatures due to its woolly coat; the Narwhal or "Unicorn Horse," and the Sperm Whale, which will not be described here for obvious reasons.

Still, these majestic steeds are popular in cinema and horse movies such as Free Willy and Moby Dick remain popular to this day. Live shows such as the Lipizzaner Whales also draw large crowds, and many families like to own whales as amusements for their children, or for professional whaleback riding. Be sure if you elect to own a whale that you feed it regular bails of hay, and register it with the United States Trotting Association.

WHIP

The sound of a whip cracking is made by the fracture of the whip's spinal column. A whip can only be cracked about 50 times before it dies.

WILSON, WOODROW

Woodrow Wilson never had children. He gave birth to adults.

WIND

Wind was once thought to be the farts of sky fairies. Hurricanes were thought to be the results of their visits to Mongolian Grills.

WIND CHIME

The Markedness Wind Chime is notable in that it only makes noise while motionless.

WINDMILL

The oldest windmill in the world is still in operation, milling wind as it has for thousands of years.

WINE

Red wine is made from the blood of the grape, while white wine is made from its lymph.

WINNIE THE POOH

Everyone remembers that it's Winnie the Pooh but it is in fact Winny the Pooh. This misconception has caused many to believe that they once existed in an alternate universe.

WISCONSIN

There's a game called Wisconsin Roulette where you place five cheddar cheese curds and one rock of sulfur on the table and take turns eating them until someone bursts into flame.

WIDSOM

Wisdom differs from knowledge in that one can know wisdom, but cannot wise knowdom.

WIG

Wigs can cause itching of the hair. Not the scalp, the hair itself.

WOLF

The wolf is nature's version of the dog. Most wolves cannot bite, and must rely on the queen wolf to chew their food and regurgitate it into their mouths.

Though capable of hunting in dark conditions, wolves merely adopted the darkness. Wolfsbane was born in it, molded by it.

WOLVERINE

The Wolverine is not actually a wolf, nor is it even a mammal or an animal at all, nor has it ever actually been proven to exist in any state of matter, or have been imagined by anybody ever.

WOOD, ED

Ed Wood was the pen name of Steven Spielberg for the black and white films he made before he was born.

WORD

There are three types of words in English: English words, Loan words, and Foreign words. The differences are as follows:

An English word, such as English or is or an, is an English word. A Loan word, such as loan or word, is an English loan word, as in is English an English word or a loan word, which is an English word, not a loan word. Foreign words such as such and are are neither loan nor English words like English or words, but are foreign words like but or like. Because like and but are Foreign, if if is an English word or a loan word like word or Foreign like such, then there are really no ifs ands or buts about it, which is an English word.

WRESTLING

In 1904, modern wrestling was codified into the sport we now know. But before that year, wrestling was played by all kinds of rules, varying greatly from country to country and continent to continent. In some countries the objective was to choke the opponent to unconsciousness. In others, to wrangle them into or out of a circle. In yet others, to disrobe them.

But what's strange is that these various proto-wrestling sports did not evolve independently of each other. They all in fact developed from a single sport played in the city of Suhag around the year 150: Wreithlisting.

It should be noted that "Wreithlisting" is a British historian's paraphrase of the original Egyptian name, "Ra-Th-Lis-Thi" which translates most accurately as, "The Grabby-Rolly Game."

The rules of Wreithlisting were rather complex compared to the modern sports derived from it. Most of these rules have analogous iterations in modern sport, but some are wholly forgotten and alien to the current wrestling institutions.

For instance, in the Papyrus of Sekh-Ankh, the following rules are given top priority:

-Whosoever grabbeth their opponent by their belt shall be pummeled with figs until such time as the belt is released.

-Whosoever grabbeth their opponent by their hair shall be tickled with feathers of the ibis that they may laugh uncontrollably in the manner of Set-Hakh-Ru-Ubis, by which he died but not unto their death, nay, but until they letteth go of the hair, or the hair detaches from the scalp.

-Whosoever grabbeth their opponent by their toes shall be licked by the tongue of the Setesh and the skin shall be thusly dissolved from their body, for they hath taken the toes which belongeth only to Set, and defiled them for sport. They shall also forfeit the match, though they may not care, for their skin hath fallen off like the rind of a rotten prune.

-Other rules included punishments for sneezing during a match, setting ones opponent on fire, cursing an opponent with plague, and singing when victorious.

Wreithlisting cannot be played by its full original rules today owing to the extinction of several animals mandated by the original papyri, and the illegality of several acts, including the proscribed victory move, the "Su-Buri-Utat," roughly translated, "The Spine Pretzel," but the Wreithlisting United Team (WUT) of Sacramento is devoted to playing the sport as closely as possible to its original version, right down to the fig pummeling.

WRITING ADVICE

Want to improve you writing style? Check out these easy tips!Very you're sentence structure. Add periods randomly and extend other sentences unnaturally to make them longer, more repetitious, and longer.

EXAMPLE: Bob went. To the market to buy some dogs.

Use descriptive word. Sentences are boring without some good, strong, interesting, useful, descriptive description.

EXAMPLE: Don't just say "She looked with her eyes," say, "She looked with her round, spherical, moist eyes."

Use obejctive tone. This means using a voice in narration that objectifies you're characters. When you characters are more like objects it's easier to write them because you don't need to give them human stuff like emotions and motives. They can just act to fit the plot.

EXAMPLE: Carla went to her morning class at school and when the aliens attacked she joined them in fighting Earth.

MAke up words when you don't know the right one. This will not only ornaclate your readers, but they will also think your smarter because you know words that they don't.

EXAMPLE: Richard felt he had to obfuscate the truth.

Use "passive" voice. This means when you get to a word that could be an action verb, instead "pass" the word over and use a better word, like "nestle" or "sponge." These are good words. They are mine but I will let you use them.

EXAMPLE: There was a plot to sponge the king, but it was nestled by the knights.Now you know writing. Go froth and write using these laws and you will write a good every time.

WUTHERING HEIGHTS

The real Wuthering Heights is nothing like the one in the book. In reality it's not very high up, and hardly even wuthers.

-X-

X

No words begin with the letter X, not even X-Ray, which really begins with an "L."

-Y-

YAM

Yams are technically a meat, as the Yam tree is technically an animal rather than a plant.

YARN

Authentic yarn is made with mango fiber, in accordance with the Holy Bible. Pronouncing the word "Yarn" is actually slightly damaging to the vocal cords.

YAWN

When you yawn, your brain stops working completely for about two seconds.

YOUTUBE

If all the footage on YouTube was transferred to 35mm and projected, the film related would be the exact same size as the solar system.

-Z-

ZARATHUSTRA

Thus Spake Zarathustra was the first composition in a musical trilogy that continued with Also Sprach Zarathustra, and concluded with Zarathustra Ran Out Of Things To Say.

ZEBRA

The zebra is the only mammal to lay eggs. Its eggs are striped.

ZELDA

"The Legend of Zelda" was originally going to be called "The Legend of Link" but the name had to be changed because "Link" is considered a bad word in English.

Every Zelda game contains an easter egg. That is not to say something is hidden in the gameplay, but that the cartridges have actual dyed eggs in them.

ZIPPER

Zippers are considered torture devices by the United Nations.

ZOMBIE

Zombie films up to the late 60s depicted zombies as living humans under mind control. It was not until the classic "Night of the Living Dead" that they were all depicted as giant bats.

ZOO

Zoo fences aren't meant for keeping the animals in, or even for keeping the visitors out, but for keeping the fence industry subsidized.

The proper plural of "Zoo" is "Zooyim."

ZWAGGERBEETLE

In 1999, Professor Herman T. Zwagger of the Florissant Fossil Foundation announced the discovery of a previously unseen insect that died out in the Jurassic Period. The fossil belonged to a bug over three feet tall.

Professor Zwagger's students named the organism a "Zwaggerbeetle" in his honor. According to one student who asked to remain nameless because he is wanted by the FBI for smuggling a fossilized trilobite out of the Smithsonian in his rectum, "The Zwaggerbeetle may be the largest insect the world has ever known. It likely fed on land-krill through orifices on its feet, and though it could not fly, it could jump well over 20 feet with its massive hind legs."

This concludes the book, which contains all the knowledge of the universe. You now know everything there is to know.

www.ingramcontent.com/pod-product-compliance
Lightning Source LLC
Chambersburg PA
CBHW060005100426
42740CB00010B/1404